KU-602-152

Theatre and Cultural Struggle in South Africa

Robert Mshengu Kavanagh

Zed Books Ltd.

Theatre and Cultural Struggle in South Africa was first
published by Zed Books Ltd., 57 Caledonian Road, London N1
9BU, in 1985.

Copyright © Robert Mshengu Kavanagh 1985
Copyedited by Roger Hardy
Typeset by Jo Marsh
Proofread by Ros Howe
Cover design by Magenta Design

Printed by The Pitman Press, Bath

All rights reserved

British Library Cataloguing in Publication Data

Kavanagh, Robert Mshengu
   Theatre and cultural struggle in South Africa.
   1. Theater — Social aspects — South Africa
   2. Theater — Political aspects —
South Africa
I. Title
792'.0968   PN 2049

ISBN 0-86232-282-0
ISBN 0-86232-283-9 Pbk

US Distributor
Biblio Distribution Center, 81 Adams Drive,
Totowa, New Jersey 07512

QM LIBRARY
(MILE END)

PN 2984 KAV

WITHDRAWN
FROM STOCK
QMUL LIBRARY

QM Library

23 1389731 7

Theatre and Cultural Struggle in South Africa

Robert Mshengu Kavanagh

To Workshop '71
and to Thembi, my wife, who shouldered the
responsibilities this book forced me to
neglect.
Angisoze ngikhohlwa, dudu.

My thanks to Martin Banham and Janet
Woolf of Leeds University who supervised the
research for this book.

Contents

Map Diagram of South Africa and the Witwatersrand

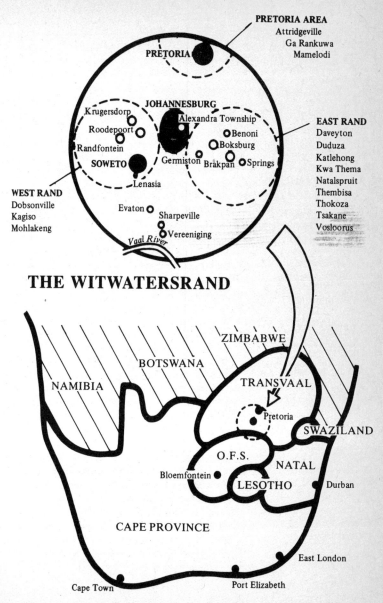

PRETORIA AREA
Attridgeville
Ga Rankuwa
Mamelodi

PRETORIA

JOHANNESBURG
Alexandra Township

Krugersdorp
Roodepoort
Randfontein
SOWETO
Lenasia
Germiston
Brakpan
Benoni
Boksburg
Springs

EAST RAND
Daveyton
Duduza
Katlehong
Kwa Thema
Natalspruit
Thembisa
Thokoza
Tsakane
Vosloorus

WEST RAND
Dobsonville
Kagiso
Mohlakeng

Evaton
Sharpeville
Vereeniging
Vaal River

THE WITWATERSRAND

ZIMBABWE

BOTSWANA

NAMIBIA

TRANSVAAL

Pretoria

SWAZILAND

O.F.S.
Bloemfontein
NATAL
LESOTHO
Durban

CAPE PROVINCE

East London

Cape Town
Port Elizabeth

SOUTH AFRICA

List of Abbreviations

AMDA	African Music and Drama Association
ANC	African National Congress
BCM	Black Consciousness Movement
BPC	Black People's Convention
NUSAS	National Union of South African Students
OHSA	Oxford History of South Africa
PAC	Pan Africanist Congress
PET	People's Experimental Theatre
SAIA	South African Information and Analysis
SASO	South African Students Organization
SATO	South African Theatre Organization

Preface

My ancestors, with the unfortunate exception of an English grandfather, were Celts. The English grandfather was a missionary — to the Xhosa and the Tonga. The first of them came to South Africa towards the end of the last century — some to build and man the railroads, others to seek their fortunes in the diamond fields. My grandmother achieved great fame as a singer, earning herself the distinction of being called 'The Belle of Kimberley'. In actual fact, she rejoiced in the 'professional name' of Madame Laughton-Rivers.

I myself was born in more prosaic circumstances, in that 'last outpost of the British Empire' — not to be confused with the Falkland Islands — Durban, in 1944, the son of a life insurance agent who travelled the length and breadth of the country to send me to the top white private schools and subsequently to Cape Town University. It was at my first school that the acting began — the Queen of Hearts in *Alice*, Tamburlaine, Faustus and Mark Anthony, all before the age of twelve.

In Johannesburg where my mother was living I learnt Zulu and then, on becoming a student in Cape Town, Xhosa. It was about this time that some-one phoned up asking, in Zulu, to speak to Mr Mkhize. I said Mr Mkhize was not in. He then asked who I was. I said: 'Mr Shabalala'. The next day he asked Mr Mkhize who this Mr Shabalala was and the name stuck. Later the *isithakazelo* 'Mshengu' was added — 'Msheng' uyashelela!' — by a (Johannes-burg) *Post* journalist as a matter of fact and from then on I was Mshengu.

With the language went the music and the old songs of that time: 'Ngilahlekelwe insizwa yokugcina', 'Cindy sithandwa sam' ' — and *King Kong*, which made a great impact on me. With the language and the music, people and then inevitably politics — of the liberal sort, also inevitably. I was acting and reading poetry at Cape Town, got a first in Honours, was playing rugby and cricket for the university, was on the S.R.C. This combination of 'academic excellence', sport and liberal politics was calculated to meet with the approval of the Rhodes Scholarship selection committee and in 1966 I duly 'went up' to University College, Oxford.

My drama activities continued there — in the Oxford University Dramatic Society (OUDS) and the Experimental Theatre Company (ETC) — and also the politics. I wrote a play, *Train from Pretoria*, which won the ETC Play

Competition in 1969 or thereabouts, about a sabotage operation in South Africa. However, who could remain unchanged by 1968? The answer: many, in fact. But my politics began to move . . . left – a little. Labour Party in Britain, Mao in the Third World. Far enough left anyway to suggest to me that theatre should be used in South Africa as a means of mass organization, mobilization and conscientization.

So I went back to South Africa, looking for a job that would take up a negligible part of my time and yet pay me enough to finance my theatre plans. On the face of it rather difficult it would seem, but a lectureship in the English Department at the University of the Witwatersrand turned out to be just the thing.

At that time the Institute of Race Relations in Johannesburg was anxious to start a drama workshop in order that 'people of different races' could get together and have 'contact'. I had previously done some work at an Anglican youth workshop on the theme of Simon and Garfunkel's 'Bridge Over Troubled Water'. It was all meant to be about the beauty of racial harmony and understanding. A white priest showed us the air-conditioned disco in the church basement while the visiting youth from Soweto and other un-air-conditioned places wryly absorbed the lesson about the brotherhood in Christ as practised by the Christian church in South Africa.

Our group's improvization had a white priest preaching a sermon of peace, love and brotherhood while a black priest 'translated' this into Xhosa. He spoke of the less beautiful and harmonious realities – suffering, oppression and resistance. The audience was split. Those who understood no Xhosa sensed something was cooking and got jumpy, but they had to contain their butterflies until the end, and ask those who did understand Xhosa to explain what had been said. This was a salutary and refreshing reversal of the usual roles. On the strength of this work I was invited to run the workshop at the Institute of Race Relations.

We started work by adapting the medieval morality of the old play, *Everyman*, to the realities of life in black Johannesburg, an extremely dangerous part of White City Jabavu in Soweto called Crossroads in particular. We researched the life of Lefty Mthembu, the notorious gangster of the Msomi-Spoilers era in Alexandra Township (Dark City). Our play became *Crossroads*, our Everyman Lefty and the workshop was called Experimental Theatre Workshop '71 because it was founded in 1971.

We still had problems with the Institute and its 'race relations' approach. These problems got in the way of our work. To the Institute, 'contact' with 'other races' was conducted within the parameters of white colonial middle-class culture and patronage. I remember the elderly lady, a member of the Institute staff, who rasped out at one of our members who was leaning against an Institute wall that he should get away from it. 'Why?' he asked. 'Er . . . it's not good manners to lean against walls', she faltered. This kind of attitude revealed itself in many other incidents.

Usually, in those days, in 'multiracial' activity the whites did most of the talking. In our Workshop we made it a rule that any member of the group was free to improvise and to make a contribution to the discussion in any major South African language. This tilted the balance. Instead of listening to long 'authoritative' opinions in English from various well-intentioned but not too knowledgeable individuals from the 'kitchens' (the white suburbs) everybody was able to create and talk with equal ease and authority. No longer able to dominate 'contact' many of the whites were chagrined, and slowly left. Incidentally, in the process I had to learn Sotho/Tswana and Tsotsitaal in addition to the Zulu and Xhosa I already spoke; virtually everyone in the group was able to speak a similar combination of languages. Others could actually speak more — Venda and Shangane as well, for instance.

Well, the rest is at least a little documented. I mean, the plays — *ZZZIP!* (a musical adaptation of Ben Jonson's *The Silent Woman*) *uHlanga — the Reed*, Credo Mutwa's *uNosilimela* and *Survival* (the last two were published in Kente and others, *South African People's Plays*, which I edited) — and *S'ketsh'* magazine. What is not documented is the labour, the struggle, the rough and tumble, which most battling unfunded theatre groups working against the system in Johannesburg went through. There was the painting of endless cloth banners to advertise each performance in the 'townships'. Late at night, after rehearsals and after delivering the cast — all workers — to far-flung parts of Soweto ('deep Soweto', 'the Wild West' etc.) and Lenasia, we drove around key points and climbed on to the old Ford Transit roof and hammered the banners on to the telephone poles. It was sometimes difficult to find any wood on the pole to put a nail into, it was so studded with those of past productions. Next morning, often, half the banners would be down already, stripped by rival groups or just some night roamer feeling cold. Once or twice we saw in the early grey of the morning some such figure, *ZZZIP!* or *Lifa* or *Mahlemola* scored across his back, gripping a banner tightly round his shoulders.

Then the police. Our kind of theatre and the police somehow just kept bumping into each other, sometimes on the verge of tragedy, at other times crude comedy. Not only white police. Once there were stories of a particular carload of gangsters that specialized in forcing cars off the road and robbing, sometimes killing the passengers. A kind of mugging on wheels. So when a car came up fast behind me one night and tried to get me to stop, I 'poured fat' — as they say. Unfortunately I was cornered in waste ground in Mofolo. I had to stop. Suddenly the warm muzzle of a revolver swayed unevenly in through the window. 'Sorry', I say in Tsotsitaal, 'I thought you were the *kgathas*' — a disrespectful word for the police. 'We *are* the *kgathas*! Get out! You should have respect!' shouted the policeman, referring to the fact that I had refused to stop. He questioned me. We spoke Zulu and ended up pissing into a ditch together, the best of *bras* (brothers). 'Don't be shy', says the *kgatha* as we piss 'you've got the same *thing* as me.'

Or the night of the party when the young man who played the drums in *ZZZIP!* stole somebody's *s'lamba* (lumberjacket). Just as we were leaving the party he comes back with his mates and we're surrounded by knives, *baksteens* (broken bricks) and an axe. We escape with sweet talk; but at another party in the white suburbs we're not so lucky. A local gate-crasher, frustrated because our girls from Soweto don't take him — a domestic worker from Zululand — seriously, went off in a huff and came back with a Zulu *impi*. Going to the rescue of 'I'm-not-the-fighting-type' Seth Sibanda, *I* end up on all fours in a very dark alleyway with my back being pounded resonantly by *isagila* (knopkerrie). Lucky it was only my breath and not my life I lost.

In Mayfair — Afrikaans labour aristocracy district — at bar-closing time, we stopped after a performance. The men went to the café for take-away Russian and chips. I stayed in the van with all the girls. Then out of all the bars come these drunken *graspapiers* — a name for red-necks, well-earned by stupidity. The story goes that on account of the difficulty of getting the recruits in the white army to march in time and tell their left from their right, they strap grass to the left and paper to the right and *'Gras! Papier! Gras! Papier!'* — off they go marching in step at last.

Now these *graspapiers* see me inside the van with all these black ladies. They don't like it. Or perhaps they're just jealous. *'Sies, jong'* they say, *'hoe kan jy dit doen?'* Whistles. Jeers. 'You think you're Casanova, hey?' bellows a more erudite *graspapier*. So I try and play it cool by rolling down the window to facilitate conversation when an extremely accurate fist pistons right through it on to my nose. I begin to leap gallantly but suicidally from the driver's seat to do battle, when the girls save me by putting their arms around me — something that in any other situation I would have really enjoyed. *'Ungaphumi, Mshengu! Bazokubulala!'* (Don't get out, Mshengu, they'll kill you) they say — and I had to agree with them. So I reversed the Transit and charged out of a situation in which making oneself scarce was definitely the better part of valour.

I survived and most of my comrades survived. Not all.

In 1976 *uHlanga* went to the Royal Court Theatre, London, *Survival* went to the States and I went to Leeds University to do the research which finally became this book. After a four year dose of life in Britain, in which hardly a day went by when I did not want to smash the TV screen and push my fingers up some non-existent wires till they emerged at the other end and sought out the throat of the newsreader, expert, intellectual or other creep white-washing blackguards and falsifying facts in the name of big business, I (married now, and a daddy) left for Ethiopia where for another four years I was in — and for two years was chairman of — the Theatre Arts Department at Addis Ababa University. There we found another struggle, of an altogether different order. 'Ethiopia — trailblazer of the African Revolution' — as someone put it. I learnt Amharic. Even acted Captain Cameron, Her Imperial Majesty Queen Victoria's Consul to the Emperor Tewodros of Ethiopia in Tsegaye Gebre-Medhin's *Tewodros* — in Amharic.

Now we are in Zimbabwe. *'Abyot yemayakwarit inkisikase new!'* The revolution is an unstoppable movement. From Zimbabwe where? Pamberi!

Robert Kavanagh
Zimbabwe

Introduction

The founders of Marxism emphasized that art was an important weapon in the ideological struggle between classes. It could re-inforce just as it could undermine the power of the exploiters, could serve to defend class oppression or, on the contrary, contribute to the education and development of the consciousness of the toiling masses, bringing them closer to victory over their oppressors. Marx and Engels therefore called for a clear distinction to be made between progressive and reactionary phenomena in feudal and bourgeois culture and put forward the principle of the Party approach to art — that it be evaluated from the position of the revolutionary class.

> From the Preface to Marx and Engels' *On Literature and Art*
> (Moscow, 1976)

What is the principle of party literature? It is not simply that, for the socialist proletariat, literature cannot be a means of enriching individuals or groups; it cannot, in fact, be an individual undertaking, independent of the common cause of the proletariat. Down with non-partisan writers! Down with literary supermen! Literature must become *part* of the common cause of the proletariat . . .

> From *Party Organization and Party Literature* by V. I. Lenin

Whereas the political, sociological and economic aspects of the South African situation have received a great deal of attention, culture and the arts have not. There are many studies of culture in the traditional societies but few of contemporary culture. To date there is no history of South African literature and virtually nothing on non-colonial theatre. Yet an understanding of the nature and interplay of cultural forces in South Africa and how they express themselves in art and literature is essential for those who wish to understand the society and above all for those who wish to change it. No strategy for change in the pre-revolutionary period is complete without a theory and analysis of South African culture. A lack of a theory of culture in the period of socialist reconstruction after the revolution can be extremely dangerous, as my present experience in Socialist Ethiopia confirms.

Such a theory and analysis will not, however, be of much assistance if it is not based on the social perception that South Africa is not only a racialist state but also, importantly, a capitalist state, characterized by particular conjunctures of race, nationality and class.

Recently a number of historians and economists have attempted to correct the liberal insistence on the racial factor in South African history and politics.[1] They often refer in their analyses of state domination to the importance of ideological and cultural mechanisms. None of these writers, to my knowledge, has attempted to analyse these mechanisms as they operate specifically in the field of art and culture.

The literature of the South African liberation movements understandably stresses political issues to the exclusion of cultural ones – though since 1976 the cultural upsurge in the country has been reflected in articles on black poetry and literature in party periodicals. Consciousness of the importance of the cultural dimension in political struggle has advanced beyond the bad old days when it was possible for Joe Slovo of the ANC to say: 'The radicalizing role of drama or any other art in a society is negligible. Change comes through human action informed by political awareness and exacerbated by intolerable humiliation, suppression and depression.'[2]

These developments have paved the way for revolutionary analysis in the field of culture. I have written this book therefore because a strategy for revolutionary change in South Africa requires a cultural analysis, and because this cultural analysis needs to be a Marxist one for it to be genuinely directed towards meaningful social transformation.

It is one thing to acknowledge the importance of cultural analysis in the South African situation, another to undertake it successfully. It is a complex situation, full of apparent paradox and contradiction. The guidance in crucial areas of writers such as Raymond Williams, Amilcar Cabral and Paulo Freire is only partially helpful in the cultural analysis of South African society. The position is made all the more difficult by the fact that this book concentrates on theatre, which is only a small part of the complex workings of culture, without the support that a comprehensive analysis of South African culture along the lines of, say, Raymond Williams' *The Long Revolution* would provide.

Nevertheless a start has to be made and what is more we have the great advantage of a sound and scientific social theory as communicated to us by the founders of Marxism and the many who have contributed to its development, Lenin to name but one. Also what I have written is not only based on this great body of theory but also on many years of praxis – first-hand observation and involvement in cultural activity in South Africa. To a large extent this book is a record of the development of my own consciousness and the realization that the analysis with which we South African cultural activists worked prior to the 1976 uprisings was not adequate. As a result, it is likely that much of our work had quite opposite results from those we intended.

This explains why in this book I concentrate to a large extent on theatre activity that took place in the Johannesburg area before and up to 1976, i.e. the area and period in which I myself, as a member of the Johannesburg theatre organization Experimental Theatre Workshop '71, was active. It also explains why I consider the primary consideration in revolutionary cultural analysis to be *function*. Form, content, intention and aesthetic criteria ultimately give way to the fundamental consideration of function. If our aim is to bring about revolutionary transformation through our work in threatre (or the other arts), the theatre we create and perform must be revolutionary in function.

In order to assess whether this is the case, an analysis of intention, content and form by themselves is clearly inadequate. A detailed socio-political understanding of the society in which the work is performed, of the individuals and structures that produced it, of the way in which theatre operates as a medium, of the nature of the audiences, the performance conditions — all this is necessary for an assessment of function or, in other words, of the extent to which it is a revolutionary or a reactionary act. I believe that this constitutes the only useful evaluation process for a revolutionary Marxist.

A Marxist analysis of society enables us to determine the function of a work in a given society with some precision, and the critic should use this analysis to identify exactly what functions *for* and what *against* the revolution. The revolutionary artist should use it to determine as far as possible that what he is creating becomes in fact an *effective* contribution to the revolutionary struggle. And in the context of the South African revolution an effective contribution is considered to be that which operates in the interests of the *fundamentally* oppressed classes, the workers and peasants. As it is these classes who *fundamentally* oppose the ruling bourgeoisie, it is these classes who are the real revolutionary classes in the society. In this book these classes are referred to as 'the majority', distinguishing the term from its purely nationalist usage according to which 'the majority' is taken to mean the black people of South Africa in general.

I have written this book for those in the revolutionary movements in order that they may have more information and, I hope, insights with which to formulate correct cultural strategies for revolutionary transformation and reconstruction. I have also written for cultural activists everywhere, but especially for those working in South Africa who may derive from this book an understanding and a consciousness which may help them be more effective in their struggle for a better future for the majority in our country than we who came before.

1. Culture and Social Relations in South Africa before 1976

'Objective Facts not Abstract Definitions' – Mao Tse-tung

In 1960 the population of the Union of South Africa, as the republic was then still called, was 16 million. Of these, 10.9 million were classified as 'Bantu', 3 million as 'white', 1.5 million as 'coloured' and 0.5 million as 'Asiatic'. In 1970 the figures were: 'Bantu' 15 million, 'white' 3.8 million, 'coloured' 2 million and 'Asiatic' 620,000. Thus in 1960 68% of the total population was classified as 'Bantu'. In 1970 this figure had increased to 71.4%. In 1976 it was estimated to be 71.5%. By 1976 the white population was estimated to have increased from 3 million in 1960 to 4.3 million.

In 1960 47% of the total population and 32% of the total 'Bantu' population lived in urban areas. 46% of the total urban population was classified as 'Bantu'. By 1970, despite strenuous efforts to reverse the trend, this figure had increased to 50%. Also in the same period the percentage of black Africans who lived in urban areas rose by 1.3% against the total black African population. The figures relating to black population in urban areas are notoriously conservative. For instance, official estimates of the black African population of Johannesburg in 1946, 1953 and 1957 were 395,231, 400,500 and 432,900 respectively. In the same years the Non-European Affairs Department of the Johannesburg City Council, which administered the area, estimated unofficially that there were 400,847, 516,620 and 541,521 respectively. Non-governmental estimates usually put the figures as much higher.

By 1976 of South Africa's 9.7 million workers 71% were black. The following table shows the population economically active between 1960 and 1970:

	Mining	Manufac- turing	Com- merce and Finance	Profes- sional, technical and related	Administ- ration and Mana- gerial	Clerical and sales
1960 White	61,748	210,702	255,648	137,858	58,889	373,987
'Bantu'	548,317	308,583	188,829	48,487	5,716	48,161
1970 White	62,790	279,810	418,900	202,390	69,850	579,750
'Bantu'	605,240	511,540	349,260	93,300	3,400	207,160

During the 1950s trading and general dealers' stores owned by black Africans increased steadily. In the Johannesburg area alone up to June 1958, 1,683 licences had been issued. In 1955 the African Chamber of Commerce was established and a number of finance corporations formed and larger commercial enterprises undertaken.

The above statistics have been quoted in order to illustrate a number of things which are central to an analysis of South African society and culture. First, they indicate the extent to which the population of South Africa, black and white, was urbanized by 1976. Second, they show the important fact that, though whites are outnumbered by blacks, the ratio of white to black is relatively high and over the period 1960-1976 relatively stable. Third, they illustrate the determining factor of race in the occupational structure but also point to a process of class differentiation among blacks.

The size of the white population, the degree of urbanization and the nature of the occupational structure and class formation among blacks characterize social and cultural relations in South Africa in the period up to 1976 and therefore determine the nature of the analysis of art and culture in the country.

Racial Segregation, Economic Exploitation and Political Oppression

The four major racial groups that live in South Africa — black Africans, whites, 'coloureds' and 'Asiatics' — are by no means homogeneous. Each group is divided and differentiated in various ways. For instance, in 1960 the white group was divided into 1.8 million Afrikaners, 1.2 million English-speakers and whites of various nationalities, among them Dutch, Germans, Italians, Portuguese and Greeks.

The black African population of South Africa is also heterogeneous. In 1960 black Africans were divided into 3 million Xhosa, 2.7 million Zulu, 1.3 million Sotho, 1.1 million Tswana, 0.5 million Tsonga and 0.2 million Venda. Whereas the heterogeneity of the white group is officially ignored, that of the black African group is emphasized in legislation and policy.

During the 1950s and 1960s government policy and legislation, reinforced by race prejudice on the part of the vast majority of whites, segregated the lives of blacks and whites as far as possible given their economic inter-dependence. In the rural areas blacks were swept up from their homesteads in areas designated 'white' and dumped in those designated 'black'. The major towns and cities consist of a central business and shopping area exclusively reserved for white business or residence, a sprawl of white residential suburbs and industrial estates or mines, and usually well removed from the white city and suburbs, separate 'townships' for 'Bantu', 'coloureds' and 'Asiatics'.

In the early years of urbanization blacks lived in areas relatively close to the town centre and in these areas there was a large degree of racial integra-tion. African 'coloureds', 'Asiatics' and poor whites lived as neighbours and intermarried. By 1958 these racially integrated inner-city areas had been largely destroyed, along with many of the segregated 'locations' which had grown up on the outskirts of the towns, and the process of removing the black groups to the segregated areas, now called 'townships', was well under way. For instance, in 1955 Sophiatown near Johannesburg was cleared, its inhabitants removed to South-Western Native Townships (Soweto) and converted into a white residential area.

Despite official policy, there was always some social interaction between whites and blacks. Lewis Nkosi describes a multiracial 'Bohemia' in the 1950s in which certain black intellectuals and professionals fraternized with small numbers of 'liberal' whites. The state exerted pressure in order to stop such contact and this was reinforced by white public opinion. The journalist Bloke Modisane, who was a part of this 'Bohemia', in his book *Blame Me on History*, described his despair as his white friends began to succumb to the fears and pressures and stopped coming to visit him in Sophiatown.

Nevertheless such mixing was very much the exception. The vast majority of blacks and whites lived apart, were educated apart, recreated apart, were buried apart. In the daytime they met at work in the town centre or on the industrial estates. There too they were kept apart. Blacks did different, inferior jobs — often in segregated areas in the factory or the office. They used different facilities, for example lavatories, and at lunchtime or teatime whites could eat in restaurants and tearooms while blacks ate 'take-aways' or lunchboxes at the workplace, in the street or in one of the very few, crude, 'blacks only' eating places in the seedier parts of town. At the end of the day the whites returned to their suburbs, blacks to their 'townships'.

What they returned with on pay day was different too. In 1959 the average worker of the black African group in private industry, the best-paid sector, was paid £174.6 a year. The average white worker in the same sector was paid £948 a year. In 1972 the overall average monthly wage of whites was R316, that of blacks R48. In 1976 the figures were R467 and R101 respectively. Black workers tended to be paid weekly, white workers monthly, hence the special significance of Friday in black urban culture:

The ward was like a battle-field
victims of war
waged in the dark alley
flocked in cars, taxis, ambulances, vans and trucks
. . .
'So! it's Friday night!
Everybody's enjoying
in Soweto.'
[Oswald Mtshali] [3]

In the discrepancy of wages lay the key to the relations of black and white wage-earners. The Federated Chamber of Industries put it quite frankly in 1925 when in evidence to a commission it said: 'White wages have been paid, and are being paid, largely at the expense of native workers.' What was in 1925 industrial practice was by 1960 government policy. As a Nationalist MP explained in that year, all the government was trying to do

is import labour into South Africa (i.e. the 'white' areas), and when those labourers have completed their work here, they return to their homeland, where they have their roots, where their future lies, where they can realize their ideals and where they can get their rights. They only come here to supply labour. They are only supplying a commodity, the commodity of labour . . . As soon as the Opposition understands this principle that it is labour we are importing and not labourers as individuals, the question of numbers will not worry them either.

Or as the poet Sipho Sepamla saw it:

To Whom It May Concern
Bearer
Bare of everything but particulars
Is a Bantu
The language of a people in Southern Africa
He seeks to proceed from here to there
Please pass him on
Subject to these particulars
He lives
Subject to the provisions
Of the Urban Natives Act of 1925
Amended often
To update it to his sophistication
Subject to the provisions of the said Act
He may roam freely within a prescribed area
Free only from the anxiety of conscription
In terms of the Abolition of Passes Act
A latter day amendment
In keeping with the moon-age naming
Bearer's designation is Reference number 417181
And (he) acquires a niche in the said area

As a temporary sojourner
To which he must betake himself
At all times
When his services are dispensed with for the day
As a permanent measure of law and order
Please note
The remains of R/N 417181
Will be laid to rest in peace
On a plot
Set aside for Methodist Xhosas
A measure also adopted
At the express request of the Bantu
In anticipation of any faction fight
Before the Day of Judgement.

This relation of economic exploitation was organized and maintained by legislation which determined that the political relations of blacks and whites were those of oppression, in which the minority governs the majority without its participation in any meaningful way, without its consent and without consultation.[4] Thus the distinctive characteristics of South African society before 1976 were racial segregation, economic exploitation and political oppression. In other words, the major social forces operative were those of race, class and nationality. It is to the peculiar conjunctures of race, class and nationality that we now turn.

Race, Class and Nationality

In complex modern societies the analysis of class and occupational structures is difficult at the best of times. In South Africa it is further compounded by the difficulty presented by factors of race and nationality. Many analysts writing about racialist or so-called 'plural' societies reject class as a relevant factor. Others insist on class as the primary factor and reject the importance of race. Few take the factor of nationality into consideration and even fewer attempt to understand the dynamic, dialectical relationship of all three factors.[5]

In the previous section it was suggested that the three distinctive characteristics of South African society before 1976 were political oppression, economic exploitation and racial segregation. It is our contention that to concentrate on one of these and neglect the others results in an unreliable analysis. We intend to take all three factors into consideration as important social forces, without attempting to demonstrate the primacy of any one of them.

In the analysis of social structures, particularly those related to culture, two aspects of Marxist theory are particularly important and useful. These are the model of the base and superstructure and the concepts of 'class consciousness' and 'false consciousness'. Marx explains the former thus:

> In the social production of their life, men enter into definite relations which are indispensable and independent of their will, relations of production which correspond to a definite stage of development of their material productive forces. The sum total of these relations of production constitutes the economic structure of society, the real foundation, on which rises a legal and political superstructure and to which correspond definite forms of social consciousness. The mode of production of material life conditions the social, political and intellectual life processes in general. It is not the consciousness of men that determines their being, but, on the contrary, their social being that determines their consciousness. [*Selected Works*, p.101]

Engels himself and recent Marxist writing have been at pains to reject vulgarizations of this idea. The model is not a wooden construct and much harm is done when it is treated as such. Engels wrote:

> According to the materialist conception of history, the *ultimately* determining factor in history is the production and reproduction of real life. Neither Marx nor I have ever asserted more than this. Hence if somebody twists this into saying that the economic factor is the *only* determining one, he transforms the proposition into a meaningless, abstract, absurd phrase. The economic situation is the basis, but the various elements of the superstructure . . . also exercise their influence upon the course of the historical struggles and in many cases determine their *form* in particular. (Engels to Joseph Block, 21-22.9.1890)

And again:

> Political, juridical, philosophical, religious, literary, artistic, etc., development is based on economic development. But all these react upon one another and also upon the economic base. It is not that the economic situation is *cause, solely active*, while everything else is only passive effect. There is, rather, interaction on the basis of economic necessity, which *ultimately* always asserts itself. (Engels to W. Borgius, 25.1.1894)

Raymond Williams, in *Marxism and Literature*, devoted considerable space and attention to the attempts of various Marxist theorists to interpret the model flexibly and to the concept of 'hegemony' as developed by Antonio Gramsci. When we refer to the model we shall assume that there is a constitutive interaction between base and superstructure. We shall assume that consciousness determines and is determined by social being, and that social being determines and is determined by consciousness, but we shall situate our analysis of this interaction within a firm appreciation of the nature of the material base of the society and its class structure.

The main usefulness of the model in the analysis of culture in South

Africa is that it enables us to distinguish between 'material life conditions', 'social being', etc. and 'social, political and intellectual life processes', 'consciousness', 'ideology', etc. In the main it is this distinction that provides the key to the differentiation of 'false consciousness' from 'class conscious- ness', or between what individuals and groups think they are and what they objectively are. Georg Lukacs defined these concepts thus: 'Class conscious- ness' is 'the appropriate and rational reactions "imputed" to a particular typical position in the process of production'. 'False consciousness' is 'the sum (or) the average of what is thought or felt by the single individuals who make up the class' (Lukacs, 1971, p.51).

The determination of what an individual or a group's objective interests are is made with reference to the relation of that individual or group to the economic base *as well as* to the legal, political, ideological, cultural, etc. superstructure of society. By making this reference the analyst is able to recognize the function of a group within society and thus determine its real interests, distinguishing these from 'false consciousness', from its hopes, aspirations and affiliations based on what it imagines its interests to be.

We are concerned with culture and ideology, and more particularly with cultural domination, and therefore primarily concerned with superstructural phenomena and with 'false consciousness'. We must, however, examine these things in the context of the interaction between them and the structures and forces of the economic base of society and 'class consciousness'. It must be reiterated at this early stage that the consequence of analysis of this kind is that it is the *function* of human beings and their actions, the *function* of theatre in the society, that is taken to determine in whose interests they operate. Though individual motives or what people *imagine* to be the nature and consequences of their thoughts and actions are important factors which ought not to be excluded from the total analysis, they must be distinguished from the real function, the actual consequences, of their thoughts and deeds. As Engels wrote:

> The many individual wills active in history for the most part produce results quite other than those intended — often quite the opposite; their motives, therefore, in relation to the total result are likewise of only secondary importance. On the other hand, the further question arises: What driving forces in turn stand behind these motives . . . [*Selected Works*, p.613]

Apartheid *appears* to be primarily a racial structure. This is how it is commonly regarded by most people within South Africa and by liberal scholars and writers. Recent analysis has, however, offered a different under- standing of it. It is now suggested that 'Apartheid is "economic" no less than political.' These are the words of Harold Wolpe, one of those who is working to produce a Marxist analysis which effectively demonstrates the importance of class and economic factors in South African society.[6]

Wolpe views apartheid as 'predominantly . . . an attempt to order the non-white (*sic*) working class in terms of specific demands of different classes and sectors of classes'. He stresses the class structure of the society:

> An analysis of the abstract class categories and relationships (in South Africa) leads to its characterization as a capitalist society. At the concrete level, the specific form of these relationships is defined by the content of Apartheid. The 'colour bar' in the economy may be the result of political decisions but it nevertheless defines the relationship between classes (and sectors of classes).

Like Eugene Genovese writing in the context of the United States, Wolpe believes that the established racial interpretation of the society obscures this fact. The ascription of the position of 'Africans' in society and in the occupational structure to race prejudice 'tends to obscure important changes in the social relationships within the society'.[7]

The liberal contention that there is a fundamental contradiction between the 'laws' of a capitalist economy and the racial structures of apartheid is not true, according to Wolpe. The racial structures of the society constitute the effective organization of that society in the interests of the capitalist class. Racial structures are the essential means of sustaining and reproducing cheap labour. He demonstrates that, as the needs of capitalism have changed, so has the official ideology. In particular, he notes the transition from segregation to separate development, a process which was intended more efficiently to ensure the reproduction of cheap labour and which led to the transformation of the official ideology of racial inferiority to one of 'separate but equal peoples'. One of the important concomitants of this process was the need to prop up certain traditional African social and cultural forms.

He goes on to show that when capitalism required a cheap semi-skilled and skilled labour force as well as a cheap unskilled labour force, racial legislation relating to job reservation and the industrial colour bar was relaxed. He identifies the different fractions of capital, i.e. mining, manufacturing, agricultural and state capital, and, importantly, notes their relations.

Writers of the liberal tradition, on the other hand, and the so-called 'pluralists' such as Pierre van den Berghe, though they discount the importance of class and are not able to see beyond the racial structures, are not entirely unhelpful. The reason for this is that, as already mentioned, superstructural areas and the values and expressions that make up 'false consciousness' are of particular importance to the cultural analyst. In South Africa the thinking of the entire society is dominated by racial perspectives. These racial perspectives are an essential element of 'false consciousness'.

Race, then, is an important social force, especially in the superstructure, and Wolpe, among others, has demonstrated the importance of class and economic factors as determinants of social structure and change in South Africa. It remains, then, for us to determine the importance of nationality and the relations between the forces of class, race and nationality.

Historically the structures of modern South Africa derive from the inescapable facts of conquest and colonization.[8] These facts remain important today. First, there was the invasion of the area now known as South Africa, the defeat and subjugation of the indigenous peoples by British and Boer forces, and the seizure of the land and its resources. Then there was the protracted struggle of the Boers or Afrikaners to establish their conquest of the indigenous people in states independent of British rule, their defeat in war and their political struggle to reverse that defeat. Third, there was the struggle of the African nationalists for political rights and then hegemony in the land that had been wrested from their forebears.

Racial structures in South Africa have to be understood in the light of these facts *as well as* in the light of the economic development of the region. In other words, class and economic factors alone are not sufficient to account for such structures. Apartheid *is* a structure which in important ways ensures the provision and reproduction of cheap labour for the capitalist class. It is, however, also a structure which ensures the continued domination of an alliance of two minority national groups over the majority, the descendants of the original possessors of the land. The factor of nationality has to be insisted on, as only by taking cognizance of it can one fully understand that the white minority is made up of two 'national' factions which have historically been, at one and the same time, in alliance and in conflict. They have been allies in the face of the threat from the third important group, the black Africans, but they have competed against each other for hegemony. Racial segregation and the fostering of ethnic divisions among black Africans were largely mechanisms created for the purpose of weakening that group and perpetuating the 'national' domination of the black African people by the whites.

Factors of nationality were particularly important in the earlier phases of development in South Africa. While the economic structures of the country and its relations with other countries were predominantly colonial, factors of nationality were especially important. As the colonial economy gave way to an integrated capitalist economy, factors of nationality diminished in importance, while those of class and the economy increased in importance. The rise of Afrikaner capital in the 1960s, and the steady coming together of the English-speaking and Afrikaner sections of capital, reduced the contradiction between the interests of capital and those of the Afrikaner nationalist élite, a contradiction which did historically exist as the existence of two white political parties with different policies, the Nationalist Party and the United Party, suggested.[9] Significantly the United Party was dissolved in 1976.

Though we have expressed a reluctance to enter into the debate concerning class, race and nationality, we have indicated that we believe that the structures in South Africa are not static and are in the process of transformation. In the course of this transformation, the factor of nationality shows signs of decreasing in importance and the factor of class of increasing in importance. In addition, we might indicate that we believe that race as a factor and racial ideology derive their greatest importance from their being a medium of maintaining and justifying economic and political structures.

Class Formation and the Occupational Structure

Following Marx and Engels, the two most clearly defined classes in capitalist society are the bourgeoisie and the proletariat. The bourgeoisie consists of those who, not working themselves, hire labour to work the means of production which they, the bourgeoisie, own. The proletariat consists of those who own no means of production and sell their labour to those that do. In addition, strictly speaking 'the proletarian is a man (*sic*) who is unprotected from the extremes of exploitation by any special qualifications which would prevent him from being replaced by another worker with equal physical strength'. (Ossowski, 1963, p.79)

Between these two classes lie the 'intermediate classes', affiliated to the bourgeoisie or to the proletariat according to various functional attributes. For instance, there are those who do own the means of production but work it themselves. The fact of owning the means of production draws them to the camp of the bourgeoisie. The fact of working and not hiring labour or working alongside their hired labour separates them from it. Again, there are workers who do not own the means of production and sell their labour but have considerable (or slight) qualifications or privileges. In South Africa race or nationality can obviously be a considerable 'qualification'. The real interests of, say, a white artisan may draw him to the camp of the (black) proletariat proper but his 'qualifications' or advantages separate him from it. In addition to the classes created by the capitalist mode of production there are those related to other residual modes of production — traditional chiefs, peasants, etc.

In South Africa capital is divided into a private and a state sector. In the private sector there are four powerful fractions — mining, agriculture, manufacturing and finance. The proletariat consists of rural (i.e. wage) labourers in capitalist agriculture, migrant and urban workers. Between these two great classes are the intermediate classes, active in the state and private sectors, in mining, agriculture, finance, commerce, the professions, services, etc.

The white groups include no working class proper and the black African group no big bourgeoisie. Both groups, however, contain classes and the study of the relations of these classes reveals that class is an important factor not only in determining relations with others who belong to different classes (or sections of classes) within the same national or racial group, but also with those who occupy a similar class position in other national or racial groups. This will emerge clearly when we begin to look at theatre activity in later chapters.

In the white groups, the working class successfully campaigned to achieve for itself the position of a labour aristocracy, legally protected from the competition of black workers. However, despite the position of privilege enjoyed by white workers as highly paid skilled workers or overseers of black labour, there remains a considerable number who depend on state welfare and patronage to protect them from the extremes of poverty endured by the mass of other (i.e. black) workers.

Government policy, financial practice and the wage structure severely restrict the access of blacks to capital. Until recently it was government policy that black Africans should not be allowed freehold or leasehold rights in the so-called 'white' areas of South Africa. This important way of accumulating capital, i.e. through the charging of rent, was in effect denied to them. Another, the conversion of skills into capital, was chronically restricted owing to the low wages paid to blacks generally. It was also extremely difficult for blacks to get capital loans. Thus the black African group was, on the face of it, excluded because of race (or nationality) from the ranks of the national bourgeoisie. However, many members of the black African group owned property, hired labour and lived off profit. There was thus an intermediate class identified in function with the (white) bourgeoisie proper.

The important criterion in the determination of the nature of the proletariat is 'qualification' or privilege. It is this that originally marked off the white working class from the black working class. Other 'qualifications' lead to stratification in the black working class. In a situation of chronic exploitation such as obtains in South Africa the mere possession of a job is one such 'qualification' which marks off the employed, who are paid though exploited, from the unemployed (whose existence it is that enables the payment of extremely low wages to the employed). Not only does the unemployed black worker in South Africa receive no unemployment benefit, but he can be arrested for being unemployed.

Various sectors of the economy — mining and railways, for example — were traditionally low-paid and relied on migrants for their labour needs. Migrants are less protected from exploitation than those resident in the urban areas because they have no 'right' by law to seek work there. Those employed in the manufacturing sector generally earn more than those employed in other sectors, except for women, and this introduces another 'qualification', that of sex. Black women in South Africa are, as elsewhere in the Third World, the most exploited section of the proletariat. Residence in Johannesburg, where wages are higher and job opportunities greater, is another 'qualification'. Of course, more conventional 'qualifications' do apply. Semi-skilled and skilled workers are protected by their skills and training.

Thus in the black urban areas there existed a graded working class, consisting of a basic extremely exploited stratum and other strata variously protected by 'qualifications' such as sex, the right to reside in the urban areas, skills etc. The intermediate classes, i.e. intermediate between this graded working class and the (white) bourgeoisie, included those who own neither the means of production nor property, who sell their labour but whose particular qualifications provided them with a relatively greater capacity to earn and thus acquire status — e.g. teachers, priests, policemen, salesmen, clerks, government-employed professionals, journalists and some artists; those who

11

own neither the means of production nor property but who do not sell their labour — e.g. petty traders, hawkers, some artists; those who own their equipment or even their business premises, who do not sell their labour or hire labour but work themselves — e.g. doctors and dentists in private practice, barbers, photographers, some artists; and those who own property and equipment and hire labour — e.g. big traders and businessmen, gangsters and theatre and entertainment entrepreneurs.

One group, common to all national or racial groups and most important in the analysis of culture and cultural domination, is the intellectuals. We shall be looking at them and their function later.

Class in the black African urban areas is complemented by an additional factor, that of social strata determined according to the estimation the community has of itself. A number of criteria determine the composition of these strata. For instance, the community sees itself as consisting of élite and ordinary people; educated and uneducated people; westernized — i.e. ascribing to, and to some extent being able to afford and live up to, the lifestyle of the white middle class (or rather the Black American middle class in recent times) — and non-westernized; 'English blacks' and those who habitually speak the vernacular; the wealthy and the poor; the 'clevers' and the 'moegoes', etc. Various combinations of these criteria determine status.

Status groups should not, however, be confused with classes or sections of classes, though sometimes they are related. Class is determined by the objective relation of groups to the means of production; status is determined by what groups or the society imagine to be important, valuable, prestigious, desirable, etc. Status has therefore an ideological base and is often a consequence of 'false consciousness'.

2. The Struggle for Social Hegemony

Britain, the colonial power, had granted South Africa a form of self-government in 1910 which left whites firmly in control of blacks, but did not decide the relations of the English-speaking and Afrikaner sections of the white group or of the mining capitalists, the farmers and the urban workers. The following years saw a battle to determine these relations.

Initially the English-speaking capitalists and British investors dominated the economic and state structures. English-speaking workers received special treatment at the hands of employers and the state, in the civil service, on the railways, in the mines, etc. Afrikaners were discriminated against. Unskilled and newly proletarianized when they arrived in the towns, they found themselves in circumstances remarkably similar to those in which the proletarianized black worker found himself. There was therefore the distinct possibility that in these circumstances solidarity between black and Afrikaner workers might develop. This possibility was viewed by the petit-bourgeois Afrikaner nationalists with alarm. H. J. and R. E. Simons describe the situation and how it was dealt with:

> Urban conditions developed close relations between humans of different types, assimilated them into social classes, promoted the growth of sub-cultures, and broke down the barriers between ethnic groups. To prevent assimilation, Afrikaner leaders made racial segregation compulsory and formed a wide range of separate voluntary associations. Afrikaner schools, universities, churches, press, political parties, occupational and cultural societies — chambers of industry and commerce, clubs, boy scouts, and the like — insulated Afrikaners from British or radical influences and cultivated a colour consciousness that inhibited the growth of class consciousness. [p.517]

'Colour consciousness' was not the prerogative of the Afrikaner alone. The English-speaking worker considered the cheap labour of black workers to be an extremely dangerous threat. He observed with alarm the efforts of the mining companies to employ black workers in jobs 'customarily' done by 'civilized labour' and organized a militant campaign directed against the bosses and against the employment of 'uncivilized labour'. This combination of socialist and racialist objectives received its historical expression in the slogan: 'Workers of the world unite, and fight for a white South Africa.' The struggle of the white workers led to the Rand Rebellion of 1922, which was ruthlessly suppressed by a government which represented the interests of the mining companies and capital generally.

A direct result of the rebellion was the alliance of white labour and Afrikaner nationalism, which enabled the latter to win power in the 1924 general election. The white labour movement gained the legal guarantees of its privileged industrial position which it had demanded, and in return supported the nationalists whole-heartedly in their efforts to entrench racial discrimination and the political oppression of the black majority. Having achieved its main objectives, the white labour movement rapidly lost its influence in the political affairs of the country.

The Afrikaner nationalists had been able to support the white labour movement because, by so doing, they divided their own workers from those of the black African group and restricted the growth of a black working class, whose integration into important sectors of the economy was an unacceptable threat to Afrikaner hopes for hegemony. Their relations with capital at this stage were ambivalent. The Afrikaner nationalists aimed at total hegemony, and the continuing domination of the economy by the English in South Africa and abroad was an obstacle they were determined to remove. They were therefore able to unite with the white labour movement against English capital. On the other hand, as Wolpe has explained, their own segregationist policies, intended by them primarily at that stage to ensure the effective suppression of the black Africans and to elicit the support of their own working class, were at the same time an effective means of securing for capital the cheap labour it required. Therefore in this area there was no basic contradiction between the interests of Afrikaner nationalism and capital.

Between 1924 and 1948 the struggle for political hegemony between capital and Afrikaner nationalism remained undecided. In 1948, however, Dr Malan's 'purified' Nationalist Party was voted into power. The Afrikaner nationalists used this decisive opportunity first to entrench their political position and then to move towards full hegemony over both the English-speaking white group and the black groups. In the 1950s this process was not yet complete. The key, therefore, to the understanding of the operation of cultural domination during this period is that the hegemony of the white groups as a whole over the black groups was being militantly challenged by the African National Congress, and later the Pan Africanist Congress, at a time when the Afrikaner nationalists had not yet established full hegemony within the white groups.[10]

The English-speaking whites retained certain important residual powers as a result of their continuing domination of fractions of capital, e.g. mining and manufacturing. This explains the apparent anomaly that in South Africa during this period capital and the state were sometimes at variance and appeared to have different interests. It also provides the political reason for the rapid and ruthless implementation of the policies of separate development.

By the end of the 1960s, however, the Afrikaner nationalists established virtually total hegemony within the white groups and in the society as a whole. A powerful Afrikaner capitalist class came into being, and the 1970s saw the beginning of a rapprochement between Afrikaner and English sections of capital, in the process of which their common class interests began to take precedence over their national differences.

'Rule' and 'Hegemony'

Up to now we have been using the word 'hegemony' in its conventional sense of political and economic predominance. We now need to introduce certain other meanings. As Raymond Williams explains:

> The traditional definition of 'hegemony' is political rule or domination, especially in relations between states. Marxism extended the definition of rule or domination to relations between social classes, and especially to definitions of a *ruling class*. 'Hegemony' then acquired a further significant sense in the work of Antonio Gramsci, carried out under great difficulty in a Fascist prison between 1927 and 1935. Much is still uncertain in Gramsci's use of the concept, but his work is one of the major turning points in Marxist cultural theory. [Williams, 1977, p.108]

Groups or classes that are politically predominant rely only partly on legislation and the direct instruments of political power and enforcement — or, as Gramsci put it, 'rule'. To a large extent, their domination takes the form of a 'complex interlocking of political, social and cultural forces'. Gramsci, developing the conventional meaning of the word, called the operation of these forces 'hegemony' or 'social hegemony'.

According to Gramsci, 'social hegemony' is:

> The 'spontaneous' consent given by the great masses of the population to the general direction imposed on social life by the dominant fundamental group; this consent is 'historically' caused by the prestige (and consequent confidence) which the dominant group enjoys because of its position and function in the world of production.

This he distinguishes from 'rule', which he defines as:

> The apparatus of state coercive power which 'legally' enforces discipline on those groups who do not 'consent' either actively or passively. This apparatus is, however, constituted for the whole of society in anticipation of moments of crisis of command and direction when spontaneous consent had failed. [Gramsci, 1971, p.12]

Raymond Williams puts Gramsci's distinction between 'rule' and 'hegemony' succinctly:

> 'Rule' is expressed in directly political forms and in times of crisis by direct or effective coercion. But the more normal situation is a complex inter-locking of political, social and cultural forces, and 'hegemony', according to different interpretations, is either this or the active social and cultural forces which are its necessary elements. [Williams, 1977, p.108]

In the advanced capitalist countries, the 'normal' situation is one in which the ideological domination of the ruling class is effected without recourse to direct coercion. The operation of hegemony thus involves an apparently 'spontaneous' consent and also a process of 'legitimation' which constantly, all-pervasively, ensures the acceptance of the dominant ideology as legitimate and other rival ideologies as illegitimate.

Gramsci's analysis and subsequent developments of his and Marx's own theories have cast new light on the role of culture (in both senses) in the social hegemony of the ruling class.[11] Just as the ideology of the fundamental ruling class is 'legitimated', so is its culture. Other classes in the society are persuaded to accept the culture of the ruling class as legitimately that of the society as a whole. This process, which elicits the respect and support of the whole society for the values and tastes, ways of living, etc. of a section of it, acts as a powerful instrument of psychological oppression and reinforces the willingness of other classes to accept the leadership of the ruling class.

This is particularly true of the art, literature, theatre and music, etc. that is projected by the ruling class as that of the society as a whole. As it is not actually theirs, the other classes do not appreciate the official culture. A special (inferior) culture therefore comes into being and is purveyed to them by the ruling class and its agents for their consumption. Though often based on or incorporating elements of these classes' own 'illegitimate' constitutive culture, the culture manufactured for them tends to be non-critical, passive and anaesthetizing. Such a culture is imposed on the working class and needs to be distinguished from the dynamic, constitutive culture in which the working class expresses its objective self.

If South Africa were a fully integrated capitalist industrial state, the above analysis of hegemony and the role of culture in the operation of hegemony would be an adequate guide in itself. However, as already pointed out, it is not. First, South Africa is a society in transition and characterized by uneven development. Second, it is a society in which factors of race and nationality are important determinants of social structures and change.

In consequence, there exists a system of domination which differs in at least two important respects from that described in the above analysis. First, the element of 'rule', i.e. direct coercion, is proportionately greater in South Africa than in the Western 'democracies', and the 'crisis' situation Gramsci refers to, in which the state relies on naked coercion, is virtually the 'normal' situation. The absence, for short periods in particular areas, of large outbreaks of visible or reported defiance and suppression should not be confused with 'spontaneous' consent; neither is it quiescence. The operation and administration of apartheid requires a daily police presence and psychological and physical intimidation. Second, the dominant group does not attempt to 'legitimize' its own culture in the way described by Gramsci and others. Nevertheless, this does not mean that the South African ruling classes do not make complex and intensive use of cultural and ideological forms of domination.

Again the position in South Africa has to be viewed historically. Historically, the dominant culture was that of the British capitalist class and of the English-speaking settlers in the country. This was the consequence of Britain's hegemony as the colonial power. During the colonial period the ideology and culture of this group achieved considerable 'legitimation' among blacks. This it was able to do through its control of missionary work, the churches and black education. In this, many educated blacks proved enthusiastic allies. The Afrikaners were subjected to the same cultural domination as the blacks, but launched a fierce nationalist struggle to free themselves from the political and cultural hegemony of the English-speaking whites, in which the development of the Afrikaans language and literature played an important part. The political aspect of this struggle has been touched on.

Social Hegemony in the Early Years of Nationalist Rule

Despite the attainment of decisive political hegemony in 1948, when the Nationalist Party under Dr Malan came to power, the Afrikaner nationalists were still battling in 1958 to reduce the cultural and ideological influence of the English-speaking section, which as the section of capital, both national and international, classically commanded 'the prestige . . . which the dominant group enjoys because of its position and function in the world of production' and by virtue of its historic cultural and political position. In addition, the English-speaking whites had the advantage of possessing a basic ideology and culture which enjoyed virtual hegemony not only in South Africa but in the capitalist world as a whole.

Not only were the Afrikaner nationalists still battling to reduce the influence of the English-speaking section in the white group as a whole. They were simultaneously attempting to neutralize that section's influence among blacks. They did this not so much by attempting to legitimize their own ideology and culture, but by attempting to impose on them fossilized and adapted versions of African traditional ideology and culture.

As they did not possess full hegemony in the society, and as cultural relations were, as a result of their political policies, undemocratic and racialist, there was little chance of their eliciting 'spontaneous' consent from the majority of blacks. They therefore stiffened the operation of 'hegemony' with the direct coercion of 'rule'.

Thus the cultural action of the Afrikaner nationalists was directed in three ways. The first was towards the indoctrination of its own youth and working class in a culture of nationalist racialism with a Calvinist base, derived originally from the relations in a slave society and forged in the struggle against British imperialism. The second was the indoctrination of the English-speaking whites — and to a much lesser extent blacks — in the same ideology and culture. The third was the projection of 'Bantu' culture and education, derived from the traditional forms operating in the Bantustans and based on the labour requirements of white industry.

The English-speaking whites, who in the 1950s dominated certain fractions of capital, found themselves in a particularly complex situation. Certain fractions of capital, such as mining, required cheap unskilled labour. The government's separate-development policies provided efficient structures for supplying that, but did not deal adequately with the need, especially of the growing manufacturing industry, for a stable but cheap skilled and semi-skilled labour force and for local mass markets. Apartheid as a system created in the cities a restless, politically volatile labour force with no stake in the system. Therefore the government's policies, cultural and political, though acceptable in the rural areas, were quite unrealistic in the urban industrial areas. In these areas capital favoured quite different policies. Later, too, apartheid was an obstruction in capital's need to expand its operations and find markets among South Africa's newly independent neighbours.

In the urban areas capital favoured the rapid abandonment of pre-modern African social forms in favour of those of capitalist industrial societies. This meant the development of a considerable 'Westernized' black intermediate and working class, and the legitimation of its own culture among these classes without permitting full integration into its social and political structures or — on a non-racial basis — into the economic structures. In effect, therefore, it favoured the normal operation of hegemony, as it operated in other capitalist societies, and hoped in this way to win the 'spontaneous' consent of the dominated groups and classes rather than relying on retrogressive cultural policies and direct coercion along racial/national lines, like those favoured by the Afrikaner nationalists. The ideology, therefore, of English-speaking capital, as it applied to urban blacks, was in the main a form of paternalistic, non-democratic, liberal multi-racialism. It attempted to 'legitimize' its culture among urban blacks in general.

Thus cultural domination, as exercised over blacks by the Afrikaner nationalists, was effected to a large extent by what Gramsci has called 'rule'. As exercised by English-speaking whites, it was effected to a greater extent by 'hegemony'. Their *apparent* opposition to the policies of the former facilitated the operation of their cultural 'hegemony' among blacks. For example, as we shall see, English was widely adopted by blacks as a lingua franca in preference to Afrikaans, which was regarded as 'the language of oppression'.

In the 1950s the ability of the Afrikaner nationalist state to impose its cultural policies on the black groups was still relatively restricted, though it already controlled school education as a result of the Bantu Education Act of 1953. The ethnic universities for the black groups had not yet been established, and black students attended the English-speaking white universities and the adult and further education 'night-schools' established by them. Radio Bantu had not yet been established. The United Party controlled the city and town councils in much of the country, and thus the state did not have complete control over such matters as housing, recreation, entertainment, etc. in the black urban areas.

The English-speaking group, on the other hand, exercised a subtle and complex form of domination, especially in the area of culture, through their special relations with the black intermediate classes. Though they had lost political power at the national level, they still wielded considerable influence in local government, industry, university education, advertising, sponsorship and the press. For instance, their control of the Johannesburg City Council's Non-European Affairs Department gave them jurisdiction over the rapidly expanding Soweto. Municipal house-building operations in the black areas under their jurisdiction — not favoured by the government — were largely financed by loans from the mining houses, in particular Anglo-American Corporation. Through the city council, English-speaking capital was able to influence sport, recreation, entertainment and art in the black urban areas. The Bantu Men's Social Centre in Johannesburg, for 20 years an extremely important centre of black cultural activity and resources, including an influential library, film shows, concerts and dramatic activities, had been funded by the mining companies and fell under the jurisdiction of the council. The English-speaking capitalist institutions also owned the newspapers read by blacks. The most influential 'black' magazine of the time, *Drum*, and the popular newspaper, *Post*, were owned by Jim Bailey, the son of the mining magnate, Sir Abe Bailey. Other newspapers for blacks were bought up by the Argus Group of newspapers, itself owned by a consortium of mine-owners. Of crucial interest to us is the financial aid extended by the mining companies to multi-racial theatre ventures, the Union of Southern African Artists in Johannesburg in particular.

So far we have been describing the complex rivalry of separate interests which marked the relations of the two main white groups. We must, however, stress that this rivalry took place within the overarching framework of their *joint* domination of the black groups. In the cultural sphere this domination was facilitated by the fact that, despite considerable variations, the dominant white groups shared a common cultural tradition, i.e. European, while the dominated black groups had others, i.e. African, Asian, etc. The exploitation of the labour of blacks by whites and the retention of the monopoly of political power were facilitated by their shared 'European' or 'Western' culture — what Steve Biko called Anglo-Boer culture. This culture was the common cultural weapon in the defence of the common political and economic interests of the white groups and in the domination of the black groups.

Crucial in the operation of cultural hegemony is the role of the intellectual.

Gramsci has provided a particularly useful assessment of the function of
intellectuals in the advanced industrial countries of the West (1971, pp.5–23).
He suggests that intellectuals can be divided into two categories – the
'traditional' and the 'organic' intellectuals. The traditional intellectuals, i.e.
the artists and scholars, 'those we normally think of as intellectuals',

> consider themselves an autonomous group, independent of the ruling
> class. They are tied to the Establishment indirectly and in ways
> sufficiently subtle to permit them to maintain illusions. If this
> indirection fosters illusions, it also creates room for independent
> thought and action.

Their true duty, according to Gramsci, is to use this independence to join the
revolutionary class, i.e. to become organic intellectuals. Those who do not,
but continue to work in the interests of the established order, do not do so
by coercion and direct methods. Rather, 'their task is to reason with the
masses, to persuade, to convince; they are the essential element in the
hegemony of the ruling class'.

The 'organic' intellectuals are those who expressly and specifically perform
the intellectual or 'intelligent' tasks that the furthering of their class interest
demands. If they belong to the dominant class, they are the technicians,
industrial managers, administrative personnel, economic advisers, members
of official 'think tanks', etc. If they belong to a dominated class, they serve
'as constructor, organiser, "permanent persuader"' in the political party of
their class. They have a crucial role to play in the establishment of the
hegemony of their class and the evolution of its theory.

In the 1950s in South Africa, though there was legislation and considerable
social pressure directed towards dividing the society into racial/national
groups, it was still possible for black and white intellectuals to operate across
racial/national divisions. The intellectuals of the Afrikaner nationalist group
tended to isolate themselves in accordance with their ideology from contact
with black intellectuals. The Afrikaner intellectual also, as can be expected,
tended to be 'organic' and fulfil the function Gramsci identified as that of
the organic intellectuals, i.e. as 'the officers' of the ruling class for the exercise
of the subordinate functions of social hegemony and political government.
They provided the legislators and administrators and increasingly the civil
servants, magistrates, police and officers of the armed forces. Among the
traditional intellectuals of this group there were 'dissidents' – just as there
were among the traditional intellectuals of the English-speaking group.

One of the functions of the organic English-speaking intellectuals was
that they administered the structures of their group's hegemony among
blacks, for example the English-speaking universities, the Non-European
Affairs Departments, the Bantu Men's Social Centre, the bureaucracy in the
black urban areas, commercial advertising, personnel and sponsorship sections
of industry and commerce, the English-speaking newspapers for both whites
and blacks, etc.

The structural position of these intellectuals is relatively easy to determine. They operated the structures established and supported by the capitalists of their group. The structural position of the traditional intellectuals of the group, roughly those commonly referred to as the 'white liberals', can best be described by Gramsci's explanation of the relation of traditional intellectuals to the establishment:

> The whole of the idealist philosophy can easily be connected with this position assumed by the social complex of intellectuals and can be defined as that social utopia by which intellectuals think of themselves as 'independent', autonomous, endowed with a character of their own, etc. [1971, pp.7–8]

He goes on to point out that liberal-idealist intellectuals are 'closely linked' to the class structure of society and 'are as much bound to the industrialists — the ruling class of the liberal society of their day of whose liberalism they are the spokesmen — as the Catholic priesthood was to the feudal aristocracy'.

Because the liberal intellectuals have a certain *apparent* independence, they appear to be more dissident in the context of the dominant ideologies and cultures of the society than other whites. They likewise enjoyed a traditionally close relationship with the black intellectuals and intermediate classes. Their activities were particularly influential in the sphere of black art, theatre and literature. Many of them worked closely with black writers and artists, often on the basis of personal friendship. It is they, for the most part, who attended performances of black or multi-racial theatre in town. It was they too whose criticism in press and publishing was decisive. They edited literary and poetry magazines to which black writers contributed.

How the white liberal intellectuals used their influence, and in whose interests, is for us to investigate, and this will be attempted in other parts of this study. However, perhaps it is worthwhile noting at this stage that it was precisely against them that the Black Consciousness movement of the 1970s directed its major criticism.

Social Hegemony Post-Sharpeville

The years 1958–66 were a major watershed in South African history. The rise of black African nationalism threatened white rule at a time when the Afrikaner nationalists were still in the process of consolidating their own hegemony in the white group as a whole. The outcome was the temporary defeat of the political challenge of black African nationalism and a decisive increase in Afrikaner hegemony in society as a whole.

Years of protest and defiance by legal and predominantly peaceful political organizations culminated in the shootings at Sharpeville and the banning of the African National Congress and the Pan Africanist Congress in

April 1960. For a short period both organizations attempted to conduct an underground armed struggle. Their efforts were neutralized by the state security forces. There followed a long period of severe repression in which the increased power of the state was utilized by the Afrikaner nationalists, not only to make more effective the apparatus of political repression vis-à-vis the black groups, but also to increase their power relative to that of the English-speaking group.

The crisis had consequences of the utmost significance for the future of the country. For a moment it actually appeared, especially from a distance, that the apartheid structure might be about to crumble and be replaced by a more democratic one in which the African nationalists would have hegemony. It was not only a crisis of political confidence for the ruling white groups. It was also a serious crisis of economic confidence. For the first time, foreign investors were forced to contemplate the fact that the golden era of profitable investment in the South African economy might not after all be everlasting. By May 1961, foreign-exchange reserves were as low as R153 million, and the monthly capital outflow in 1960 and the first half of 1961 was R12 million. In the same period, after a customary growth rate of 4.5% a year, there was no growth at all. It became almost impossible to attract foreign investment, on which the economy depended, and Harry Oppenheimer, the chairman of Anglo-American Corporation, was compelled to negotiate a $30 million loan from American banks.[12]

However, the South African state demonstrated both the will and the ability to crush its opponents and the restoration of 'law and order' and stability saw the economy recover, the investors return and the next ten years become an era of unprecedented prosperity. Between 1960 and 1970 the GNP growth rate was a real 5.9% and per capita incomes rose at about 2.9% a year. By the late 1960s South Africa was the 15th biggest trading nation in the world and her white population was more affluent, person for person, than the Californians.

Both the near collapse of the economy after Sharpeville and the boom that followed proved to be immensely advantageous to the Afrikaner nationalists. After their victory in the 1948 election they had systematically attempted to increase their financial muscle. The *arme blankedom* (poor whites) had been eradicated as a social group, having been largely absorbed into state employment. A new class of Afrikaner businessmen came into being. Above all, this period saw the growth of powerful Afrikaans financial institutions which, when stocks plummeted in the wake of Sharpeville, expressed greater confidence in the hegemony of their group than the English-speaking and foreign capitalists by investing heavily. This led to an immense increase in their power when the market later recovered.

Just as private Afrikaner capitalists benefited from the boom, so of course did the state itself. In the decade 1961–71 the government was able to use the great increase in state income, and the absence of any genuine organized opposition, in a number of strategic ways. For instance, the nationalized and parastatal sector of the economy was vastly expanded. In addition the government was able to press ahead ruthlessly with the application of its separate-development policies. The Afrikaner nationalists were thus able to strengthen their position still further vis-à-vis both the English-speaking and the black groups.

It was during this period that the primitive policy of segregation was developed into the more sophisticated sophistry of separate development. The transition from apartheid to separate development has been well described by Harold Wolpe. He writes:

> The emergence after 1959 of separate development as the mode of maintaining cheap labour in the Reserves (complementing that in the urban areas) . . . takes as given the changes in the African 'tribal' economies and erects, under the overarching power of the capitalist state, an institutionalized system of partial political control by Africans. That is to say, the practice and policy of Separate Development must be seen as the attempt to retain, in a modified form, the structure of the 'traditional' societies, not, as in the past, for the purposes of ensuring an economic supplement to the wages of the migrant labour force, but for the purposes of reproducing and exercising control over a cheap African industrial labour force in or near the 'homelands', not by means of preserving the pre-capitalist mode of production but by the political, social, economic and ideological enforcement of low levels of subsistence. [Wolpe, 1972, p.450]

Apartheid was ostensibly a system in which the races were separated wherever they might be *within one country*, which was to be ruled in its entirety by one of those races. Separate development envisaged the separation of the black African group and the white groups into allotted portions of the country, where the white groups and each ethnic section of the black African group would govern themselves as independent nations. Accompanying this change in political direction was a pronounced ideological change.

> Whereas in all its essentials Nationalist Party ideology had previously insisted upon the biological inferiority of Africans as the justification for its racialist policies, as the Government was impelled towards the Bantustan policy so it began to abandon certain of its previous ideological positions. Now the stress fell upon ethnic *differences* and the central notion became 'different but equal'.

As Wolpe further points out, this change in ideology was necessary because 'a policy of ethnic political independence (for each of the eight ethnic groups identified) was incompatible with an ideology of racial inferiority' (Wolpe, 1972, pp.450-1).

The new ideology of separate development meant a perceptible increase in the cultural hegemony of the Afrikaner Nationalists at the expense of the English-speaking whites, who to a large extent depended on multi-racial activity. Separate development tended to restrict access to the black African group. In education, for instance, the Extension of University Education Act of 1959 effectively removed black students from the English-speaking white universities and placed them instead in newly established ethnic colleges in the Bantustans. The ideological reason for this was quite openly admitted. It was necessary, the government explained, to prevent undesirable ideological developments such as had disturbed the non-white institutions not directly under the charge of the government. At ethnic colleges, sited in distant rural areas, a rigid control of student thought and expression could be maintained by the intellectuals of the Afrikaner nationalist group who administered them and formed the majority of the lecturers.

Black adult education had long been an area in which the English-speaking intellectuals had been active. Legislation between 1955 and 1962 brought all adult education activity under government control and night schools in white areas were closed down. In schools ethnic divisions were enforced and mother-tongue education in all subjects was increased. A radio service had been begun for black African listeners in 1952. By 1959 there were 12,450 subscribers. At the end of 1963 this figure had increased to over a million. All radio programmes were tightly controlled and supervised by white 'advisers' and conformed to the ideological emphases of Afrikaner nationalism. An important function of the radio service was the provision of a vernacular school programme with which it was intended to provide information and education to 250,000 schoolchildren.

This period saw important changes and restrictions in the field of entertainment, which seriously affected and eventually transformed theatre activity. This will be described fully later. Not only theatre activity was affected. Films came to be rigidly censored and, though sometimes allowed for white viewing, they were banned for blacks. Instances of the banning of films for black viewing alone were *West Side Story, Cleopatra* and *Spartacus*.

All these steps weakened English-speaking white influence among blacks, but by no means neutralized it. They still owned and controlled the press and virtually all the popular 'black' newspapers and magazines e.g. *Drum, Post, The World*. Attempts by the Afrikaner establishment to counteract this through the publication of the magazine *Bona*, published in 'Bantu' languages and distributed free in Bantu-education schools, were not entirely successful. The English-speaking whites, because of United Party majorities in key city and town councils, retained their control of important aspects of local government in black areas and were in a position to obstruct, sometimes actually counteract, government policy. In terms of culture this gave them control of censorship, municipal halls (where plays were performed) and the granting of permits to whites who wished to enter the black areas — to promote or perform plays, for instance.

Social Hegemony in the Period Leading up to June 1976

1966–76 was a decade in which the implementation of the Afrikaner nationalists' policy of separate development was at first assisted by a period of exceptional economic growth and political stability, and then put under increasing pressure by a worsening economic crisis, unprecedented political change in the Southern African region and growing dissent and defiance on the part of certain sections of the black groups.

The economic boom that followed the 1960 Sharpeville crisis continued into the early 1970s. As already stated, the growth of the South African economy depended on foreign investment. Once the political crisis was over, this was forthcoming on a gigantic scale. However, in December 1971 the rand was devalued. The reasons for this were that South Africa's trade deficit had widened alarmingly and its GDP growth rate, which had been 6.2% a year in the period 1963–71, slowed to 4% in 1971–73. By 1976 GDP was actually declining. This was an extremely serious matter for, as R. W. Johnson reminds us, 'For South Africa a rapid growth rate was not a luxury; it was essential to political and social stability' (Johnson, p.84).

South Africa in the 1970s was one of the top twenty trading nations in the world and, despite the high price of gold, it could not remain immune from world inflation. Through the 1960s inflation in South Africa had run at an average 3.3% a year. In the 1970s inflation increased dramatically. If 1970 is taken as 100, the consumer price index was up to 141.5 by August 1974. Food prices had spiralled even higher; they stood at 156.4. In other words, from 1971 onwards prices rose sharply, and as the economy slowed down, so unemployment increased. This, too, was extremely serious. As John Vorster, the Prime Minister, had said in 1971: 'Unemployment is a greater danger to South Africa than terrorism.'

The internal crisis obviously affected South Africa's external policies. Manufacturing industry was the economy's fastest growing sector. For its growth to be sustained South Africa would have to achieve new markets. It turned to Africa and initiated a détente policy with black African states north of the Zambezi. The details of this policy do not concern us here. The results, though, in terms of internal (largely cosmetic) change, do. Selected hotels and restaurants were declared 'international' and race restrictions were relaxed in them. The official attitude, so firmly adopted after the Dusty Springfield affair in 1965, towards overseas artists and black and multi-racial audiences began to soften. Permits for black audiences, even multi-racial ones, at 'white' venues in Johannesburg began to be granted. In 1975 the Nico Malan theatre in Cape Town was gradually (and grudgingly) declared open to all races, with certain restrictions still being retained on black performers performing there. In Johannesburg the Civic Theatre, whose segregationalist policy had been attacked by Athol Fugard in 1963, opened its doors for the first time to all races for a performance of 'an indigenous biblical opera'.

In other centres, representations were made and concessions granted permitting black attendance. In June 1975 the government was forced to state its policy on such matters. It declared:

> It remained Government policy . . . that the different racial groups should have their own facilities in their own residential areas. But in cases when no equivalent facilities existed for Blacks, permits allowing them to attend theatrical performances in venues for Whites would be considered if the owners or controllers of the premises were agreeable.

These relaxations of the restrictions in white areas were not matched by a similar flexibility in black areas. On the contrary, the apparatus for even tighter control was constantly being developed and operated. In 1971 an important change was made in the machinery of Bantu administration. Until then the administration of black urban areas in South Africa had been the responsibility of the town or city council. In many cases – in Johannesburg, Durban, Cape Town, for instance – these councils were controlled by the official opposition. This position was clearly unacceptable to the government, and legislation was enacted to transfer control of these areas to specially constituted Bantu Boards, which administered government policy strictly and far more rigidly and uncompromisingly than previously.

For instance, it was government policy not to encourage settled family residence in 'white' areas. The emphasis was to be placed on the accommodation of migrant and single workers in hostels. The building of family housing in established areas such as Soweto virtually ceased. Instead hostel accommodation was expanded, particularly in Alexandra Township, Johannesburg, where the government erected two enormous hostels for 'single' men and women and committed itself to an energetic programme of evicting and moving the remaining inhabitants of the township either to the Bantustans or to other urban areas. Thus migrant labourers began to represent an increasing proportion of the urban township population, while the virtual abandonment of construction for the increasing family population added worsening crowding and accommodation problems to those of inflation and unemployment.

Other external events had even more profound repercussions on the internal situation than South Africa's détente manoeuvres. In April 1974 there was a coup in Lisbon and in a matter of months the Portuguese empire in Africa collapsed. There was a Marxist government in Mozambique and another was soon to take power in Angola. South Africa prudently pursued a policy of non-interference in the affairs of the former country, but intemperately involved itself in a disastrous intervention in the latter. The combined effect of non-racial revolutionary governments in Mozambique and Angola and the undignified retreat of the South African expeditionary force from Angola was a potent psychological factor in an already volatile situation.

These are the bare facts concerning a number of important events and developments which made the period up to June 1976 one of the most crucial in the history of the country. Behind these events and developments, the relations of the major sections of the white and black groups were clearly in the process of changing and this resulted in important developments in the struggle for social hegemony.

For instance, this period saw a gradual rapprochement between the power structures of Afrikaner nationalism and capital. Two factors were responsible for this. The country's economy, contrary to the government's intentions, came to depend increasingly on gold production. The Afrikaner nationalists had developed their own powerful capitalist interests in both the private sector and the state and parastatal sectors. There was thus bound to be a coalition of interest between the old foes. It was no coincidence that the major opposition parties, representing English-speaking capital, abandoned old commitments to a unified South Africa and began to experiment with and espouse federalist solutions. On the other hand, Afrikaner nationalists found themselves favouring certain measures which had long been advocated by the representatives of English-speaking capital (such as Harry Oppenheimer), even when they conflicted with stated government policy. The most obvious example of this was the rapid, but unofficial, breakdown of job reservation in industry and later in the mines.

Capital needs markets. This prompted the détente policies of the early 1970s and a significant relaxation (once again largely unofficial) of petty apartheid. The relaxation of restrictions concerning visits by black entertainers and the attendance of blacks at 'white' venues served two useful purposes. It was good for South Africa's image abroad and in Africa, but at the same time it was what white commercial managements had been clamouring for for years.

As capitalist big businessmen of the Afrikaner and English-speaking white groups came together, so did the smaller men and the workers of these two groups. The basis for their rapprochement was, however, quite different. They were alarmed at the increasing dependence on black labour and the removal of restrictions against its employment in semi-skilled and skilled categories. Afrikaners and English-speakers alike vigorously opposed these tendencies.

Thus a government formed on racial/national lines began to reveal growing contradictions. These contradictions were largely confined, both in the Nationalist Party and between it and the English-speaking opposition, to matters concerning the black group in 'white' areas. On the basic principles of Bantustan policy there was greater agreement. Capital clearly favoured the integration of a stable, semi-skilled and skilled urban workforce into a paternalistic capitalist state in 'white' South Africa, but was happy to leave the generation of cheap labour power in the hands of the ruling hierarchies of balkanized 'independent' black states nearby. White labour opposed the integration of the black proletariat in the 'white' state.

The result of these changes was an ideological situation of some confusion. In certain areas it seemed as if the ideology of Afrikaner nationalism – i.e. separate development and Christian national culture and education – was to continue its all-conquering progress, despite the rapprochement of Afrikaner and English capital. The direct pressure of Afrikaner nationalist ideology was felt by both the English-speaking whites and blacks as a whole. For instance, South African television became a potent instrument of aggression against traditional English-speaking values and political attitudes. In education, too, the teaching of English-speaking children at school in all subjects, including English itself, was increasingly dominated by Afrikaans-speakers.

The tendency (already described in our account of the post-Sharpeville years) for the ideological and cultural hegemony of the Afrikaner nationalists over the black group to increase, as that of the English-speaking whites decreased, continued at an accelerated rate. This was especially the case in black education, where Afrikaans and the vernacular languages were constantly promoted at the expense of English. Strenuous efforts were made to restrict the exposure of blacks to English-speaking culture from whatever source — films, radio, books and cultural activities in 'white' areas. The new Bantu Boards of course greatly facilitated this. For instance, one of the functions they took over from the town and city councils was the granting of permits to whites who wished to enter black areas. In this way the boards could decide which white individuals and organizations would be allowed to take part in cultural and educational activities with blacks in black areas.

Increasingly the homeland (i.e. the Bantustan), with its ethnic culture and local traditional loyalties, was projected to blacks as their spiritual and cultural home rather than the urban black areas or the English-speaking dominated towns. The ethnic Radio Bantu, the organization of 'townships' and schools on ethnic lines, ethnic universities — all were intended to assist in this process. In the black urban areas the ideology of separate development continued to be imposed with vigour.

Simultaneously, the Afrikaner nationalist establishment waged an intensified war against the workings and influence of English-speaking culture. It had removed from the control of the English-speaking whites the administration of culture in the black urban areas, and had restricted liberal activities of a multi-racial nature in towns. It then began to take action to inhibit, and if possible destroy, certain key instruments of English-speaking ideological and cultural influence. In February 1972 parliamentary commissions of inquiry were set up to enquire into the activities of the University Christian Movement, the National Union of South African Students, the Institute of Race Relations and the Christian Institute and, following the completion of their report, steps were taken to put an end to or restrict their activities. In three major areas, however, the government was not able seriously to diminish the cultural control exercised by the English-speaking group in the society in general and in the black African group in particular — namely, commercial advertising, the press, and art and entertainment in white areas.

The ideology of advertising directed at black urban consumers was dictated by the realities of the market and flatly opposed some aspects of the official cultural policies of separate development. Advertisements that operated within the parameters of 'Bantu culture' simply antagonized the black urban consumer. Many firms had already begun employing black copywriters whose experience of black urban culture enabled them to appeal more accurately to the aspirations and status values of urban blacks.

Because of the economic weakness of the black African group, most aspects of recreation and entertainment in the black areas depended on sponsorship provided by white firms. Boxing and soccer, among sports, were particularly well supported by both Afrikaner-dominated and English-speaking firms, especially tobacco companies and breweries. Furniture and clothing retailers, cosmetics firms and beverage manufacturers (e.g. Teaspoon Tips tea and Coca-Cola) not only sponsored ballroom competitions, beauty contests, concerts and theatre but also organized their own public events — music competitions and fashion shows, for example. In the early 1970s the Soweto Show was started as an annual event, and a wide variety of white firms exhibited there.

The press was still owned, directly or indirectly, by the mining companies. This was an area which saw considerable expansion in the 1970s. All the English-speaking newspapers greatly increased their black African readership and to facilitate the process took on to their staff an increasing number of black African journalists. The *Rand Daily Mail* and the *Sunday Times* introduced special black editions. *Drum* re-emerged and *The World* expanded. The East London *Daily Despatch*, under the editorship of Donald Woods,[13] began as a white paper but developed a majority readership of blacks. All these papers included substantial coverage of theatre and entertainment, both black and white. White theatre critics especially exercised an important influence on black African theatre, especially 'town theatre' (see below, p.54). The Afrikaner nationalists made strenuous efforts to reduce the monopoly the English-speaking press exercised in this field, even to the extent of clandestinely attempting to buy up English papers and establishing with state money an English-speaking daily, *The Citizen*. The Afrikaans papers began to include coverage of black news and hired black journalists to provide it, but without much acceptance from the black readership.

The white arts and entertainment industry was virtually the monopoly of the English-speaking section, both in the importation of foreign 'hit' plays or 'stars' and in the local commercial sector. Professional theatre in Afrikaans did not thrive, although indigenous original material was being written and performed. Commercial theatre in English, though it relied almost exclusively on the importation of British and American comedies, musicals and thrillers, was relatively successful. Managements were, however, anxious to integrate their theatres in order to facilitate their access to overseas material and to attract a larger audience. They had already, in some instances, taken advantage of government relaxation of controls concerning performances by black casts to white audiences and produced a number of black 'tribal musicals', such as *Ipi Tombi*, *Kwa Zulu* and *uMabatha*, which were commercially extremely successful.

There were distinct signs that the government was preparing to move in their direction. The rapprochement of English and Afrikaans capital meant that the official policy of cultural segregation in accordance with separate development was being challenged by a tendency towards forms of integration and, in terms of culture, by a process of 'legitimation'. The black intermediate classes were being invited increasingly to participate in the general European culture of capitalism. Concerts, music, ballet and other white cultural activities were being opened to blacks, sometimes even to multi-racial audiences.[14]

In other words, the contradictions within the ruling Afrikaner nationalist section, especially where reinforced by a strong English-speaking capitalist presence, as in Johannesburg or Cape Town, translated themselves into the emergence of an alternative strategy for the operation of hegemony, opposed, in some areas, to the official one of separate development. This alternative strategy was that favoured by Oppenheimer and similar to that described by Gramsci. Its political and economic corollary was the establishment of a modified form of European-type capitalist 'democracy'. It is only when one is fully aware of the impact of both cultural strategies, i.e. that of Afrikaner nationalism and that of the capitalist establishment, that one can begin to understand the complex cultural developments that characterized the pre-1976 and continue to characterize the post-1976 periods.

3. Alternative Hegemony in the Making

So far we have been describing the rivalry of the two main white groups, the English and the Afrikaner nationalists, to establish dominance in South African society. As has been pointed out, the relations between these two groups expressed themselves as, at one and the same time, a partnership in dominance over blacks and, within this overarching joint domination, a struggle for overall hegemony within the society as a whole. Set against this is the struggle of the oppressed groups in the society to adjust to, or resist, the overall dominance of the white groups and in the process develop the basis for an alternative hegemony in a future society in which they will no longer be oppressed. It is this struggle to which we now turn, not expressly in its political form but in its social and cultural form.

By the 1950s the various peoples who were the original occupiers of the land had, through a process of military defeat and political and economic dispossession, become a vast reservoir of cheap labour for South African capitalism. Historically, this process brought into play forces which tended to dissolve the ethnic barriers, and instead lead to a consciousness of being, not separate peoples, but one black African nation with a common history of dispossession and a common cultural heritage. It experienced a common political oppression as both a race and a national group. However, the process at the same time brought forces into play which developed and accelerated class formation. By the 1950s there existed a developing and dynamic black proletariat, underdeveloped but growing intermediate classes, a rural proletariat and a malformed and enfeebled subsistence section. Thus though the entire group was politically, socially and economically disadvantaged, its economic disadvantages were experienced differentially according to the relation of individuals to production, i.e. according to their position in the class structure.[15]

This conjuncture of race, nationality and class expressed itself in the 1950s in still rapidly developing and complex cultural characteristics. Before the conquest, the black peoples of South Africa were socially and culturally closely related. Their traditional cultures were basically similar, though they spoke different (though closely related) languages and different historical circumstances had produced variant social and cultural forms.

The conquest itself retarded the constitutive processes of these peoples' culture and introduced a struggle between constitutive and imposed processes. The common cultural traditions which black Africans owned as a racial/ national group were being rapidly transformed within the dialectic of constitutive and imposed processes. In addition, the proletarianization and urbanization of the group was producing two basic consequences: first, the traditional culture was being transformed and, second, the economic forces were tending to introduce new heterogeneous elements into the process of social change.

Thus it was possible to say that the group possessed a common historical culture in which there were inherent and developing heterogeneous elements. African nationalist movements tended to stress the homogeneous elements. The dominant white groups conversely tended to stress the heterogeneous elements, e.g. ethnic divisions, 'tribalism' and vernacular languages. Only the Communist Party was in a position to take due cognizance of both class and nationality, and while pressing for a socialist South Africa, at the same time evolve the historic concept of the Black Republic.

The culture of rural blacks varied considerably, from the miserable acculturated lot of workers on white farms to the vestigial traditional subsistence survival of those working on their own land. The question of culture in the rural areas of South Africa has been greatly complicated by the policy of forcibly removing blacks and dumping them into rural reservoirs of unemployment and starvation, and by the efforts of the government to revive an ossified but convenient distortion of traditional society in the framework of its Bantustan policies. The whole question requires a separate study. We shall be concentrating on the urban experience, as it is largely in the urban areas that theatre and other art forms have been used as instruments of cultural struggle.

In important senses all classes of urban blacks occupy and activate one culture. This sense of cultural unity — particularly evident in the plays of Gibson Kente — is reinforced by the shared racial/national aspects of their social existence and, in so far as government policy has been based on racial/ national considerations, this policy has contributed to inhibiting the process of social differentiation.

On the other hand, the massive expansion of the South African economy in the 1960s, and equally its crisis in the 1970s, led to a process of rapid class formation and the development of class consciousness among the black urban proletariat. This has taken place despite the influences to the contrary touched on in the previous paragraph.

In addition, government policy, though in some respects inhibiting class formation, was particularly directed at weakening the black intermediate classes and at reducing the influence of English-speaking liberal culture in these classes. In the process, this led indirectly to a corresponding strengthening of the working class vis-à-vis its intermediate classes, and to the creation of black intellectuals relatively independent of both white groups.

This meant that it became increasingly possible to note cultural or ideological characteristics which differentiated the black intermediate classes from their proletariat, and the older generation of black intellectual from the new.

Factors Inhibiting the Development of Class-Based Cultural Differentiation

Education
Before the introduction of Bantu education in 1953, black education was largely in the hands of the 'European' churches, who dispensed to a minority a liberal Christian education in the medium of English. This resulted in an ideology which was élitist and individualistic and a culture which was based on that of the white English-speaking intermediate classes in South Africa and elsewhere. It was characterized by belittlement, or at best patronization, of the historical culture, religion, music, art and languages of black Africans. It tended to regard the culture of the urban proletariat — to the extent that it was regarded at all — with similar feelings. For instance, Peter Rezant, a popular band-leader of the intermediate classes in the 1930s, said of the urban working-class *marabi* music: 'the upper-class, the non-white, didn't want to associate with the type of music this band was playing . . . They thought that it was music of no significance.'

Those educated before 1953 received one form of education, directed apparently towards their assimilation into 'civilized society'. Those educated after 1953 received quite another, specifically directed towards their exclusion:

> My department's policy is that education should stand with both feet in the Reserves and have it roots in the spirit and being of Bantu society . . . there is no place for him [the Bantu] in the European community above the level of certain forms of labour.
> Dr Hendrik Verwoerd, then Minister of Bantu Education [Roux, p.394]

However, if the Bantu Education Act meant the introduction of an educational system designed to inculcate servility, it also made education available to thousands whom the previous system had excluded. In effect, education, albeit of an inferior brand, became available not only to the children of the intermediate classes but to those of the working class and peasants. An élite education of a minority for assimilation was replaced by a broad, inferior education for the majority directed at unskilled labour categories. Bantu education thus acted as a social leveller and struck a blow against the increasing prestige and leadership of the educated élite within the black African group.

Group Areas
The abolition of freehold rights and the group-areas policy has until recently inhibited residential segregation along class lines. The Sophiatown removals

in the 1950s are an example with implications similar to those relating to the introduction of Bantu education. In Sophiatown the intermediate classes owned property and rented it out to tenants. When these rights were abolished and the people of Sophiatown were removed to government townships, the effects were felt differently by owners and tenants. For the owners their loss was great. For the tenants the removal often meant an individual house instead of a room in a crowded yard, and a much smaller rent payable to the government rather than to a private landlord. The effect of the removal and the abolition of ownership and renting rights was clearly another socially levelling phenomenon, having similarly weakening effects on the black intermediate classes' position in the black community.

Not only were the latter forced now to pay rent to the government or the city council along with the rest, but they had only very restricted ability to determine which house would be allotted them. There was very little difference between the houses they could rent and, with the exception of one or two areas such as Dube in Soweto, the intermediate classes had little possibility of separating themselves residentially from other classes. Plots were small and the possibility of extension restricted.

Restrictions on Economic Advancement
The government's emphasis on unskilled labour opportunities and restrictions against employment of blacks in a wide range of better-paid jobs meant that educational advantages did not translate themselves into better salaries, and earning differentials among blacks remained comparatively small.

Outside government employment or employment in the private (white) sector, opportunities of advancement were limited. Trading and business was a case in point. Although there was an expansion in these activities among blacks, government policy placed severe restrictions on them unless they were conducted in the 'homelands'. In a circular letter to local authorities the department concerned informed them that trading by blacks in areas outside the 'homelands' was not 'an inherent primary opportunity' for them. In such areas only stores providing the basic daily necessities were to be allowed. Local authorities were to be sparing in the granting of licences and in giving permission to build or expand. They were to discourage larger undertakings such as dry cleaners and garages.

These restrictions on the commercial intermediate classes applied in different ways to all sections of these classes and were another factor inhibiting class formation and differentiation.

Factors Making for Class-Based Cultural Differentiation

Economic Expansion
As a result of the post-Sharpeville economic boom, industry expanded and black wages in all sectors (except mining) rose in real terms. More black

workers were sucked into the industrial and service machine, and the new demands for semi-skilled and in some cases skilled labour began to be met, despite official government policy to the contrary, by the employment of black workers. The economic expansion accelerated the pace of class formation and strengthened the working class.

Economic Crisis

As the economy began to experience crisis in the 1970s, inflation spiralled and unemployment increased. By 1974 the economics departments of three Afrikaans universities warned that black unemployment was rising at about 100,000 a year. As inflation increased, black wages fell further and further behind. In October 1972 'the dam broke and a great wave of strikes began, centred on workers in the manufacturing sector in and around Durban. Soon there were 60,000 on strike' (Johnson, p.85).

The outlook for South Africa's black workers – in 1976 71% of the total – was by no means propitious: rising prices; wage increases (where achieved) eroded by inflation; fewer jobs; growing unemployment; strikes and redundancies. The position in the Bantustans was worse. The pre-capitalist mode of production and subsistence had all but collapsed in many areas and jobs were extremely scarce. Though by 1976 an estimated 60% of all economically active blacks in 'white' areas were male migrants, their wages were appreciably lower than those of urban resident black workers. These resident workers, wretched as their condition was, found themselves mocked by a situation in which it was possible to call them a 'labour aristocracy' – like their privileged 'comrades', the white working class of old.

Whereas expansion had created an ever larger working class, inflation and unemployment precipitated them into a fight with capital, and this struggle began to form a consciousness based not only on the fact that they were black and African, but also on the fact that they were workers exploited by capital.

The Intellectuals

Before Black Consciousness

Earlier black African intellectuals had aided the Christian missionaries in suppressing indigenous culture and religion. In the 1950s they still tended to project the culture of the English-speaking intermediate classes and oppose both the traditional and the syncretic modern cultures of the proletariat. Where the English-speaking group was influential, they collaborated as the purveyors of that group's culture, for example as journalists on English newspapers and magazines or as ministers of religion. Where the Afrikaner nationalist group dominated, they acted as agents of the ideological and cultural purposes of that group, for example as teachers, interpreters, clerks, etc.

Among blacks themselves they used their political, social and intellectual leadership to promote actively the culture and ideology of their own classes. This was in the earlier period in important respects identical to that of the English-speaking white intermediate classes. Clearly this was an indication of the affinity that developed, on the basis of class, with the English-speaking white liberals. However, if we take the ideology of African nationalism and the political action it produced, it is possible sometimes to make the distinction. As an ideology, African nationalism was directed against the hegemony of the entire white group, and was concerned both with removing the barriers to the advancement of the black intermediate classes and with the widespread poverty and exploitation of blacks as a whole.

Many intellectuals and individual members of the intermediate classes refused to act as agents of Afrikaner nationalist hegemony. For instance, in 1953 many teachers resigned their posts rather than teach in Bantu-education schools. The Afrikaner nationalists had themselves successfully established an alternative hegemony to that exercised over them by the British. This they did by a vigorous nationalist political and cultural struggle. The black African group likewise attempted to establish an alternative hegemony by waging a nationalist political struggle but, significantly, without the cultural dimension. In other words they attempted to establish their hegemony by opposing 'rule' alone.

Four factors therefore hampered the efforts of those black intellectuals who rejected their role as agents of white hegemony. First, before the Black Consciousness movement there was little enunciated understanding of the cultural dimension of oppression and the subtle process of 'social hegemony', as opposed to the more direct oppression of 'rule'. Second, following from this, the function of the traditional intellectuals of the English-speaking white group, i.e. the white liberals, had not been widely recognized. They were regarded as allies in the struggle against domination rather than as dominators in their own right.

Third, the intermediate classes were underdeveloped and therefore unable to act effectively on their own. Yet they were unable to involve their proletariat effectively in the nationalist struggle. Few intellectuals existed at this stage who were ready to make the historic identification which Gramsci refers to and throw in their lot with their proletariat. Fourth, economic weakness made alternatives to 'white' employment, and therefore independent action, hard to find.

Black Consciousness
In the late 1960s and early 1970s, i.e. roughly 15 to 18 years after the introduction of Bantu education, a new generation of young students in schools and universities emerged. Bantu education had wrenched them from the intellectual penumbra of the English-speaking white liberals. Legislation had drastically reduced their contact with them in all spheres. At the same time they had been brutally exposed to that brand of servile, second-rate education their Afrikaner nationalist rulers and university lecturers deemed fit for them. They reacted no longer in terms of English liberalism, but in

terms of their alienation from both white groups, i.e. in terms of Black Consciousness.

The Intermediate Classes

The black intermediate classes, though underdeveloped and to a large extent relatively recently formed, exercised considerable influence in the urban areas by virtue of their status as an 'élite' and through the agency of the intellectuals associated with them — journalists, writers, artists, academics. Being, however, underdeveloped and of recent formation, their cultural characteristics revealed much heterogeneity and disparity. Also, because of the weakening of their traditional ties with the English-speaking whites and because of the racial polarization of South African society — the result of the Nationalist government's policies — and in the world in general (with, for instance, the black-power and civil-rights movements in the United States) certain sections of these classes began to identify with black as opposed to white intermediate-class lifestyles and values, namely those of black America.

A prime example of the Soweto élite's cultural orientations was the Inn Club, a select group which met in a private home in Dube, the small section of Soweto where the élite were able to achieve a degree of residential segregation. Members of the Inn Club were professional men, teachers, traders, people involved in banking and commerce, nurses, etc. The Inn Club entertained businessmen, diplomats and politicians from abroad who wished to familiarize themselves with 'Soweto opinion' and 'to meet the black community'.

The business section of the intermediate classes could claim membership of this élite by virtue of their wealth, without in some cases having much formal education. This meant that, whereas the educated intermediate classes eschewed traditional culture, the uneducated but affluent business section often maintained strong links with it. This expressed itself in the speaking of traditional languages and in the development of ties between themselves and the rural hierarchies in the Bantustans and elsewhere. For instance, Ephraim Tshabalala, the Soweto 'tycoon', married his son to one of King Sobhuza of Swaziland's daughters.

Of all the urban areas in South Africa, Soweto was the most prestigious. It was also comparatively privileged. In it was concentrated a high proportion of the black intermediate classes. Wages were higher, business was better. Soweto was like a mini-capital, in comparison with which the other urban townships — near Durban, East London, Port Elizabeth and on the Witwatersrand — were provincial. It was Soweto which established cultural trends and fashions throughout the republic. The urban culture of Sophiatown had in the process of removal to Soweto maintained a degree of continuity within a general atmosphere of change.

The intermediate classes of Soweto and many workers (not including migrant workers) while they still practised certain aspects of the traditional culture, nevertheless affiliated themselves to the cultural idioms and values of urban black America and their own eclectic urban South African culture. According to generation, this meant in terms of music either jazz or soul music.

The black-power movement of the 1960s, black writers like James Baldwin and Eldridge Cleaver, 'soul music' and the visits to South Africa of popular black American singers such as Percy Sledge, Brook Benton and Wilson Pickett, the 'black-is-beautiful' culture, 'Afro' hairstyles, fashions and cosmetics, American films and advertising showing blacks living glamorously, combined to present, especially to the young, an alternative culture to that of the whites which was at the same time sophisticated, affluent and *black*.

In the 1970s many of the youth carried their identification with American soul culture further and adopted the clothing, music and jargon of American anti-Vietnam 'hippy' culture. In Soweto these were called *o-love-and-peace*. A feature of the entertainment of this group was the *akulalwa* (no-sleeping) all-night 'gigs'. The older jazz culture had expressed itself in English or especially American English, and a conventional form of *tsotsitaal*. The new soul culture tended to express itself in American English or a vernacular language, especially Sotho. This is not to say, however, that many did not remain close to the traditional culture and prefer the music and languages of their ethnic group.

The Proletariat

Social change, as Raymond Williams warns, is not determined solely by independent inhuman forces. Human beings have a constitutive capacity to effect and take part in social change. The urban proletariat was not the passive clay out of which the forces of the traditional society and of the urban industrial society moulded a culture. The formation of the urban proletarian culture was the result of the dialectic referred to earlier of constitutive and imposed forces, and involved the energy and adaptive/creative capacity of human beings to affect or even restructure their relationship with their environment, exemplified by the development of new languages, e.g. *tsotsitaal*, new cultural forms such as the *stokvel* and new genres of music and dance such as *umbhaqanga, ngomabusuku* and *marabi*.[16] One of the problems in the analysis of proletarian culture is how to distinguish the authentic, constitutive elements from the imposed ones, i.e. those imposed by economic exploitation, racial discrimination, political oppression, manifestations of cultural domination, etc. Such a distinction is important because it is probably in these authentic constitutive elements that the basis for an alternative democratic hegemony is to be found.

As previously differentiated, the proletariat consists of various grades of workers and is broadly divided into resident, migrant and lumpen sections. In the 1950s the culture of the resident section, being that of classes in the process of formation, was at one and the same time strongly influenced by, and strongly determined to leave behind, the traditional culture. Though the forms of traditional medicine, divination and magic were widely practised and Christian rites celebrated in forms derived directly from the traditional culture, though the backyards of the old residential areas, such as Sophiatown, possessed a social organization closely resembling that of the traditional homestead or village, and though the traditional languages were spoken rather than English, the urban environment and integration into the industrial economy produced cultural forces which impelled this section of the proletariat into new forms, values, practices and structures. As the economy expanded in the 1960s, the influence of the traditional culture decreased markedly, and as the economy went into crisis a class consciousness and a culture based on class increasingly effaced the traditional.

The second section of the proletariat, the migrant labourers, in the same period became more and more decisive, and this meant that their cultural influence in the urban areas increased correspondingly. This manifested itself in an adherence, quite unlike that of the resident section, to traditional cultural forms and the developments these forms had undergone in the urban areas. They spoke traditional languages, and preferred either authentic traditional music and dancing or their developed forms, such as *umbhaqanga* and *ngomabusuku*. Whereas the settled workers were strenuously opposed to ethnic associations or divisions, and unsympathetic to many aspects of the traditional culture, the migrant workers tended to preserve ethnic divisions and adhere to traditional customs. Those, however, who lived in hostels in Soweto showed between 1968 and 1976 a distinct tendency to move from antagonism towards Soweto residents, often on an ethnic basis, towards identification with them and a rejection of ethnic differentiation.[17]

The culture of the lumpen youth, or *tsotsi*, was another influential sub-culture which was shared to some extent with all those of school-going age. This was an eclectic, almost totally non-English, original mode of social behaviour, dress, talking, courting, dancing, etc. which adults of all sections might observe but were essentially excluded from. This exclusiveness expressed itself in the mid-70s in a new language called *isiCamtu*. Unlike *tsotsitaal*, as spoken by older generations, *isiCamtu* contained very little Afrikaans and not much English. It was an almost exclusively vernacular-based slang.

The strength of the black proletariat — resident, migrant and lumpen — revealed itself increasingly in the cultural field, where many previously despised working-class forms were being 'legitimated' — the popular music form, *umbhaqanga*, for instance. The influence of these classes was nowhere more clearly felt than in the area of language. As this is an extremely important factor in the analysis of culture and a central problem in cultural action, especially theatre, it needs to be discussed in a little detail. As Frantz Fanon wrote: 'A man's whole world is expressed and implied by his language.'[18]

Language

The 'official' languages in South Africa are English and Afrikaans. These are the languages in which the fundamental relations between blacks and whites are conducted. There are seven major African languages. The problem for black people in South Africa, stated simply, is that if both English and Afrikaans are rejected as the languages of the conquerors and oppressors, what alternative to ethnic isolationism exists? Blacks could not be expected to master all seven African languages, and any attempt to choose one of the seven would be resented by the speakers of the other six. A lingua franca is required.

Government cultural policy enforces the use of African languages, e.g. in primary schools after 1953 and in the courts. As these languages were found as yet unable to cope with the demands of a modern industrial society, government committees were set up to bring them up to date. Thus not only were the separate African languages imposed on blacks, but the official direction and development of the languages was taken out of the hands of the people who spoke them and artificially 'planned' by white government committees and institutions. The result was that children were taught 'Bantu languages' — ersatz languages — which their own parents could not always understand. The state's overall intention in the context of Afrikaner nationalist domination was stated clearly in a Unesco report published in 1967:

> In South Africa, however, the policy of apartheid has had recourse to the choice of the mother tongue as the main medium of instruction at the primary level (beyond which, it has been shown, the vast majority of African children do not pursue their studies) in order to reinforce the linguistic, social and cultural isolation of the African population within the country as well as from the world at large. [Unesco, p.67]

The particular problems posed for the educated sections of colonized peoples in Africa and elsewhere have been described in detail by a number of writers. Historically in South Africa the lingua franca of educated blacks has been English. The traditional languages have generally been rejected because the language of education (and status) is English; the use of traditional languages is ethnically divisive; it is government policy that black Africans should use them; and English is an international language, a language with a large literature, which enables communication with the educated of other parts of the world. Thus educated blacks speak English.

The proletariat were forced to master the basics of communication with their employers, officials, the police, etc. They therefore possessed at least a rudimentary knowledge of English and/or Afrikaans or, in the mines, Fanagalo. They did not, however, like the educated, converse habitually in English. They conversed in black African languages. In this case, the question arises — how did they solve the problem of the seven major languages?

Of the seven, two — Venda and Shangane (Tsonga) — were spoken by small and relatively unurbanized peoples. In the industrial areas of Natal and the Cape language is no problem, for the workers there speak Zulu and Xhosa respectively. In the Witwatersrand, however, the problem is acute. All major languages are spoken there, but in fact the linguistic situation is a classic example of the dialectic between constitutive and 'imposed' cultural forces. Though African languages are being 're-planned' by the government committees in order to be not only modern but also 'pure' — i.e. in order to strengthen ethnic barriers — they are being developed organically by the urban proletariat in the Witwatersrand in functionally quite a different way. The need and willingness of people of different ethnic groups to communicate with each other is reducing the five basic languages to two, and at the same time developing two alternative linguae francae. A Zulu/Xhosa (Nguni) conglomerate and a Sotho/Pedi/Tswana (Sotho) conglomerate are coming into existence. A new language, *tsotsitaal*, and a popular form of English, colloquially called 'Soweto English', have been developed.

Indeed, this process of reduction shows signs of going still further with the use of words in one language conglomerate derived from the other. For example, though a Sotho-speaker might use *ho bapala* (Sotho), *go raloka* (Pedi) or *go tsameka* (Tswana) for 'to play', the Nguni word *ukudlala* has tended to become standard in the form *go dlala*. The tendency towards the development of one urban black African language has been further facilitated by the flexible and copious use of English and Afrikaans words, as in the following sentences:

> *I'm sure* ukhona (Maybe he is there/here).
> *Miskien* o tla ba *busy* (Perhaps he'll be busy).
> A *never* a kgone (He'll never be able to).

The italicized words are borrowings from English and Afrikaans. Often the original meanings are modified or altered altogether, as in the case of 'I'm sure'.

Tsotsitaal was originally an Afrikaans dialect used by criminals, but it has been taken up by other sections of the black groups in the urban areas, for example by the youth, musicians and journalists. It became virtually the accepted idiom of the *shebeen* sub-culture. Its basic grammatical structure is that of Afrikaans, substantially modified by that of Sotho and Nguni, and its vocabulary, though basically Afrikaans, is extremely eclectic and inventive. For example:

> *Jy sien, mfanakuthi, das die s'gog'lady wat hulle se is Doreen Lamb.*
> *Sy maak uit sy het ons klaa gegoni. Sy wil nou net kom bandage.*
> (You see, brother, there's this old lady called Doreen Lamb. She seems to think she has already knifed us. All she needs is to come and bandage us.)[19]

Here, *jy sien*, pronounced *jay seen* instead of orthodox *yay seen*, is from Afrikaans, while *mfanakuthi* is from Xhosa. *Das die* is varied from Afrikaans *daar is die*, and *s'gog'lady* is a *tsotsitaal* neologism in which English and Zulu elements combine. *Wat hulle se is* is a literal translation into Afrikaans of the Sotho phrase *ba re ke* — i.e. 'who they say is', meaning 'called'. *Goni*, meaning 'knife', is a *tsotsitaal* neologism; like many *tsotsitaal* neologisms its etymology is uncertain. The language is constantly in the process of being added to. There is the ever-present likelihood that a speaker will expand, enrich or at least modify the language every time he/she speaks it.

It was unlikely that *tsotsitaal* could be associated with the government and its policies, despite its Afrikaans content. It transcended ethnic divisions. It was uniquely capable, being organic, of coping with the specific nature of the black African group's experience of modern urban existence. It linked sections of the intermediate classes with sections of the proletariat and, significantly, linked sections of the black African proletariat with the proletariat of other black groups, i.e. 'coloureds' and 'Indians'.

Thus the intermediate classes tend to speak English and to oppose Afrikaans, the traditional languages and the organic languages of the proletariat. In effect, this cuts them off from their proletariat and links them instead to the English-speaking intermediate classes in South Africa and elsewhere. The proletariat, on the other hand, is developing languages which tend towards the dissolution of ethnic barriers, which retain links with the rural classes and which stretch out beyond national/cultural divisions to the urban proletariat of other black groups. In other words, there are in the constitutive and organic uses of language made by the black urban proletariat cultural elements which suggest a movement towards the concept of 'majority', i.e. the proletariat and peasantry, as developed in the conclusion of this book.

4. The Development of Theatre in South Africa up to 1976

Not very long ago Africans and non-Africans alike believed that African history began with the arrival of Europeans on the coast of West Africa. Similarly many thought — and still do — that African theatre began with the first European-inspired dramatic performances in the early 20th century.

Ruth Finnegan, author of the copious *Oral Literature in Africa*, though enlightened in her perceptions concerning the nature of oral literature in Africa, did not show a similar enlightenment about the nature of drama when she wrote:

> With a few possible exceptions, there is no tradition in Africa of artistic performances which include all the elements which might be demanded in a strict definition of drama — or at least not with the emphasis to which we are accustomed. [Finnegan, p.516]

Could she really be so sure that 'there is no tradition'? Did she really expect to find in Africa exactly what she was 'accustomed to' in Europe?

Nevertheless an increasing amount of information has already come to light concerning the existence of theatrical forms in historical Africa. It is not important to apply 'strict' definitions of what constitutes drama with the emphases to which Europeans are accustomed. What is important is to describe as accurately and scientifically as possible the theatrical forms to be found in traditional African societies and allow definitions — if and when they are required — to arise from the scientific description of the forms themselves.

Traditional Drama

To many working on the production of Athol Fugard's *No-Good Friday* in 1958, or in the Union of Southern African Artists' *King Kong* in 1959, their work seemed like a beginning. A beginning it was, of a sort, but not that of theatre in South Africa. This took place almost certainly centuries earlier.

The black Africans of present-day South Africa trace their earliest ancestors to the 'great family of peoples which spread out from an original centre, possibly in the region of the Cross River, and gradually occupied most of sub-Saharan Africa south of a line from the Bight of Benin to the horn of Somaliland'. It is probable that the section of these peoples which came to constitute the majority of the population in modern South Africa entered the region south of the Limpopo around the 12th century AD (Omer-Cooper, p.10).

The task of reconstructing the culture (and drama) of traditional societies in South Africa, even quite recent ones, is complicated by many factors. Some of these societies were still developing in southern Africa independently of European rule as recently as the early 19th century. Yet we know surprisingly little about their culture and still less about their art. It is true that a fair amount has been written, especially about the customs and social forms of South African peoples. Unfortunately the rapid and comprehensive destruction of these societies has meant that researchers in this century have recorded cultural practice in societies which are in an advanced state of collapse. Descriptions of traditional culture based on these records are not adequate. Those who were fortunate enough to observe cultural practice at a time when the traditional societies were still dynamic often understood little of what they saw. In addition to these factors, the prejudiced, often racialist, viewpoints of white observers, the absence of black African researchers and a lack of experience of (or interest in) theatre on the part of researchers has contributed to research or reporting tending to obscure rather than reveal the true nature of the dramatic activities of traditional societies in South Africa.

The above problems notwithstanding, there is sufficient evidence to suggest that there existed in the early societies rich and varied dramatic forms. Hottentot and Bushman communities possessed certain forms which included mime, music, dance, costume, props, make-up and ritual. Similarly the Nguni-speaking peoples practised various forms of a dramatic nature, including the dramatized solo narrative, *intsomi* in Xhosa and *inganekwane* in Zulu. Other peoples had their equivalents. For instance, the Sotho praise-poems, *liboko*, like the Nguni *izibongo*, included definite dramatic elements.[20]

H. I. E. Dhlomo and Credo V. Mutwa contend (and cryptic references in early descriptions of festivities at the court of the Zulu king Dingane seem to support the contention) that there were developed dramatic forms in existence in the early traditional societies. Dhlomo examined an extant *ingoma* (a choral dramatic dance, accompanied by drum) and reconstructed from it a brief but lucid historical dance drama. He claimed, too, that the *izibongo* of pre-Shakan Zulu society were actually dramatic texts from which the stage directions had been removed.[21]

Mutwa, too, attempted on the basis of his own studies and extensive travel in southern and central Africa to reconstruct the form of early African theatre for which he used the Zulu word *umlinganiso*. His play, *uNosilimela* (first performed in 1973) was based on this reconstruction.[22]

Drama before 1950

By 1906, the year of Bhambatha's rebellion, the process of defeating and subjugating the indigenous peoples of South Africa was complete. The process of transition from pre-capitalist forms of society to capitalism was accelerated. The culture of the conquered peoples entered into a parallel phase of transition. As the social base of the traditional structure was destroyed, so the culture declined. As more and more of the traditional population left their homes to sell their labour in the towns, so a new urban culture came into existence.

How the new proletariat expressed its own reactions to this process of transition in the first half of the century is only partly recorded. We know something of the new slang they evolved, of their dress and their music. The rest, because it was oral and 'beyond the pale', remained unrecorded, except for one or two scraps of evidence that suggest that there was some kind of popular dramatic activity and that the forms and content of traditional culture were sustained, adapted and developed. One remarkable example of popular theatre which has been recorded is the theatre of Esau Mthethwa and his Lucky Stars from Natal.[23]

The Lucky Stars began performing in 1929 with a repertoire of original didactic and satirical comedies in Zulu, based on Zulu traditional life, employing much music and dance. Their plays were improvised and extemporized on stage when the spirit moved or a crisis demanded it. The titles of two of their plays were *Umthakathi* (Witch) and *Ukuqomisa* (Courting). *Umthakathi* was a piece of domestic satire illustrating the differences between *umthakathi* (witchcraft) and *isangoma* or *inyanga*, in other words between 'witchcraft and legitimate traditional medicine and soothsaying'. *Ukuqomisa* showed how to win a young girl's love with the aid of charms, and illustrated the traditional usage which forbids the marriage of a younger sister until the elder sisters are wed.

The Lucky Stars toured Natal, the Witwatersrand and other parts of the country, performing in Zulu to whites and blacks. In 1936 they attracted much attention at the Empire Exhibition in Johannesburg. In the end 'some interested white producers . . . offered them trips overseas under their auspices. After this, however, they ceased as an organized company'. Significantly for this study, it is recorded that 'they greatly influenced Johannesburg Location productions'.[24] Unfortunately it is not clear whether this refers to productions by the educated or by the urban proletariat.

Much of the early drama of the educated has been recorded. It was literary as opposed to oral, and was often oriented towards publication rather than performance. The educated wrote in the new forms made available to them by their European education — verse, novel, play, etc. — and these they usually first practised in school. There had been dramatic activity in the schools since the last century. The earliest recorded examples are the dramatized animal satires of Job Moteame and Azariele M. Sekese in Lesotho in the 1880s. Another early example is the activity at Marianhill mission school in Natal in the 1920s, where sketches were improvised by teachers and pupils in both English and Zulu. One of the students involved, Francis Mkhise, continued his dramatic activities after leaving Marianhill. It is possible that Mthethwa and the Lucky Stars were inspired and influenced by the Marianhill beginnings, especially as it is recorded that their example had inspired other schools in Natal to perform drama. The foundation for non-literary theatre, based on improvisation and group authorship and incorporating music, was thus laid early in South Africa.

A number of plays by playwrights from all over the country were published, in both English and black languages, before 1950 — starting with Guybon Sinxo's Xhosa work, *Imfene ka Debeza* (Debeza's Baboon), published in 1925. The activities connected with the Bantu Men's Social Centre in Johannesburg and the work of H. I. E. Dhlomo and Ezekiel Mphahlele were particularly important.

By 1924, the year in which the Social Centre was founded, a sizeable group of educated black Africans had come into existence in the Witwatersrand. The Social Centre served as a focus for their cultural activities. It was founded for the purpose of 'helping young native men to devote their leisure time to the best advantage in healthful recreation and good citizenship, the development of worthy character, and the promotion of real sympathy between Europeans and non-Europeans'. Drama did not begin there as an organized activity until 1933, when the Bantu Dramatic Society was formed 'to encourage Bantu playwrights and to develop African dramatic art because Bantu life is full of great and glorious incidents and figures that would form the basis of first-class drama'. Their first production, however, was Goldsmith's *She Stoops to Conquer*, followed by *Nongqause*, a play written in Xhosa by a white woman, Mary Waters. Oscar Wilde's *Lady Windermere's Fan* came next. It is possible that the society also performed *Iziganeko zomKristu*, an adaptation in Xhosa of *Pilgrim's Progress*.

It is not certain whether the Bantu Dramatic Society was connected in any way with the Bantu People's Theatre. The latter put on a production of Eugene O'Neill's *The Hairy Ape*, directed by the well-known Belgian socialist director, Andre van Gyseghem,[25] in which Fanagalo, a hybrid language developed between white and black workers of different language groups in the mines, was used to represent American slang. This was an early indication of the critical problem of language in black and multi-racial theatre.

H. I. E. Dhlomo was the first black Librarian-Organizer of the Carnegie Non-European Library, based in Germiston with a branch at the Social Centre. We have already referred to his theories about the nature of traditional theatre. Unfortunately, much of his original dramatic writing has never been published. We hear of a play about Shaka, which was to be grouped with others about Cetshwayo and Moshoeshoe and collectively called *The Black Bulls*. A play about Dingane exists in mimeographed form. Vilakazi speaks of a play called *Ruby*, which was 'acted and produced by the author himself'. Dhlomo wrote another unpublished play called *The Pass*, about the corruption of the pass system. It is unfortunate, then, that the one play which *was* published reflects so unflatteringly on this intelligent and gifted man. *The Girl Who Killed To Save*, published in 1935, was the first published play in English by a black South African. It is about Nongqause and re-interprets this disastrous episode in Xhosa history as a triumph for Christianity and 'civilization'. *The Girl Who Killed To Save* is evidence of the effectiveness of the hegemony of the English-speaking whites over black intellectuals at that time. It would only be fair to say, though, that in Dhlomo's case total identification with Christian European civilization seems to have been temporary. His later theoretical writings show much independence and originality of mind, and he left African playwrights an inspiring challenge:

> The African dramatist has an important part to play. In the story of African Travail, Birth and Progress, lies an inexhaustible source of African literary and dramatic creations. We want African playwrights who will dramatize and expound a philosophy of our history. We want dramatic representations of African Oppression, Emancipation and Evolution. [Gerard, p.229]

Ezekiel Mphahlele 'developed a passion for dramatics' at school in Johannesburg. He later dramatized *A Tale of Two Cities*, which was performed at various venues in the Transvaal. When he became a schoolmaster at Orlando High School in 1945 he introduced 'dramatics' to the school, encouraged by Norah Taylor, later to become the director of AMDA, the drama school of the Union of Southern African Artists. He formed the Syndicate of African Artists in order to 'bring serious music and the arts to the doorstep of our people, who were not allowed to go to white theatre or concert halls'. The syndicate performed *Lady Windermere's Fan*, scenes from Shakespeare, adaptations from Dickens and 'folktales'.[26]

Taken as a whole, black and multi-racial theatre in the transitional period before the 1950s anticipated what were to become some of the most important features of later drama. There was the importance of song, music and dance, improvisation and group creativity. The potential of mobile popular theatre had been demonstrated, though it was not until virtually 30 years after Mthethwa's Lucky Stars that touring companies such as Kente's were able to make it the basis of a successful professional theatre. The crucial problem of language had been raised. Mthethwa's company had performed in Zulu. Fanagalo had been used in *The Hairy Ape*, and the educated intermediate classes had performed in either English or Xhosa. The effect on black theatre of white commercial management with its promises of tours abroad had been revealed in the case of the Lucky Stars. An early attempt had been made to organize African artists in Mphahlele's Syndicate of African Artists. Finally, a slender tradition of theatre as protest or satire had been born and survived precariously during the period, for example in the animal fables of Moteame and Sekese, *The Pass* by H. I. E. Dhlomo and in political theatre in Cape Town in the 1930s initiated by Trotskyites.[27]

Much of the drama of the period sprang from collaboration between blacks and whites. Father Hess was responsible for the early experiments at Marian-hill. Mary Waters wrote a play about Nongqause which was the second production of the Bantu Dramatic Society. Andre van Gyseghem worked with the Bantu People's Theatre. Mphahlele was advised and encouraged by Norah Taylor.

Drama before the Entertainment Segregation Laws

Though the 1950s were essentially a period of continuity in terms of the forms of theatre that were practised, they were marked by an increase in the scope of activity, particularly of multi-racial activity organized by whites, and by the commercialization of both white and black theatre. Some theatre collaboration was undertaken in the context of the efforts of English-speaking white and black African intellectuals to resist the pressures brought to bear on their association by the state, and to resist the growing hegemony of the Afrikaner nationalists.

The published drama of the educated intermediate classes was seriously affected by the introduction of Bantu education in 1953. Many writers and intellectuals shunned the system and consequently were no longer published; they were no longer prepared to write in African languages or, as they were now called, Bantu languages. This meant that they either ceased to write or channelled their energy and inspiration into performed drama. There was no shortage of writers, however, prepared to write plays on traditional themes in Bantu languages, suitable for use in Bantu-education schools. The importance of this aspect of Afrikaner nationalist hegemony — i.e. the continued publication of suitable plays in Bantu languages under the government's auspices and published by companies owned by the growing Afrikaner capitalist section — should not be underestimated. They were read as prescribed texts in schools throughout South Africa, and many of them were later performed publicly to black audiences in the urban areas.[28]

The tradition of educated or 'serious' theatre, based on European models, as practised by Mphahlele's Syndicate of African Artists, continued in this period but came increasingly under white direction. For example, in the early 1950s, Ian Bernhardt, manager and actor in a white amateur dramatic society, the Dramateers, formed an all-black drama group, the Bareti Players, whose first production in 1955 was *A Comedy of Errors*. Athol Fugard, together with certain black intellectuals including Lewis Nkosi, Nat Nakasa and Bloke Modisane, produced *No-Good Friday* in 1958. Fugard went on to produce *Nongogo* and *The Blood Knot*, and founded the Rehearsal Room group at the Union of Southern African Artists' premises at Dorkay House in Johannesburg. This group explored the European and American avant-garde, performing works by Beckett, Pinter, Sartre and Steinbeck.

Popular theatrical activity based in the traditional culture hardly existed at all in the Witwatersrand, except in comic sketches interpolated between musical items at concerts. Traditional elements were present to a greater or lesser degree in the commercial theatre of the early 1960s, especially in plays that originated in Natal or the Cape or were directed towards white audiences. An example of the first was *Sponono* by Alan Paton and Krishna Shah, and of the second, *Dingaka* by Eddie Domingo and Bertha Egnos. The bulk of popular theatre was based in the urban culture, and during the 1950s much of this activity was sucked into the concert packages of Alf Herbert and the Union of Southern African Artists, culminating in 1959 in the musical *King Kong*.

Dramatic activity organized by whites was extended from the schools into other instruments of hegemony in the black African urban areas, such as youth clubs. In the early 1950s one 'JP', 'a well-known personality who has been the mainspring behind the establishment of Girls' Clubs for Young Natives living in many industrial townships along the Reef in the Southern Transvaal', had attempted to develop what he termed 'True African Drama'. He and others set about organizing the members of their girls' clubs to do 'simple scenes, such scenes including a little dialogue, some tribal singing and dancing', some of which were performed at the University of the Witwatersrand Great Hall.[29]

This sort of initiative on the part of English-speaking whites was exemplified on a greater scale by the establishment by the Union of Southern African Artists of the African Music and Drama Association (AMDA) in 1960. The main activity of AMDA was the running of a drama school under the direction of a Johannesburg drama teacher, Norah Taylor, who had been Mphahlele's mentor. Student plays at the school, sometimes performed in public, included original texts developed by the students themselves under the direction of their teachers on traditional and 'township' themes. The AMDA school projects, initiated by Bob Leshoai,[30] often included this material in their repertoires. AMDA's activities were less highbrow than those of the Rehearsal Room group and contained many popular elements. These derived from a combination of the relatively low formal educational qualifications of the students, the use of improvisation from everyday experience and the condescending concept of 'African theatre' entertained by the school's director.

There were three major new developments in theatre activity in the 1950s: the establishment of a substantial professional and amateur white theatre; the formation of the Union of Southern African Artists; and the popularity of black variety concerts with white audiences.

White theatre on any scale is a comparatively recent development. It was possible, for instance, in 1958 to write that 'ten years ago [i.e. in 1948] theatre was confined almost entirely to an occasional musical company from Britain or a Christmas pantomime'. Though white theatre had expanded by 1958 — 'in Johannesburg four professional managements fight for the rights of plays' — its repertoire was still predominantly foreign and 'the development of indigenous drama [i.e. local white drama] was then still in its infancy' (Kavanagh, 1958, p.182).

This expansion of white theatre was one of the factors that provided the foundation for the domination of black theatre and entertainment by the English-speaking whites in this period. For instance, in the early 1950s the white amateur group, the Dramateers, performed a play in aid of the Alexandra Township anti-TB Association. One of the black members of the association went further than expressing his thanks for the financial support and asked if blacks might be permitted to see the play itself. The committee of the Dramateers felt the play, which included rape and murder, would not be suitable for black audiences and so they produced a series of 'suitable' one-act plays which toured in black urban areas. This led to the establishment of the Bareti Players, which in turn resulted in its founder, Ian Bernhardt, becoming chairman of the newly formed artists' union, the Union of Southern African Artists, which ultimately produced *King Kong*.

The establishment and later development of the union will be described in some detail later. Briefly, however, the union was founded in 1952-53 at a meeting of black African artists and musicians to protect their rights. Initially it organized lectures, held members' evenings and gave free legal advice. By 1958 the union had become one of the most profitable promotional bodies in entertainment in the country. This transformation was associated with another development in the period, the popularity with white audiences of black variety concerts.

Before 1952, the year in which Alf Herbert, a white promoter, 'discovered' the legendary Dolly Rathebe and other talented musicians and dancers and began his presentations of African jazz and variety, popular urban black music and drama was largely despised by the black intermediate classes and virtually unknown outside black areas — except, that is, to certain recording companies and promoters who marketed it in the black African market. Following Alf Herbert's example, the union organized Township Jazz concerts in the white areas and soon dominated the market. It was the possibilities suggested by these shows which inspired the union to stage *King Kong* in 1959.

The years between *King Kong* and *Sikalo*, Gibson Kente's first successful musical, were dominated by the union. It produced *Sponono, Back in Your Own Backyard, Emperor Jones, King of the Dark Chamber*, plays performed by the students of the AMDA drama school, jazz concerts and talent contests. Others attempted to emulate its success. Wilfred Sentso, leader of the musical group the Synco-Fans, produced *Washerwoman*, Prince Skosana produced *Black Boy*, Morris McHugh produced *Mgodoyi* and Bertha Egnos produced *Dingaka*, of which only the latter was financially successful, a film being eventually made from it. There were musical plays in other parts of the country too, including Alf Herbert's *Shebeen* and Union Artists' *Mr Paljas*, written by Harry Bloom, the author of the *King Kong* script. These plays were first staged in Cape Town. In Durban there were *Chief Mambo* and Alan Paton's early effort, *Mkhumbane*; in Port Elizabeth there was *Shantytown*.

Theatre before 'Soweto'

The Union of Southern African Artists was a powerful instrument of English-speaking white hegemony. As we have seen, during the 1950s the Afrikaner nationalists were attempting to consolidate and extend their hegemony within the country by, among other things, imposing their own cultural policies on and neutralizing the influence of the culture and ideology of the English-speaking group over black Africans. Their decisive defeat of African nationalism's challenge to their hegemony in 1960-61 enabled them to intensify their efforts, and one of the results of this intensification was important changes and restrictions in the field of entertainment. As a result of these restrictions, it eventually became impossible for the union to function effectively, and by 1965–66 it was losing its dominance of black theatre and entertainment to black entrepreneurs.

In the 1940s and 1950s it was still possible to organize multi-racial activity of many kinds, though apartheid inhibited and obstructed it at all levels. The government did not forbid multi-racial audiences, for instance. Legally, there were comparatively few restrictions. Nevertheless other pressures were operative. Mphahlele describes how the the government refused to give the Syndicate of African Artists funds unless it ceased its performances to multi-racial audiences. The government, he wrote, was content 'to wag a finger of cold war at white patrons'. 'Whites were too scared to attend because multi-racial audiences were now the focus of the Nationalist Government's wrath' (Mphahlele, p.182). Black writers such as Nkosi, Nakasa and Modisane describe how they were barred from attending white theatre and entertainment.

By the 1960s this position had deteriorated markedly. The Afrikaner Nationalist government introduced a series of laws which made the separation of the races more effective. These laws inhibited the ability of whites and blacks to associate or collaborate outside working hours and working relationships. New legislation banned black audiences from attending public performances in white areas and black performers from performing there. A series of proclamations and laws against mixed audiences and black performers culminated in the 1963 Publication and Entertainment Act, by which the specially constituted Publications Control Board was empowered to prohibit public entertainment for a number of flexible reasons. In 1958 a proclamation had prohibited the attendance of blacks at cinemas in white areas without the minister's permission. Another, in 1965, extended this to apply to 'any place of entertainment'. In that year black audiences were banned from the Selbourne Hall at the Johannesburg City Hall, venue of numerous black concerts and musicals including the Union of Southern African Artists' Township Jazz concerts in the 1950s. Union Artists were forced to cancel a tour by the black South African jazz pianist Dollar Brand, because 'it would not pay to bring him out for an all-white audience'.

These restrictions on multi-racial audiences provoked a playwrights' boycott in Europe and America. The English-speaking white commercial theatre was particularly hard hit by the ban on performance in South Africa of commercial hits from the West End and Broadway. Also in 1965 the English singer Dusty Springfield refused to sign a declaration that she would not perform to mixed audiences and was deported. British Equity and the British Musicians' Union took action to prevent their members performing in South Africa.

It was now virtually impossible for the multi-racial theatre of the past to survive. In May 1965 Golden City Follies and Golden City Dixies closed down. Fred Langford, the impresario, explained that he could no longer get blanket permission to play to mixed audiences throughout the country. In the same month Alf Herbert complained bitterly about the laws closing in on him: 'The complexities of the Group Areas Act clamping down on the travels of his cast, the tough no-mixing rules on audiences (are) threatening to destroy him at the box-office' (*Post*, 9–16 May 1965).

In the following year the screw tightened further. The 'non-racial but all-white' musicians' unions of Natal, the Transvaal and the Cape called on the government to ban black entertainers in white hotels and nightspots. With the doors now closed or closing on performances by black artists to white or mixed audiences in theatres, public halls, hotels and nightclubs, the white managements which had hitherto marketed black entertainment in the white cities either went out of business or were forced severely to curtail or adapt their activities. Those white-controlled organizations that still survived, such as the Union, were faced with increasing problems and contradictions. None of these companies had based their activities primarily in the black areas or on black audiences. In fact, no management had yet been able to base a commercial theatre company solely on support from black audiences.

Thus, in short, the new government legislation threw black artists out of their jobs in white-controlled entertainment. They were forced by law to perform in black areas to black audiences at a time when the conditions for them to do this with limited success were in the process of coming into existence — namely, increased urbanization and greater spending power and therefore a potential audience capable of supporting, albeit on a small scale, professional entertainment; separate development, which favoured the growth of such activity because it broke the monopoly of the English-speaking whites by making performances in town impossible and by cutting the links between black and white urban areas; and finally the work done by the Union of Southern African Artists and various theatrical ventures all over the country, which had provided blacks with dramatic skills and models and the confidence and the taste for making and managing plays.

This led to the development of independent black theatre and an important tilt in the cultural relations of black and white in the theatre. From now on those white producers who wished to involve themselves in black theatre or entertainment on a commercial or other basis would have to produce a product which pleased black, not white, audiences. In the earlier situation, when such material was specifically designed for white consumption, white directors and writers were at an advantage and black artists sought to collaborate with them. When, however, the situated changed, whites found themselves at a disadvantage. Thus though there were sporadic efforts by white directors and writers to exploit the black theatre market, none of them were successful. Black playwrights and directors, on the other hand, were conspicuously more successful.

Black African artists had early begun to challenge the monopoly on direction and playmaking exercised by whites in the union. For instance, the musical *Back in Your Own Backyard* was devised by Ben Masinga. Bob Leshoai managed the AMDA schools project and wrote *Morati of Bataung* for the drama school. One or two members of the union went abroad for training as directors and on their return became resident directors for the union. Two members of the union, Cornelius Mabaso and Gibson Kente, eventually withdrew and functioned independently by basing their activities in the black urban areas. They were not alone in working independently of the union. However, with the exception of Sam Mhangwani's *The Unfaithful Woman*, which was first performed in May 1965, none of these was quite as significant as Mabaso's Soweto Ensemble and Kente's stage company.

Mabaso had been a member of the Rehearsal Room group and before that had played Guy in Fugard's *No-Good Friday*. In 1965 he founded the Soweto Ensemble, which rehearsed and performed mainly in black areas. Their first production was a rather academic *Shaka*, based on a book by one X. Gorro. It enjoyed a long and successful run. In January 1966 the ensemble announced plans to perform Anouilh's *Antigone* and Sartre's *In Camera*. Later productions included Pinter's *The Dumbwaiter* and John Mortimer's *Dock Brief*.

The main development in this period, however, was the growth of black commercial theatre or what has been called 'township theatre', best exemplified by the work of Gibson Kente and Sam Mhangwani's *Sea Pearls*, but practised by a growing number of professional and semi-professional groups throughout the country.

Also towards the end of this period there reappeared a theatrical form much favoured by the early élite and later used importantly by the Black Consciousness movement. This was the poetry reading format in which recitation is accompanied by or interspersed with music.

Black Consciousness Theatre

In 1969–71 students under the influence of the Black Consciousness movement began to forsake the foreign avant-garde models of recent 'serious theatre' in favour of black material — American, West African or Caribbean — and their own adaptations or indeed creation of material 'relevant to the black experience' in South Africa.

The ideology of the movement required expressly that they perform to blacks only in black areas. Thus the segregation legislation had given rise not only to black commercial theatre independent of English-speaking white management but also to a form of 'serious' political theatre which completely rejected the earlier forms of collaboration with English-speaking whites.

Town Theatre

This collaborative tradition did not, however, die and in the changed circumstances of the early 1970s, it in fact underwent a renaissance. Elsewhere I have referred to this form of theatre as 'town theatre'.[31] Athol Fugard had in effect founded the first 'town theatre' group, along with Lewis Nkosi and others, with the performance of *No-Good Friday*. When legislation in the 1960s made multi-racial collaboration extremely difficult, Fugard nevertheless continued in Port Elizabeth with a group of black amateurs. This group, the Serpent Players, was flourishing in the early 1970s when other similar groups came into existence all over the country. In Johannesburg in 1967, after the formal dissolution of the Union of Southern African Artists, Ian Bernhardt and Barney Simon developed Phoenix Players (originally a white experimental group) into a new black theatre group in the tradition of town theatre. In 1971 Experimental Theatre Workshop '71 was founded. Imita Players in East London, the Ikhwezi Players in Grahamstown and later the Sechaba Players in Cape Town were other 'town theatre' groups.

Initially, Phoenix Players had confined performances of their plays to private showings to invited audiences and performances in black areas. In the early 1970s the 'town theatre' groups began to perform to invited mixed audiences at church, university and club venues. With the general relaxation of government restrictions in the wake of détente, these groups became increasingly bold until by 1975, at such venues as the Box Theatre and the Nunnery Theatre at the University of the Witwatersrand, and in 1976 the Market Theatre in Johannesburg, they operated no restrictions at all on attendance.

Other Forms

The legislation of 1963–65 had empowered the minister to grant permits at his discretion. As already described, in the early 1970s such permits began to be forthcoming for performances of a certain kind to segregated audiences in 'white' areas. Thus another form of theatrical activity began to flourish, the so-called 'tribal musical', of which *Dingaka* and *Mzumba* had been early examples. In the 1970s white managements produced, among other musicals, *uMabatha, Meropa* (later *KwaZulu*), *Ipi Tombi* and *Mma Thari*.

Des and Dawn Lindberg, well-known South African folksingers and entertainers, began a struggle to extend this commercial activity to multi-racial casts and audiences. Though they experienced much harassment and found it difficult to get permits for black and multi-racial audiences, they successfully staged *Godspell, Pippin* and *The Black Mikado* with multi-racial casts.

The Struggle for Control

During the 1970s black theatre became a crucial area of cultural and commercial conflict. As it increased in scope, so various interests competed to control it for their own commercial or ideological purposes. The competing groups included: forces of the state, which wished to control it in the interests of Afrikaner nationalist hegemony; white, largely English-speaking, theatre managements and impresarios; black theatre managements and businessmen; white English-speaking intellectuals; and organizations of the Black Consciousness movement.

Their rivalry and struggle cannot be described in detail here. Briefly, however, the state attempted, through legislation, the police and its new direct control of black urban areas in the form of the Bantu Boards, to censor, harass, proscribe and ban what seemed to endanger its political and cultural interests. Thus the activity of the Black Consciousness groups was seriously curtailed in 1973-74 by a series of arrests and trials culminating in the SASO trials of 1975-78. It used its powers, too, to encourage and even introduce new forms of theatre activity which were more amenable to its interests. It attempted to form a monopoly arts and entertainment organization, membership of which was obligatory to all who wished to perform in venues under the boards' jurisdiction. The West Rand Bantu Board went so far as to set up a cultural section in 1975 which, among other things, 'advised playwrights to change their scripts' and attempted to stage its own production, *Shaka*, written and directed by the section head, a certain Mr H. Pieterse.[32]

The white managements attempted to found a multiracial theatre organization, South African Theatre Organization (SATO). Their aim was clearly to legitimize their own segregated theatre activities in white commercial theatre, and to breach the overseas playwrights' boycott by promising to aid 'township theatre' through SATO. But shortly afterwards the government was already making life easier for the white managements by granting them permits for visits by black 'stars' from abroad, for the attendance of blacks at some of their shows and for the promotion of profitable 'tribal musicals'.

Black theatre managements and businessmen reacted in various ways to the threat posed by the other interest groups. Kente Productions held a near monopoly of popular commercial musical theatre in black areas throughout the republic and thus contented itself with protecting that monopoly and refusing to be drawn into various attempts made, from time to time, to form either multi-racial or black theatre associations. Sam Mhangwani, Kente's chief rival, gathered about him a cluster of smaller commercial companies and formed the People's Theatre Association. Kente was able to resist the efforts of the boards to bring him under their jurisdiction and often refused to use their venues rather than submit his scripts for censorship or join an official organization. However, so serious did he consider the threat posed by the board's public statement at the end of 1974, that it intended to set up an organization which would exercise a monopoly over entertainment in black areas, that he summoned a meeting of black groups and personalities to discuss the crisis.

Mhangwani's People's Theatre Association, however, was formed with the express purpose of negotiating with the West Rand Bantu Board in order to streamline the bureaucratic procedures that hindered black commercial theatre. None of the groups affiliated to the People's Theatre Association dealt with radical political material. On the contrary, much of their material implied a positive endorsement of the ruling white group's ideologies. They therefore had little to fear from censorship except that in some cases action was taken against member groups on account of pornographic elements in their work, for example G. Raletebele's *Adultery* (1974). From time to time, black businessmen were prepared to put up funds for commercial theatre undertakings, but this was rare and was often the cause for complaint amongst black companies, who had to rely on white business for sponsorship.

The intellectuals of the English-speaking white group operated almost exclusively in the sphere of 'town theatre'. Their interest was predominantly ideological, rather than commercial, and paternalistic in intention. Their collaboration with black artists tended, with some exceptions, to follow the traditional class lines of such collaboration in the past, i.e. to be with the educated sections of the intermediate classes, and within the framework of the liberal or avant-garde cultural traditions of Europe and the United States. The repertoire of the Serpent Players reflected this. By 1972 they had performed plays by Sartre, Camus, Euripides and Machiavelli, among others. Most 'town theatre' groups worked exclusively in English.

As noted, there were exceptions to these general rules. Sechaba Players, for instance, produced a powerful evocation of Xhosa history, *The Sacrifice of Kreli*, written by Fatima Dike. Workshop '71 developed its own material, too, and acted it in the languages spoken in the Witwatersrand. Its repertoire, at least after 1973, reveals too that it began to move away from the cultural influence of the English-speaking white group in the direction of first an Africanist and then a socialist aesthetic.

There were activities in the category of or associated with 'town theatre' which closely approached in ideological allegiance the aims of the Black Consciousness movement. Credo V. Mutwa's epic play *uNosilimela* (1973), which was presented by Workshop '71, was one example. *S'ketsh' Magazine* was another. It was funded by Robert Amato, a liberal industrialist and founder of the Imita and Sechaba Players, and edited by Mango Tshabangu and myself (both members of Workshop '71) until 1975 when the editorship was handed over to the poet and playwright, Sipho Sepamla. It was the only journal outside the Black Consciousness movement which attacked the cultural domination of whites in the theatre and supported, albeit critically, the activities of the Black Consciousness theatre organizations such as Mdali and Mihloti. For instance, it condemned *Ipi Tombi*, 'a tribal musical' by Bertha Egnos (who had earlier produced *Dingaka*), because it projected cultural stereotypes and was exploitative. At one stage, it opposed the performance of black plays to white audiences.

The organizations of the Black Consciousness movement were likewise concerned to influence this important area of cultural activity for ideological not commercial reasons. It is obvious therefore, given this and the movement's assessment of the role of the traditional intellectuals of the English-speaking white group, i.e. the white liberals, that they saw in the activities of 'town theatre', including at least initially *S'ketsh'*, one of their principal enemies.

They were also aware of the immense threat posed by the pressures of the state. They also opposed the so-called 'non-white' commercial activity of Gibson Kente and Sam Mhangwani. The major efforts made by those loyal to the ideology of Black Consciousness to organize resistance to the other interest groups active in the field were the formation of the South African Black Theatre Union (SABTU) and Mdali, the holding of black cultural festivals in different parts of the country and the publication of cultural and theatre newsletters.

Radicalization and Protest

By 1974 the overall pattern of theatre activity was again in the process of transformation. It was a period of increased militancy and raised political consciousness. As we have seen, unemployment had reached crisis levels. The ideology of the Black Consciousness movement had made its mark, especially among the school and university students. The combination of these two factors meant that large numbers of young people in the urban areas could not find employment, and in any case were not inclined to work for the white bosses in town. Theatre provided them with a semi-professional independent alternative. In it they could remain away from the whites, hope to earn something of a living and at the same time express in performance to others what they felt about their shared oppression and what they considered should be done about it.

Black African theatre audiences had gradually changed in social composition over the years since 1959 and, particularly in Soweto, theatre-going was no longer primarily an occupation for the educated intermediate classes. In fact, a majority of these classes now shunned the popular musical plays of Gibson Kente and others. An important new section of the audience was the youth, potentially the most militant group in the black urban population. Some were still at school, receiving what they knew to be an inferior education but one which nevertheless enabled them to make a crude but essentially accurate analysis of the political situation. At the same time, they were facing the prospect of being unemployed when they left school. Others were students who had been 'locked out' en masse from their universities in the Bantustans. Yet others were both uneducated and unemployed, with no stake whatsoever in the system, i.e. *tsotsis* and criminals.

In this climate of increasing tension and defiance, the various sections of black theatre activity began to coalesce. Some groups, it is true, resisted the tendency. Sam Mhangwani's People's Theatre Association remained committed to the presentation of commercial, professedly 'apolitical' material. Fugard and the Serpent Players, Phoenix Players, breakaways from Phoenix Players, Workshop '71, various 'township theatre' companies and, most important, Gibson Kente himself reflected, at times participated in, the growing tide of political defiance. The tide, and the radical theatre that accompanied it, continued to rise until in 1976 the uprisings broke out in Soweto and in other black urban areas.[33]

As this brief account of black and black/white collaborative theatre activity up to 1976 reveals, there is ample scope for an important analysis of the interplay of cultural and ideological forces. In Chapters 4 and 5 we shall be concentrating on collaborative theatre, 'serious' and commercial, in the 1950s, namely the plays *No-Good Friday* and *King Kong*. Thus for the later period, although an analysis of 'town theatre' in the 1970s, for instance, would be informative and important, we have decided instead to concentrate in Chapters 6 and 7 on expressly non-collaborative, black theatre, i.e. the popular commercial theatre of Gibson Kente and the 'serious' political theatre of the Black Consciousness movement, represented respectively by the two plays *Too Late* and *Shanti*.

5. 'No-Man's Land' — Fugard, and the Black Intellectuals

'Bohemia' — Black and White Intellectuals in the Late 1950s

The writings and lives of the journalists that worked at various times on the staff of *Drum Magazine*, and its sister paper *Post*, have been taken by commentators to be both a reflection and the expression of a new black urban culture. These journalists included Can Themba, Casey Motsisi, Ezekiel Mphahlele, Henry Nxumalo, Todd Matshikiza, Nat Nakasa, Bloke Modisane and Lewis Nkosi.

It is not possible for us to describe or analyse in detail the activities of this group. A study of these writers and the new urban culture they arose from and embodied has already been made — by David Rabkin.[34] Unfortunately it deals with the phenomenon without paying sufficient attention to class. This may epitomize the way in which the vast majority of South Africans and foreign observers see the South African situation. It is, after all, how the dominant ideology of apartheid persuades them to see it. But a more precise analysis of the *function* of this circle of writers in the context of the cultural relations of the groups and classes in the Witwatersrand requires us to include in our examination factors of class as well as race and nationality.

We have already referred to the connection between *Drum* and mining capital. This is a connection Rabkin notes as well:

> At no time did it turn its scrutiny on the system of migrant labour or upon the working conditions and pay of the hundreds of thousands of African mine-workers. These workers are among the lowest paid and worst treated in South Africa. To this oversight, Jim Bailey's connection with the Chamber of Mines is perhaps not irrelevant. [p.57]

Anthony Sampson, when editor of *Drum*, noted that black readers suspected that the magazine belonged to the Chamber.

Drum was clearly an instrument of cultural persuasion, i.e. of hegemony, owned by English-speaking capital and directed at blacks. In the operation of this hegemony the black journalists on the staff were equally clearly the 'agents' of that hegemony. To what extent therefore their writings reflected or expressed the authentic culture of urban blacks is a question which would need a scrutiny more exacting than Rabkin and others have afforded it.

By and large, *Drum* opposed racialism and certain aspects of apartheid and situated its stories and news within the culture produced by the urbanization of blacks. It did not oppose the practices of mining capital, and its attitudes to the African nationalist organizations were ambivalent to say the least. It opposed the communists. Both *Drum* and *Post* concentrated at least as much on 'cheese-cake, crime, animals, babies' as on politics. As Anthony Sampson declared: 'The workers of the world were united, at least, in their addiction to cheese-cake and crime' (Sampson, p.30). He omitted, to continue his own metaphor, to confess in whose interests the addiction was being administered and by whom.[35]

The role therefore of the black journalists as 'agents' in the operation of what was clearly a form of English-speaking white hegemony not only placed them in a difficult position vis-à-vis other blacks, but also vis-à-vis their image of themselves. Rabkin notes that, with few exceptions, the journalists on *Drum* were estranged from the black political organizations, and at least some of them expressed from time to time misgivings about the nature of the reporting required of them and the editing of the copy they handed in. On one occasion, Modisane had been assigned to write an article on independent African churches, very much a mass movement in the towns as well as the country. 'Because of the training I had received on *Drum*,' he writes, 'I approached the story with all the detachment and cynicism of a hard-boiled journalist. I was superior, the whole movement was a circus.' This attitude, Modisane claimed, was determined by the editor, Sylvester Stein, who headlined the article 'Ducking for a pretty convert'.[36]

Some of the journalists, Casey Motsisi and Can Themba in particular, reacted to their isolation by identifying with the culture of the urban majority. 'The *tsotsis* saw us as their cousins,' wrote Themba, and Motsisi was renowned for his evocations of the atmosphere and chat of the *shebeen*. Others, like Nkosi and Modisane, courted, and were in their turn courted by, the white liberal intelligentsia. Nkosi in *Home and Exile*, a collection of his essays published in 1965, praised the Jewish intelligentsia and professional classes for tempering 'this harsh social order of apartheid' (pp.18–19). Modisane wrote in his autobiography, *Blame Me On History*, that when he fully realized that his white friends no longer invited him to their houses because they were afraid of banning and that they were 'accommodating this intolerable situation', the country 'began to die' for him (p.11).

For Nkosi at least, the world inhabited by the journalists of *Drum*, by other black artists and intellectuals and by their white liberal friends appeared for a while to be an alternative society in the making. Here the fraternization on class cultural lines tended to transcend race and racial nationalism. Nkosi wrote: 'Everywhere, members of my own generation, both black and white, were beginning to disaffiliate from a society organized on a rigid apartheid design. We began to sense that we were being deprived of a profounder experience; a sense of shared nationhood.' *No-Good Friday* was a part of this

'profounder experience' — a collaboration between white and black
intellectuals in a 'no-man's land' Nkosi called 'Bohemia'.

Before attempting to analyse the function of the activities and writings
of these individuals, it is perhaps as well to re-emphasize that objective
function should not be confused with intention or conscious purpose. An
'agent' of the hegemony of ruling or dominant groups is not always
conscious of his function. Often he is simply doing his best, as a person with
human desires and enthusiasms, to be happy, to survive, sometimes even to do
good. The 'Bohemia' of Nkosi and the others should be seen in this light.
For them, these were exciting times. Their association with white intellectuals
and their own participation in the apparently 'international' culture of the
'beat generation', 'the angry young men engaged in anarchic gestures against
their society', was exhilarating in its own right. It also appeared to them to be
a positive attempt to break down the barriers of narrow racialism. To them,
both the Afrikaner nationalists and the Africanists appeared to be bigoted
and much less splendid in spirit than the 'Bohemian' culture which they
appeared, if only effervescently, to inhabit.

It was within this milieu that Athol Fugard's first play, *No-Good Friday*,
was created. The core of the group which created it consisted of Athol Fugard,
Nat Nakasa and Lewis Nkosi. They were joined by others, including in particular Bloke Modisane and Corney Mabaso. Though Nakasa took part in the
improvisations from which the play developed, he did not in the end act in
it. Nkosi did not act either until at a later stage he was persuaded to take
over Fugard's part when the latter was not permitted to perform at the
Brooke Theatre. Both Modisane and Mabaso acted, the former playing Shark
and the latter, Guy. We shall be concentrating on three central figures,
Fugard, Nkosi and Modisane, though we will refer to the others whenever
necessary.

Modisane lived in Sophiatown and, as we have seen, worked as a journalist
on *Drum*. His marriage to the grand-daughter of the author Sol Plaatje was not
a success for, as he admits, he hated his wife because she was black. In *Blame
Me On History* Modisane referred to his cultural roots as 'my own culture
of the shield and assegaai, of ancestral gods, drums, mud huts and half-naked
women, with breasts as hard as green mangoes' (p.178). Though once a card-
carrying member of the ANC Youth League, he became disillusioned and burnt
his membership card 'and retreated into the political wilderness' (p.139).
He claimed to have favoured the PAC but reports that he himself was regarded
by them as a playboy dilettante. With almost abject frankness, he confessed
his real yearning to be admitted fully into white society:

> I want acceptance in the country of my birth, and in some corner of
> the darkened room I whisper the real desire: I want to be accepted
> into white society. I want to listen to Rachmaninov, to Beethoven,
> Bartok and Stravinsky: I want to talk about drama, philosophy . . .
> [p.218]

He must have been delighted indeed when Sheila and Athol Fugard came to see him 'with a bottle of brandy and the request to fill a replacement' in *No-Good Friday*. The part of Shark appealed to him – 'a violent little man with an external charm and eruptions of violence which were locked inside the man' (p.289). He says no more about Fugard except that when Fugard was banned from playing the part of the white priest at the Brooke Theatre and Lewis Nkosi had to take over the role, there was a confrontation. 'Athol Fugard had accepted the principle without consulting with the actors.' But the actors did not persist with their objections – 'we became sentimental and relented because it seemed to be his whole life'. There was 'disappointment on his face'. Modisane writes that Fugard argued that the banning should be complied with because the play was 'a big break' (pp.290–1).

Nkosi, like Modisane, was a journalist on *Drum*. Rabkin classed him with Modisane as a 'situation', i.e. an intellectual standing between the black masses and the white world, with a 'pass' into the world of the liberal intelligentsia, but regarded with contempt by African nationalists. The latter could hardly be expected to have approved of a precocious young journalist who saw himself and his multi-racial circle of artists and intellectuals as the creators of 'a new and exciting Bohemia', a 'new "fringe society"' coming together in a spirit of tolerance and occupying a "no-man's land" between the two warring camps' and who actually seemed to believe that 'art might yet crack the wall of apartheid'.

Nkosi's Bohemia is depicted in his play, *Rhythm of Violence*, written at Harvard after Nkosi had left the country. The action takes place at a multi-racial revel at the white University of the Witwatersrand, and turns on the dilemma of two brothers, Gama and Thula. Gama belongs to a multi-racial revolutionary party which has just planted a bomb under the stage of the City Hall, where the Afrikaner Nationalist Party is to have a rally. Thula meets a young Afrikaans girl, Sarie Marais, and they fall in love. He discovers that her father has gone to the rally – to submit his resignation from the party. Thula perishes in the attempt to rescue Sarie's father. Even Gama, though he wishes the operation to go ahead, says: 'It's just that she's made everything that was right seem wrong suddenly' (p.64). Earlier in the play Thula offers his belief in the power of multi-racial co-operation, in a speech which probably comes close to expressing Nkosi's own attitude at the time: 'That is why it's so important for people who think alike, both black and white, to form a united front against the government, so that the fight will not be black against white but right against wrong' (p.49).

Like *Rhythm of Violence*, his short stories written in South Africa, 'As for Living', 'Holiday Story', 'Musi' and 'The Prisoner', all concentrate on or include sexual relationships and encounters between black and white.[37] Later in Paris, the United States and London, Nkosi evolved different cultural and political attitudes. In his 1965 collection of essays, though he writes enthusiastically and optimistically about the artistic ferment of the 1950s, especially the theatre, including *King Kong* and Township Jazz, he curiously does not say a word about *No-Good Friday*, in which he actually took part.

However, in *South African Information and Analysis*, which he edited from Paris, he gives a full assessment of Fugard and his three early plays. This assessment constitutes some of the best criticism of Fugard's early work.[38]

Nkosi and Nakasa were working for *Post* and *Drum* and had already discussed the idea of starting a theatre workshop where actors could be trained and playwrights try out their work, when Fugard came up from Cape Town 'in a van', recalls Nkosi, 'which seemed to contain all his worldly possessions, which, to put it a little less bleakly, were not very many'. He subsequently turned up at the newspaper officers to discuss the formation of a group and Nkosi told him: 'Yes, that's precisely what we have already been discussing.' For a long time the three of them, Nkosi, Nakasa and Fugard, moved around the city and Sophiatown together 'drinking, sleeping at each other's places' and discussing. Nkosi wanted to write. Nakasa wanted to act and write. A nucleus of actors gathered together, and the group began to act out 'situations' — 'like the situation we were very conscious of, the power of the gangsters in the township'. The script was developed in collaboration with the actors. Nkosi writes:

> Fugard's manner of writing the play had been partly to have actors improvise and then later to improve on their lines or the other way round: to write the draft-scenes and try them out with the actors, changing the material when necessary to fit a new situation.

However, it was Fugard who, in the last analysis, 'shaped the script'.

Fugard has talked and written about his early life and development as an artist on a number of occasions. For our purposes it will be sufficient to concentrate on a particularly detailed interview he gave in 1977.[39] From it we learn that Fugard's mother was a Potgieter, an Afrikaner. His father was Anglo-Irish. His roots were firmly in the Cape, the Port Elizabeth area in particular. His secondary school was the Port Elizabeth Technical College, where his training included a course in motor mechanics. Financed by his mother, who owned a tea room in Port Elizabeth, he studied philosophy and social anthropology at the University of Cape Town, where he was especially influenced by Kierkegaard.[40] He left the university before taking a degree and hitch-hiked through Africa for six months, was a seaman in the Far East for two years and did experimental theatre work in Cape Town with his wife. He then left for Johannesburg, because 'at that point I knew that I was going to earn a living in theatre'. 'To keep myself going', he says, he took a job as Clerk of the Court of the Native Commissioner's Court. 'I knew,' he says, 'that the system was evil, but until then I had no idea of just how systematically evil it was . . . Soon after our arrival [in Johannesburg] we were introduced to Sophiatown by a good friend, Benjamin Pogrund, now a very courageous journalist.' The idea of the play stemmed from this 'introduction'.

Fugard was right when he told the cast of *No-Good Friday* that it was 'a break'. The play had far-reaching consequences, not only for the theatre in South Africa in general, but for the individuals involved in it. Fugard, Modisane,

Mokae, Mabaso, Rachilo, Moloi, Gampu and Poho all went on to careers in theatre and film, some with considerable success. Fugard got a job in the all-white National Theatre Organization as a stage manager. Mokae continued his association with Fugard by acting in his next two plays, *Nongogo* and *The Blood Knot*, the second of which he performed in New York with Fugard. Mabaso worked at the Rehearsal Room with Fugard as well as acting in *Nongogo* and stage-managing *The Blood Knot*.

When in 1970 Mabaso directed a revival of *No-Good Friday* in Soweto, he described his first impressions of Fugard. When discussing the characters, Mabaso recalled, Fugard would suddenly make a comparison with 'real-life folks in "Softown", man.' This was another type of 'lanie' [white]. Fugard, he said, had three attributes, 'humility, truth and sincerity'. He was

> a dream director for the actor. He will sit hours on end listening, letting you try things for yourself, even jumping on to that stage to demonstrate how he thinks it should be done if everything else has failed . . . Yes, Fugard, the man who taught me to work and think, the man who taught me to live. Theatre is life. Hell! What can a man say about this guy! [*Post*, 19 May 1970]

No-Good Friday

No-Good Friday lies in the tradition of cultural collaboration between black and white dating back to the activities at Marianhill in the 1920s. In its time it seemed original in that it was written by a South African and based on a South African situation. Furthermore it was about the lives of blacks and especially about the lives of blacks in the *urban* situation. Whereas previous multi-racial dramatic activity directed by whites had been based on foreign scripts or situated in the traditional culture, *No-Good Friday* was an original play set in urban Sophiatown. Also the earlier intellectuals, H. I. E. Dhlomo, the Bantu Dramatic Society and Ezekiel Mphahlele and the Syndicate of African Artists, for example, had derived inspiration and instruction from the works of Shakespeare, Goldsmith, Wilde and Dickens. The new generation collaborated in *No-Good Friday* to create not only something original and indigenous (at least, in content), but a work that was shaped by more modern American and European influences – by, for example, playwrights such as Sartre, the 'Method' school of acting, Marlon Brando and American gangster films. This interest in modern American and European literature and drama ushered in a new phase in the theatre activity of black intellectuals and artists.

In terms of the relations of racial groups in South Africa, *No-Good Friday* was an original and significant phenomenon. Many believed that such instances of multi-racial collaboration, rare though they were and involving only a few people, were important blows in the struggle to resist apartheid and therefore operated in the interests of blacks in South Africa generally.

Fugard affiliated to the liberal, avant-garde tradition of European philosophy and art — what the critic Georg Lukacs termed 'modernism'. Nkosi and Modisane at that time were black intellectuals who aspired to enter this world. In Modisane's case, at least, this aspiration sprang from a somewhat intense feeling of rejection of the traditional culture of his group. Though both Nkosi and Modisane adopted a more ambivalent stance towards black urban culture, they nevertheless both had their noses pressed to the glass of the cultural world Fugard inhabited and ascribed to.

If this, then, is the broad ideological and cultural perspective of their collaboration, what we need to assess is the extent to which this perspective reveals itself in, and affects or shapes, the piece of theatre they, with the others, produced.

Plot Synopsis

The action of the play takes place in a backyard in Sophiatown. It begins on payday, Friday night, notorious in the urban townships for muggings and murder. Every Friday night Shark, the gangster, extracts 5s from each resident as protection fee. On this particular Friday Father Higgens, a white priest, brings a man recently arrived from the country to the yard in the hope that someone there will be able to find him a job. Willie, an office worker, doing a correspondence course for his BA, agrees to help him, albeit after much persuasion.

When at 8 p.m. precisely Shark and his gang arrive to collect their fee, and Tobias, the man from the country, does not understand what is required of him, he is stabbed to death. At the instigation of Father Higgens and after a considerable struggle with his conscience, Willie does the unthinkable and reports the death to the police. The inevitable confrontation takes place between Shark and Willie on the next Friday night. Willie is told either to pay up as usual or to get out. He decides to do neither. Abandoned by all — Rebecca, the woman he had been living with and who had borne the brunt of his frustration and doubt, his friend Guy, the jazz musician, and all the other residents of the yard — he waits for the coming of Shark. Only the blind Moses keeps him company.

Willie: Moses, is it true what they say about blind men, can you hear better than those that see?
Moses: Yes.
Willie: Moses . . .
Moses: I know, Willie . . . I'll tell you when I hear them coming.
(Willie moves back to the house. Guy's saxophone music is heard in the background.) Curtain.

Culture

The Sophiatown 'backyard' tended to create social homogeneity, breaking down the barriers of ethnic group, language, status and to some extent even class. Thus in the particular yard in which the play is set, there is an office worker, Willie, studying for his BA. His surname is Seopelo, which is Tswana.

He habitually speaks English. With him lives Rebecca, about whom we know little except that she is Willie's 'woman' and is not as educated as he is. Guy Modise is a struggling jazz musician whose surname is Sotho. Mr Watson is a politician, possibly of Xhosa origin. The ethnic origins of Moses, a blind man, and Pinkie, who works for a firm in town as a tea-maker, are not known. Visiting briefly is Tobias, a Zulu-speaking migrant from the rural areas of the eastern Transvaal.

The lives of these characters revolve around job-seeking, charms from herbalists to bring good luck in job-seeking, education, marriage, hire purchase, politics, Friday night, pay packets, gangsters, the police, bus queues, cards, money, music, drink, the shebeen, crowded trains and death and funerals — which is a fairly comprehensive itemization of the culture of a community such as Sophiatown. It also tallies to a large extent with the images of Sophiatown culture provided by, say, Modisane in *Blame Me On History* and Trevor Huddleston in *Naught For Your Comfort*.

Central to this culture was the proletarian's need to sell his or her labour. This accounts for a number of items on the list. In fact the circumstances of labour-selling were so important to most members of the community that they virtually characterize in themselves urban existence for the majority of black Africans in the urban areas, and in some cases achieve the status of myth — for example, pay packets, Friday night (pay day), bus queues, crowded trains and night, all of which were constant images in the theatre and litera-ture of the urban areas.[41]

There were other ways of escaping the rigours of poverty besides looking for a job. For instance, there were illegal activities, such as racketeering, liquor-selling, *dagga*-running and gambling; or the pursuit of education (men) and marriage (women); religious activity and entertainment of various kinds either as a source of income or as another form of escape. Drink and sex were important anaesthetics in a lifestyle of which the shebeen was the celebrated focus. Though racketeering (the protection racket run by Shark) and politics (Watson's 'profession') were both a part of Sophiatown culture, in this play they are, as we shall see, associated — as anti-social, parasitical activities.

Both Willie and Guy also recognize that their black skin is an obstacle to survival. Guy tells Father Higgens that there is no point in reporting Tobias' death to the police: 'You can forget about the police. They protect a fellow like Shark. You see they're only interested in our passes. But a kaffir laying a charge against a criminal . . . that would be a joke. We are all criminals' (p.147).

The battle to survive produces its own ethic. In this culture the key to success or failure is what in *tsotsitaal* is called *clevergeid* — the effective use of one's native wits in the interests of survival. The corollary of this is, of course, 'the stupidity of others' — or their goodness. Hence the term *clevergeid* evolved as a substitute for 'goodness'. 'Clever' — i.e. sharp-witted, 'with it', 'knowing the ropes' — replaced 'good', which came to be more commonly associated with 'stupid' or, in everyday speech, *moegoe*. The 'clever' is not the 'BA', who in theatre is on the contrary often shown to be a *moegoe* — or, as the abbreviation is popularly interpreted, 'bloody ass'. The *clever* is the one who is fit to survive in the struggle; the *moegoe* the one who is destined to perish — or be constantly deceived, exploited and ridiculed. Tobias is inevitably a *moegoe:*

Shark: What's your name?
Tobias: Tobias. Tobias Masala.
Shark: Tobias? No, that's no good. We'll call you 'stoopid'! *(There is a pause and then Shark's voice is almost at a scream.)* Stupid! Because that's what you are. A dumb bloody ox. Okay, Harry.
(Harry and the other thugs move like lightning. A knife flashes, it is quick and sudden.) [p.140]

Survival often entailed indifference or passivity, a cultural factor expressed in the phrase 'easy come, easy go'. It is Willie who refers to the trait when he is upbraiding the others for not taking any action to stop the deaths in Sophiatown. 'We make a proud job of living,' he says. 'Let's make it easy. Let's make the whole thing easy. Easy come, easy go' (p.147).

The 'easy come, easy go' trait is, along with concepts such as 'African time', the alleged irresponsibility and indiscipline of blacks and an inurement or buoyancy concerning tragedy, a stock attribute of the racial stereotype of black culture — not only in South Africa. The question of stereotype pushes our cultural analysis into the wider context of cultural hegemony and ideology. An important factor in the development of urban black African culture is the image of that culture entertained and projected by whites. The ruling sections of the white groups in South Africa have, for at least a century, dictated and determined the physical circumstances of black existence. The moral and psychological product of such circumstances is then instanced by whites and some blacks as examples of black 'primitiveness', 'inferiority', 'racial personality', etc.

In other words, the ruling sections have constantly created structures which tend to furnish the stereotypes they require for the justification and defence of their domination. Ideology based on these stereotypes is then reinducted through the educational system, the press, radio, art and culture into the minds of the entire population, becoming part of the dialectic of imposed and constitutive cultural forces which characterizes culture formation in the dominated sections of the society.

As has been suggested, the 'agents' of this operation in the black communities were to be found in the educated intermediate classes. As it happens, *No-Good Friday* centres on the behaviour of a member of these classes, Willie Seopelo, and it is he who alludes to the 'easy come, easy go' personality trait.

The question of the attitudes expressed in the play towards the rural traditional culture is another significant ideological area. It is generally connected with the first, i.e. that of cultural stereotypes, as it is often the source of these stereotypes, even in the urban context.

Father Trevor Huddleston, on whom the character of Father Higgens is based, expresses in his book, *Naught For Your Comfort*, a characteristic liberal position vis-à-vis the relationship between the black urban and the rural or traditional cultures:

> It would be rather hard to explain the enlightenment of a policy which on the one hand constantly affirms itself based on 'Western Christian Civilization', and on the other firmly bolts and bars the door to such culture for the African. Nothing, I think, is more evil or more far-reaching in its effects than this attempt to prevent the African from entering the world of beauty in music, art and drama. [p.150]

The ideology of this extract becomes even clearer when we recall an earlier comment in the same book, made in the context of the Afrikaner nationalist justification for segregated and different education for blacks. Huddleston saw a contradiction between the need to preserve 'traditional Bantu culture' and the alleged absence of evidence that 'that culture existed or was worth preserving' (p.125).

For our purposes we need note no more than that this shows a mis-understanding of the true nature of the rivalry for hegemony in the society between the two white groups. Obviously the 'world of beauty' Huddleston refers to is that of his own group, and it was precisely this influence that the Afrikaner Nationalists were attempting to counter. It also shows that Huddle-ston saw the cultural opposition of traditional culture (or even urban black culture) and 'Western Christian Civilization' in exactly the same light as sections of the educated black intermediate classes — Modisane and Nkosi, for example. As Father Huddleston was principal of St Peter's school in Sophia-town, where the children of the intermediate classes were educated, this was only to be expected. In effect, he and they saw apartheid as blocking the civilizing and improving process of educated blacks who were attempting to pass from barbarism ('no evidence that the culture existed or was worth preserving') into 'the world of beauty', i.e. the civilization of the white English-speaking liberals. The position would seem to imply that there was no beauty either in the traditional culture or in the popular urban one that was in the process of development.

This attitude was complemented by another, expressed by both Nkosi and Huddleston, that culture and the integration of black and white within the peripheries of liberal European culture — i.e. that of the traditional English-speaking intellectuals, the white liberals — could prove a potent weapon in the political battle against apartheid. Nkosi wrote that he and his fellow intellectuals of that time believed that 'art might yet crack the wall of apartheid'. Huddleston recorded that Yehudi Menuhin once said to him: 'Don't forget, Father, it was the negro jazz bands that first breached the colour bar in the States' (p.150). On the same page he stated: 'I have tried, in the past twelve years, to do everything possible to break this culture bar.' He promoted orchestral concerts in Sophiatown and began the Huddleston Jazz Band.

Tobias, in the play, emerges as a representative figure. He represents the rural culture. He represents the past. He is what the inhabitants of the yard (either they or their ancestors) were once and believe they are not now. They are anxious to prove that their new urban culture has little to do with the rural culture Tobias represents. There is in their attitude the assertion that their urban culture is 'superior', more 'civilized', than that of Tobias. We have seen that the black intellectuals such as Modisane and white liberals such as Huddleston shared this attitude. In the play none is more zealous than Willie, Nkosi's 'educated African',[42] in dissociating himself from Tobias:

Higgens (to Willie): Then what was he [Tobias] made for?
Willie: His quiet reserve.
Higgens: That's what they say about all of us.
Willie: I'm no simple Kaffir! [p.127]

This recalls the *Drum* journalist, Arthur Maimane, who, Sampson records, did not want to be taken for 'an ordinary Native', and the reader of *Drum* who told Jim Bailey, the owner, that 'we're trying to get away from our tribal history just as fast as we can' (pp.31 and 21).

Tobias is the embodied converse of Sophiatown's new cultural values. He is rural, traditional, uneducated (illiterate, in other words), 'simple', innocent, honest, naively brave, in short, a *moegoe* — or, as Shark calls him, 'stoopid'. As Willie says: 'This is Goli [i.e. Johannesburg], not a quiet reserve. He wasn't made for this. They flounder, go wrong, and I don't like seeing it' (p.127).

Guy, on the other hand, is an almost perfectly adjusted member of the Sophiatown community. When Pinkie agonizes over the choice between the sack and apologizing to the white man at work for something he hasn't done, Guy advises:

Now think. It's a good job. It's good pay. It's Friday night. You're going to have yourself a good time. Right? . . . This van Rensburg's not in Sophiatown. You only see him for five minutes every morning and five minutes every afternoon. Why worry about him! Apologize and keep your job. [p.131]

Guy realizes that given the realities of day-to-day survival in Sophiatown, spiritual and moral values and attitudes like pride and justice are too costly. He later gives Willie some similar advice: 'Shark's coming round . . . for you . . . in two hours' time. Are you going to wait? Answer, boy . . . Because if you can't, start running!' (p.163). When Willie contravenes the Sophiatown code, the realism of survival, Guy instinctively has recourse to the surrogate ethics of *clevergeid:*

Willie: I'm not thinking anything.
Guy: You bet you aren't, because I've never seen anything so Goddamn
    stupid in all my life. And you are the clever one, remember, the thinker!
    [p.159]

Here the cleverness of the educated man is shown, as is often the case in
Kente's work, to be different from *clevergeid* — to be in fact *moegoegeid*.
Though Guy conforms to the cultural code in these respects, and is thus
found lacking in terms of the play's moral vision, he demonstrates an integrity
in two areas — he prefers to suffer as an unemployed musician rather than
accept a menial job in town, and he treasures the relationship between
Willie and Rebecca, which Willie sacrifices. 'You and Reb,' he tells Willie,
'was one of the things a fellow could believe in . . . A good man and a good
woman.' When Willie allows Rebecca to walk out at the end, Guy says to him:
'Now? I can't call you a good man, Willie' (p.162).

It is Father Higgens who has initiated in Willie the decision to report
Tobias's death to the police and thus confront Shark. 'I know life is cheap
here,' he says.

> I've heard that sort of talk until I'm sick of it. But something inside me
> finds five shillings just a little too cheap. I was hoping you [Willie]
> might have felt the same . . . Someone must have seen what happened
> out there on Friday night. Go along to the police and give a sworn
> statement. Get others to do the same. If only we can get as far as an
> official charge. [p.146]

Father Higgens lives in Sophiatown but in important respects he is an
outsider. He is white. His income is comparatively large and stable. Most of
the characteristics of urban black life do not apply to him. Gangsters are no
threat to him. The police protect him. He observes the culture from without.
The practicality or wisdom of Father Higgens's initiative here is discussed
below. All we need concern ourselves with now is that his intervention
evokes a response in Willie, and that this response is determined by the
relations between his class and that of Father Higgens.

When Guy asks Willie why he went to report to the police, he replies:

> I went for myself. For myself. Not to get Shark. Before I even start
> reckoning with him I've got myself to think about, the part I played in
> Tobias's death. The emotion inside me is shame, not anger, shame.
> [p.154]

In other words, Willie's reaction to Tobias's death is quite solipsistic. The
death does not provoke anger or hate in him, which would be directed
outwards against Shark, and further against the perpetrators of the system
that has created Shark. Instead it provokes shame, an inwardly directed
criticism of himself. It results not in public action with others, i.e. reporting

the murder in order to bring Shark to book, or in organizing self-defence groups, or in political action. It results in introspective self-analysis and an existential act. He reports to the police in order to clear his conscience, or as he says in the next scene: 'Well, I've found something I been looking for for a long time. Peace, Guy, peace. Peace of mind . . . peace of heart' (p.163). Fugard had evidently not forgotten his Kierkegaard.

But why should Tobias of all people be the occasion of Willie's soul-searching? Curiously enough, though Willie cannot hate Shark, he can hate Tobias:

> I hated him. I hated him because I feared him. These 'simple men' with their innocence and dreams. How can we dream? When I was a child I used to lay awake at night in the room where my mother and us kids used to sleep. I used to lay awake and think. I'd say to myself, 'You're black.' But hell it was so dark I couldn't see my own hand. I couldn't see my blackness, and I'd get to thinking that maybe the colour wasn't so important after all . . . and because I'd think that I could dream a little. But there was always the next morning with its light and the truth. And the next morning used to come so regularly and make the dream so stupid that I gave up dreaming. Tobias reminded me of too much, Guy. He was going to make some money and live happily ever after. The cozy little dream . . . like this! Willie and Rebecca lived happily ever after! That's how the fairy stories end and it's stupid because out there is life and it's not ending happily. [p.155]

In other words, Tobias was a simple man, unconscious, 'natural', uncivilized. One recalls that this assessment of Tobias (and his culture) is initially the priest's. It is also that of the composer of the following verse of the African Nationalist song, 'Mayibuye iAfrika':

Mayibuye iAfrika	(Come back, Africa,
eyayithathwa ngamabhunu	which was taken away by the Boers
sisesebumnyameni.	while we were still in darkness.)

Willie is saying that in the 'darkness' of barbarism, Tobias is able to believe in simple dreams, just as in the darkness of *black* night the urban child can forget his blackness and dream. However, with the coming of *white* day — i.e. consciousness of colour and race, understanding, education, awareness of reality — it becomes impossible to believe in dreams any more. Thus even Willie's relationship with Rebecca, with her dreams of marriage and a home, loses its meaning for him.

The disillusionment of this confession, particularly with its concentration on the fact of being black, and the dismissal, as we shall see, of the political option, recall in detail Modisane's confessions in *Blame Me On History*. What, of course, links Willie to Tobias, the 'simple Kaffir', whom he rejects, and separates him from the priest, with whom he feels an affinity, is his black skin. It thus becomes the focus for Willie, as it did for Modisane, of his frustration and disillusionment.[43]

Culturally, Willie aspires to 'the world of beauty', the culture of the white liberals. He shares, then, Father Huddleston's appreciation of European culture and ignorance of, and/or condescension towards, African traditional culture. Tobias's letter to his wife, MaXulu, and his own utterances illustrate this curious mixture of ignorance and condescension, already indicated in the chronic falsification of the real situation in the country areas contained in an already-quoted phrase Willie uses twice — 'his quiet reserve'. This should become clearer when we analyse the language of Tobias's dialogue below.

As for the popular urban culture, it has already been suggested that this was in the process of formation in terms of a dialectic of imposed and constitutive elements. It was thus degraded and brutalized, but at the same time resilient and inventive. The existence of this dialectic presents the playwright with a choice which is as ideological as it is aesthetic. One can either emphasize one factor in the dialectic or the other, or one can depict the dialectic itself. In other words, the playwright can emphasize the positive elements of the culture or the negative ones, or provide a picture which shows their interaction. Though in *No-Good Friday* positive elements are included, the major emphasis thematically is on the negative ones.

In order to show this, we shall return to the backyard, which, as has been noted, plays an important role in this play, as it does in *King Kong* and other works of the time. In many of the older urban areas, freehold rights existed and it was possible for a small black landlord class to come into existence. Housing was in short supply and the influx from the rural areas was constant. The answer to the housing problem was the backyard. On the property behind the house, tenant families rented rooms or built their own shacks. Modikwe Dikobe's novel *Marabi Dance*, set in Johannesburg over a period ranging from the 1930s to just after the Second World War, provides a vivid description not only of the overcrowding, the lack of drainage, the inadequate toilet facilities, the scandal and the degradation, but also the communal life of such backyards to which in many ways the relations of the traditional culture were transferred, despite the introduction of nuclear family groupings. This communal life, which was often convivial and supportive, was of course further, but not entirely, broken down when the next stage of removals housed each family in its own house, on its own small plot, in townships like Soweto. The hostel system is the apotheosis of this development.

In *No-Good Friday* the supportive function of the 'backyard' community is reflected, as in the case of Pinkie and his work problems. The presence of other supportive strengths is hinted at, as in the sharing of food outside the family group, for example, when on two occasions Rebecca finds something in the pot for Guy. However, the major emphasis in the play is on the culture's failures to remain human — on, for instance, murder, gangsterism, rackets, drunkenness, apathy. In other words, the play emphasizes precisely the same aspects of urban black culture that were emphasized by the white-owned 'black' press, *Drum* and *Post*. One of the effects of stressing the dehumanized aspects of the culture, without at the same time at least indicating the processes of its dehumanization, is that the responsibility for the consequences of social forces is shifted from those who wield them to those who suffer them. Once again it is Willie who gives expression to the idea:

> You know, one of the ideas I've come out with? The world I live in is the way it is not in spite of me but because of me. You think we're just poor suffering come-to-Jesus-at-the-end-of-it-all black men and that the world's all wrong and against us so what the hell. Well, I'm not so sure of that any more. I'm not so sure because I think we helped to make it the way it is. [pp.160–1]

The emphasis on the culture's failings is sometimes expressed at the expense of truth. For instance, one pronounced feature of urban black culture is generous attendance at funerals. That the burial of Tobias would attract no one but the priest and Willie is not only unlikely but it involves an underestimation of the communal and supportive strengths of the community.

That certain aspects of the authentic culture of Sophiatown do emerge in the play was to be expected given the knowledge of Sophiatown possessed by the playwright and the members of the cast, who together developed the play. The emphasis on the negative aspects of the culture is the result of cultural attitudes and ideology to a large extent shared by the white and the black intellectuals, i.e. that though the urban culture is preferable to the traditional, liberal white culture is preferable to both. We shall see how the writers of the Black Consciousness movement came to recognize the political function of the cultural domination embodied in such an attitude.

If the play is not a complete reflection of the culture of Sophiatown it is, however, a remarkably accurate expression of the black intellectual's isolation in the 'ghetto' at that time, and his yearning to escape from it. Mphahlele expressed this in *Down Second Avenue*. Modisane expressed it. It is implicit even in some of Nkosi's later criticism.[44] Willie Seopelo in *No-Good Friday* expresses it thus:

> Melancholy, loneliness, despair. They all add up to the same thing. *(Pause)* The bus queue was a mile long tonight. That's a lot of people. A mile of sweating shouting bastards, all happy because there was a little bit of gold in their pockets. I've never been so lonely in all my life. [pp.125–6]

They were not Willie's people. This was not his culture. Forced by law to live amongst them, the intellectual is alone and yearns to leave.

Fugard clearly saw in the black intellectual of the time the individual alone and isolated from his community, which he later identified as the overriding thematic concern in his work.[45] There are implicit in this concern two ideological principles, both characteristic of liberal European thought. The first is the tendency to attach prime importance to individual as opposed to social needs, and the second is to see society as a threat to the freedom of the individual and consequently often to regard the individual as the guardian of truth and justice within a corrupt and corrupting society.

Willie Seopelo as a character clearly exists within this tradition. It is, however, possible to identify the emphases of this tradition at least indirectly with the emphases on the negative attributes of Sophiatown culture contained in the play. In the play the people of Sophiatown are depicted as degraded and apathetic. They have to be if the individual, Willie, is to be alone and the sole exemplar of moral virtue. In other words, it is possible to associate the liberal ideology of Fugard and his associates with the operation of cultural hegemony within the society, thus pointing to links which Gramsci believed existed between the traditional intellectuals and the established structures, despite their apparent independence and even dissidence.

This vision of the black intellectual of that time is not, however, a complete picture. Though the black and white intellectual were associated in culture and ideology, there were certain real differences in their circumstances, and these produced some contradictions in the position of the black intellectual. As genuine as his feeling of isolation, his yearning to escape, might have been, the black intellectual's cohabitation with others of his own racial/national group, in similar circumstances and suffering similar disabilities, created conflict in him. He was, at one and the same time, separate from the people and at one with them. This contradiction is illustrated clearly in Modisane's attitude to his *Drum* article on independent African churches. His training — i.e. his induction into the ideology of European commercial journalism — compelled him to regard with belittling amusement what he himself knew to be a dignified and vital part of the people's culture. He was forced to create stereotypes of the bishops and leaders of the sects in order to satisfy the image of this culture which his white editor entertained — when he knew that in reality such stereotypes were inaccurate. Thus though Modisane could be unequivocally disparaging about traditional culture, his attitude to popular urban culture, in the midst of which he lived and to a considerable extent participated in, was contradictory. His editor, however, controlled two powerful sanctions. The first was that it was he who had hired Modisane and could therefore sack him. The second was that Modisane, in order to retain status, had to identify publicly with the 'civilized' cynicism of his editor. As he acknowledged with self-criticism, 'I was superior'.

Thus though the attitudes and feelings of the black intellectual about popular black urban culture were ambivalent, he tended to collaborate with the white intellectual in projecting an image which stressed the failures of the culture. He did this because of his need to procure and retain employment, his affiliation to certain categories of European culture, and the cultural and social pre-eminence of whites generally.

Though Fugard did not exercise the *same* sanctions exactly as the editor of *Drum*, that he did exercise sanctions is testified to by both Modisane and Nkosi.[46]

Thus, to sum up, the image of the culture of Sophiatown expressed in the play, though it contains a basic content which is authentic, is modified by certain emphases given it by its main author, Athol Fugard, partially endorsed by its subsidiary authors, the black intellectuals of the cast. This modification embodied an ideology which appeared 'progressive' in comparison with that of the Afrikaner nationalists and, despite certain tensions, in the main acceptable to the black intellectuals who participated. It was, however, an ideology which reinforced the domination of the white groups in the society over blacks and especially that of the English-speaking white group. This becomes especially clear when one examines the play's substitution of political cynicism for political awareness and especially when one examines the political interpretation of crime in Sophiatown and the image of the politician that the play projects.

Politics

It would be well to recall in this context that in the year 1958 a crisis in the history of African nationalist political struggle in South Africa was imminent. On 2 November, two months after the first performance of *No-Good Friday*, the Africanists left the African National Congress to found in April of the following year the Pan Africanist Congress.

No-Good Friday contains no reference to the ANC as such, but it does present us with a portrait of a nationalist politician in the person of Watson – and he is the *only* character in the play who demonstrates any consistent awareness that the situation in Sophiatown has a political dimension.

In the opening scene, the dialogue between Guy and Watson leads up to Guy saying to Watson: 'Watson, I want to ask you something . . . How do you earn a living? You don't get up every morning at six like Willie and old Moses. You don't walk the streets looking for a job like me.' 'I make sacrifices for the cause,' says Watson.

We next see him in scene two: 'Watson, smartly dressed and carrying a briefcase, appears on his way to a meeting.' When Shark, the gangster, appears 'Watson tips his hat' and without paying the requisite 5s protection fee 'disappears' (p.138).

Two facts are suggested by the above. First, Watson would appear to be of a different class from the others, a fact which would accurately reflect the tendency of nationalist politicians to belong to intermediate classes. He does not work but is comfortably off, and he appears not to live in one of the corrugated-iron shacks 'clustered about' in the backyard. It is possible that he lives in the main house, in which case it is possible that the others are his tenants. However, if they were (and there is no mention of rent or landlord in the play) Guy would surely know where his income comes from. Secondly, the fact that he does not work but is well off, and that he does not seem to be subject to Shark's levy, begins an association in our minds – which the play develops – between the politician and the gangster.

Now the association of black politicians and black gangsters was a stock one in the minds and imaginations of whites. We shall meet another example when we come to *King Kong*. Seen from the point of view of the establishment black politicians and gangsters are anti-social forces, equally subject to police restraint and legal sanction. In moments of political crisis, e.g. in the late 1950s and later in 1976, gangsters and *tsotsis* have made common cause with the political movements, as the following popular song, sung during the Sophiatown removals testifies:

Ua utlwa makgowa a reng?	(Do you hear what the whites say?
Ha re yeng ko Meadowlands.	We should go to Meadowlands.
Ua ba utlwa botsotsi ba reng?	Do you hear what the *tsotsis* say?
Ons daak nie, ons phola hi.	We're not budging. We're playing it
	cool right here.)

If the first factor which determines our attitude to Watson and his political cause is his association with Shark, the second is that in the play he is quite obviously corrupt and ridiculous. This emerges clearly in, say, Guy's tone in the following interchange:

Guy: Ja, Watson, how's the politics?
Watson: We're fighting, we're fighting.
Guy: You been fighting for our rights today, Watson? [p.123]

The irony is obvious, especially as it all leads up to the question 'How do you earn a living?' In this first scene Watson is shown to have spent all day (in the midst of the labour of others) thinking up fine phrases for a speech at a meeting of the Organizing Committee. This kind of politician is all rhetoric and committees. Guy says he has 'never seen [him] a single day in the streets where there's a riot'. Watson, with unintended comedy, replies: 'We can't all be leaders. Some must lead, some must follow' (p.124).

When Pinkie takes his work problem to Watson, he is fobbed off. Watson is in a hurry to address 'a meeting over at Freedom Square' (p.138). Again, his solution to the problem of Tobias's murder is 'to put forward a resolution at the next congress, deploring the high incidence of crime and calling for an immediate . . .' He is cut short by Pinkie, who asks him why he doesn't 'go home' (p.160).

Watson is thus thoroughly discredited. As he is the only spokesman in the play for the African nationalist position, the effect is to discredit this too. Yet the substance of Watson's rhetoric, though he himself may be no more than a phrase-monger, remains real for all that. He talks of 'the liberatory movement', 'the heavy boot of oppression' and he calls for action and the rejection of a £3-a-week wage. These remain facts: a real liberation struggle was being, or needed to be, waged, oppression really existed and £3 a week was a starvation wage. The Sophiatown of *No-Good Friday* reflects these facts, but its political meaning obscures them.

At a crucial point in the action, when Willie and all the inhabitants of the yard are discussing Shark's final offer, Watson interposes: 'Are you denying oppression?' Pinkie supports Watson for once: 'We don't like things the way they are, Willie.' Willie replies: 'Nobody but a moron would like them. But there's a lot of it we make ourselves and a lot we accept . . . such as Tobias's death and a character called Shark' (p.161).

Here, as Nkosi points out in his criticism of the play, Willie adroitly diverts the responsibility for the suffering of the inhabitants of Sophiatown away from those who maintain and benefit from the oppressive system. For now the inhabitants of Sophiatown are themselves partly to blame. They make their suffering themselves, they 'accept' it. If Willie's criticism is accepted, two alternative responses are suggested – either 'Yes, Willie is right. We should organize effective resistance to poverty and oppression with a view to ending them', or 'Yes, Willie is right. We should try to be poor and oppressed with dignity and courage'. By suggesting that the way 'to do something about it' is to stand up to Shark, Willie makes it clear that he intends the second response.

But Shark is not the real enemy.

Shark: You done me dirty, Willie. You done me all wrong. You went along to the police like any cheap blabbermouth to cause me trouble. Did you hear that, all of you? To the police . . . the bastards who lock us up for not carrying our passes. That's who Willie went to see. You got to watch him. Because if you don't, he'll report you as well. Yes, he will. You, Watson . . . he'll report you to the Special Branch. He's ambitious, this boy . . . He'll do it. [p.157]

As the political option has been discredited by its association with an obviously inadequate figure, Watson, so it is here by its association with an obviously evil one. Shark is the villain. Willie is the hero. When Shark compares Willie to an informer and opposes his activities to those of Watson, the effect is further to discredit Watson. Similarly, the accurate analysis in this speech of the function of the South African police and its relation to the community is discredited because it is Shark, a criminal and a murderer, who expresses it. In real life the police *are* 'the bastards who lock us up for not carrying our passes'. Shark, like the real Father Huddleston, knew who the enemy really was. Huddleston wrote: 'I regard the *tsotsi* as a symbol of a rotten social order, corrupted through and through by the false ideology of racialism, of apartheid, of white supremacy.'

In Sophiatown, as in other urban townships in South Africa, gangsterism was merely an illegal facet of the struggle to survive which shaped the culture. The real enemy was the group of people who dictated the conditions of the struggle to survive. The play, by trying to concentrate the people's resentment on the gangsters, substitutes a phoney struggle for the real one, a social problem for the political one.

Father Higgens urges Willie to report the death of Tobias to the police. This he does, but not in order to expose the police or to bring the murderer to book. Willie, like Guy, knows better than Father Higgens the real nature of the police. He knows that they will not take any action, and in fact may easily be benefiting from the racket Shark operates. Reporting the death would mean, in Guy's words, asking for suicide.[47] But Father Higgens has stirred Willie's conscience. He decides to face himself, to act according to his conscience and to do this alone. In other words, he turns away from the social problem (that of gangsterism), which Father Higgens has substituted for the political problem (that of oppression), in favour of an existential one.

Now, some would argue that the death of the solitary man or woman of conscience for a right principle or idea, as in Anouilh's *Antigone*, a play that obviously fascinated Fugard, can be a potent political act. Unfortunately in Willie's case the idea is not only a mistaken one but also a distorting one, based as it is on Father Higgens' substitution of a phoney struggle for the real one. This the ending of the play implicitly acknowledges. The results of Willie's action in the real Sophiatown, or any urban township, would have demonstrated the futility of Willie's act. Wisely, the play avoids them and instead leaves the audience 'in suspense'.

When the distortions of Father Higgens and the futility and ineffectiveness of Willie's sacrifice are linked to the deliberate discrediting of Watson, the politician, and the total absence of any consideration of more effective forms of political opposition, the play's political meaning and its precise role in the operation of hegemony come into clear focus.

Language

The cultural and political distortions described above are reflected in the play's language and in its meanings relating to language.

It is noticeable that a number of the characters in the play have difficulty trying to find the words to express themselves — and by corollary to formulate difficult concepts. Tobias, for instance, admits that he has 'not got the words' (p.137). Rebecca too admits this to Guy: 'Have you ever tried arguing with Willie? . . . When you don't even know half the words for the things you want to say?' (p.149). Guy and Rebecca constantly urge Willie to put things simply, to use simple words, even when Willie's speech contains no apparent difficulty.

Language and the word are clearly associated here with education, and education means the mastery of English. Hence there is the assumption that the 'word', the instrument of forming and expressing concepts, is English. Those, then, who have not acquired the 'word' through the process of European education are conceived to be incapable of forming or expressing difficult concepts. The attitude is that of Prospero to Caliban or the colonial educator to the 'savage'.[48] The sophistication — the words — of the indigenous languages and the versatility of the urban dialects were a closed book to the early colonists — as they were to Fugard. This attitude is reinforced by the real struggle of the indigenous languages to cope with the vast influx of European objects and concepts.

In fact facility with words — i.e. flexibility, ability to borrow and adapt, inventiveness, etc. — is a notable feature of black culture in South Africa, both traditional and modern, something the government attempts to inhibit through its manipulation of the development of 'Bantu languages' in Radio

Bantu and Bantu education.

Thus the attitude of the play to the thematic problem of language is shaped by a cultural concept which is both inauthentic, i.e. not true to life, and 'colonial'.

The language the play's dialogue was written and acted in crucially affected the nature of its creation and performance, because language is a crucial element in the relations of whites and blacks generally. In the 1950s English-speaking white intellectuals were able to relate to educated blacks because of a natural affinity of class and culture, and this was facilitated by their common use of English. Such contact was rarely possible with those blacks who were not at home in English, i.e. the majority. Their culture, their ideas, their capabilities were not accessible to whites in general. This meant that in collaborative enterprises in the theatre, the culture and personality of this majority were generally either ignored or falsified, and because the language both of communication between those involved in creating and performing the work, and of the dialogue itself, was English, important meanings and textures derived from the colloquial everyday experience of the culture of the majority were invariably excluded or distorted.

The 'legitimated' language of black theatre activity at the time was English. This led to a situation which ideologically and aesthetically operated against the interests of the majority of black people. Ideally, the constituent elements of the creation and performance of a play should have linguistic unity. In other words, the language of the play should be one in which the playwright is perfectly at home, which the characters in the play and the actors in the cast speak and the audience in the theatre either speak or understand extremely well. This might sound obvious but in the 1950s and 1960s such linguistic unity did not exist.

Inevitably, the fact of working in English, allied to the black writer's relatively unsure grasp of the language and his lack of experience and expertise in the staging of plays, resulted in dependence on white English-speaking artists and intellectuals, such as Alan Paton (*Sponono* and *Mkhumbane*), Harry Bloom (*King Kong* and *Mr Paljas*) and Athol Fugard. Kente was an important exception, as we shall see.

However, though a script in English by an English-speaking writer solved one problem, it simply replaced it with another. The script would be written relatively competently in English by a native speaker with a cultural familiarity with but often no practical experience of dramatic forms; but it would deal with characters and situations from which the writer was socially and culturally estranged, and with people who spoke languages the writer himself did not speak and who in real life would not speak English at all.

As we have noted, the script of *No-Good Friday* was developed in co-operation with the actors. This method of working accounts for some of the play's positive achievements. It also points in the direction of alternative forms of play-making which later enabled Fugard largely to transcend some of the linguistic problems we are dealing with here. In this play Fugard tried 'to create a language which was comparable' to that spoken by the actors when they acted out the situations. In so doing he produced a language (which he was to repeat in *Nongogo*, his next play) which consisted of slightly bending the English by inserting a pattern of regularly repeated grammatical errors largely derived from American English.

Willie, the educated hero of the piece, is usually though not always an exception. Generally, he speaks 'correct' English. All the others do not. Rebecca, for instance, Willie's girl friend, speaks like this:

> Oh yes, and something else. Betty and Solly is engaged. They want to get married in November. I met them on the street. He asked about you. Wants to know when you are going to visit him.

Or, a few lines later:

> You wasn't listening either . . . You been learning all afternoon. . . Then give it a rest now. What you been doing? History? [p.140]

The question arises — what is Rebecca supposed to be talking? Does she habitually speak in the vernacular to Willie, or in English? She is not as educated as he is and would probably speak a vernacular language to him. Different language tendencies prevailed amongst women. They tended not to speak *tsotsitaal* unless they were actually gang members and to be freer to use a vernacular language without losing status. Is she talking American slang? Rebecca is domestically inclined, a 'decent' girl with her heart set on marriage to a BA. American slang would imply a more gregarious, slightly 'good-time' girl. Is she trying to talk English but making elementary grammatical mistakes? If so, she would make mistakes that are characteristic of English as spoken by black people in South Africa, the interposition of 'he' and 'she', for instance.

The answer appears to be that Fugard, as main author, did not know. He did not know Rebecca's psycho-cultural make-up or the language it would be expressed in. As Nkosi writes of Fugard's characterization of Queeny in *Nongogo*: 'Athol Fugard could not and really did not know anything about the life of an African prostitute' (1968, p.4). Similarly, he did not seem to know a great deal about Rebecca.

The speech of Shark, the gangster, presents another problem. In real life Shark would probably have spoken *tsotsitaal*. In this play he talks 'American'. It is true that the idiom of the criminal underworld in Johannesburg was derived from American gangster films, and though gangsters generally spoke *tsotsitaal*, one or two were noted for their American slang. So Shark's Americanisms are not inauthentic. However, the black gangster's imitation of his American equivalent was not slavish. The most characteristic and original aspects of the gangster are missing in the portrayal of Shark. In addition, he lapses from time to time into Anglicisms which recall a London 'toff' more than a Sophiatown racketeer. He says: 'Don't be vulgar, Harry. You're always thinking about money' (p.138), 'I want to report to you chaps' (p.138), and 'Hi, Willie. How's life treating you, boy?' (p.156).

The inadequacies of this depiction of a Sophiatown gangster may best be illustrated by comparing a short extract from Shark's speech with one from Dikobe's *The Marabi Dance:*

Shark: . . . I want to report to you chaps. After all you are entitled to something for your subscription. That is, other than the protection we give you. Now you boys have been paying very well and very regular. I reckon this about the best yard in Sophiatown. Isn't that so, Harry? [p.138]

In this extract from *The Marabi Dance* we hear members of the Black Cat gang from Vrededorp plotting a raid on the Bantu Men's Social Centre:

Whilst both dances were in progress, the Black Cat gang held a conference in an adjacent yard, about two hundred yards away from the main entrance. The 'Black-Jack' Municipal police did not see them because they sat in the dark, and they could not be heard even if they raised their voices.

'George has left us in the Marabi. He was our player. He has now gone to the teacher.' The Black Cat coughed and puffed dagga from his pipe and passed it over to Bitch-Never-Die.

'My cry to George is that he left me with a small baby. He now loves that Doornfontein girl.' Maria flapped her thighs with her hands.

Bitch-Never-Die looked up at the stars and puffed out long twisted smoke. She appeared in deep meditation: 'Ou Bra Black Cat,' she stopped and looked at Maria. 'Ou Bra Black Cat. Jul mors tyd.' She again looked stealthily at Maria: 'You're wasting time, Ou Bra Black Cat. I want George.' Maria twitched and extended her hand to ask for a smoke. 'Ek wil jou man hê.'

The Chief looked at Maria and laughed: 'Hoor jy, Maria? Bitch-Never-Die wants your man!' [pp.73–4]

Admittedly this gang is not in the same class as Shark's, but the atmosphere communicated by the dialogue is vivid and real. The speech is characterized by the vocabulary and inflexions of *tsotsitaal*, influences of the vernacular — 'my cry to George' — and local detail, such as the rivalry between the two urban districts, Vrededorp and Doornfontein. Shark's language is stiff and colourless when set beside this.

The language Tobias speaks not only exemplifies the inadequacies present in that spoken by Shark and Rebecca, but it also illustrates clearly what in Rebecca's case was partly hidden, namely the ideological attitude of Fugard and his collaborators towards blacks who do not speak English. Here is an interchange (chosen at random) which Tobias, 'an African from the rural areas visiting Johannesburg for the first time', has with the blind man, Moses:

Tobias: How long you been here?

Moses: A long time.
Tobias: When you going home? [p.132]

In case this is taken for the natural elision of colloquial speech one should note the first line of Tobias's letter to his wife: 'Dear Maxulu [i.e. MaXulu] , I have arrive at Jo'burg.' I think it is clear that Tobias is intended to speak broken English. Whereas in the case of Rebecca it was not clear whether her speech was intended to be broken English or a kind of American slang, in the case of Tobias there is no such doubt. Yet in real life Moses and Tobias would without doubt have spoken a vernacular language to each other. In which case there would have been no question of grammatical error unless Moses happened to be Sotho-speaking — Tobias spoke Zulu. Because the actors as black intellectuals and the author, who spoke no African language, had decided on an English script, Moses and Tobias had to be made to speak English. The genuine English equivalent of their dialogue would be more like this:

Tobias: When did you come here? *(Ufike nini lapha?)*
Moses: A long time ago. *(Sekudala.)*
Tobias: When will you return to your home? *(Uzobuyela nini ekhaya.)*

Instead the author chose to introduce grammatical errors. Why?

It is possible that because Fugard did not speak an indigenous language he was accustomed to hearing black non-English-speakers, like Tobias and Rebecca, speak broken English. Had Tobias therefore spoken perfect English, albeit shaped by the syntax and rhythms of his own language, he would not have sounded authentic to Fugard. Tobias is rural. He has no formal education. He does not belong to the same class as Fugard and the rest. He is therefore made to speak an English that is uneducated and childish. This reinforces the stereotype of an uneducated man, i.e. a non-English-speaker, which their class habitually projects. Compare a snatch of Tobias's letter with a conversation in *The Marabi Dance* in which the speakers are speaking the vernacular:

> Here also I find Sophiatown where I stay with Mr Guy Modise. I meet his friend, Mr Willie Seopelo, who will get me a job in one of the tall buildings, taking the whiteman to the top. [p.136]

and

> 'Wait, I still want to tell you something. I don't want to put a load on a person who is not the owner.'
> 'What do you mean?'
> 'You are a woman and I am a woman. You don't like to say a man is the father of your child when you know that another man is the father. It will eat you and you will get thinner and thinner until everybody says: "She has made a sin." '

'Do you mean to say you are in body?' [p.90]

In the first extract it is apparently implied that no past tense exists in Tobias's native Zulu. This quaint lapse is set in an otherwise characteristically English sentence structure. In the extract from *The Marabi Dance* the language is dignified and grammatical, but the vernacular phrases, idioms and rhythms can be heard behind it, so to speak. There is the delicacy of the circuitous, metaphorical expression indicating the carriage of another man's child. 'It will eat you', 'she has made a sin' and 'you are in body' are literal but graceful translations from the vernacular.

These examples of inadequacy in the uses of language in *No-Good Friday* are intended to illustrate how the author's estrangement from the culture of his characters and their situations, in conjunction with his particular political and ideological position, to a large extent shared by the actors he worked with, resulted in distortion and a loss of authenticity and richness.

Thus though *No-Good Friday* might appear in the context of its time, and in comparison with other political and cultural activities and events, to have been a 'progressive' phenomenon, an analysis of the culture and ideology expressed in the play and of its political meaning would seem to suggest that it functioned principally in the interests of certain sections of the English-speaking white group, while partially reflecting the attitudes and affiliations of certain black intellectuals.

The political roots of the situation in Sophiatown were obscured by concentrating the audience's attention on social evils, by discrediting political solutions and by implying that the police were potential allies in the fight against these evils rather than the enforcers of the system which gave rise to them. Though only indirectly expressed in the play itself, the adherence to liberal multi-racialism — a multi-racial society in which the structures of relations in which white capital dominates remain unchanged — was the ideology of those who collaborated on the play.

The use of improvisation, on the other hand, involving those who had an intimate knowledge of the culture and languages of Sophiatown, partly accounted for the play's cultural authenticity, to the extent that it was authentic. Fugard's sensitivity to certain aspects of the black intellectual's dilemmas at that time and the original urban context of the play accounted for other strengths.

6. 'A Tremendously Exciting Inter-Racial Enterprise'

Two months after *No-Good Friday* was staged for the first time, rehearsals for another play began 'in the large untenanted ground-floor of a warehouse' in Johannesburg, which the guitarist General Duze quickly nicknamed 'The Dungeon'. This play was *King Kong*. It was performed by an all-black cast but largely directed and produced by whites. It was set in Sophiatown, i.e. in the black urban culture. Crime and gangsters played an important part in it and the Sophiatown 'backyard' had a significant structural role. Thus in these and other ways *King Kong* and *No-Good Friday* had much in common.

There were, however, some major differences. The main one is that whereas *No-Good Friday* was produced by a temporary association of individuals, *King Kong* was produced by a structure, the Union of Southern African Artists, which was linked in real and obvious ways to other structures in the society. Thus in order to demonstrate the function of *King Kong* it will first be necessary to examine these structures.

The Union of Southern African Artists

Accounts of the formation in 1952–53 of the Union of Southern African Artists vary. Even the date is uncertain.[49] But all versions agree that Dr Guy Routh, Ian Bernhardt and Fred Thabedi played important roles in its founding. Routh was an economist 'employed by one of the Industrial Councils' and secretary of the Garment Workers' Union. Bernhardt was an advertising consultant, involved in amateur dramatics. Thabedi was an organizer of youth clubs who 'knew his way about town' and was 'working to promote African music'. Thus originally the main activities represented in the union were trade unionism, amateur dramatics and African music.

It is clear that the original intention of the black artists who wished to form a union was specifically to protect themselves from exploitation. According to one account, the occasion of the union's founding was a particularly sensational instance of such exploitation. An American group had adapted a South African song and it had become a commercial success. The group contacted a lawyer in Johannesburg and asked him to trace the whereabouts of its composer, Solomon Linda, in order that they might pay him royalties. It turned out that he and his group had been paid £5 'for both the performance and copyright of the song, which was a little above the standard rate at the time'.[50]

At first the union restricted itself to providing lectures, holding members' evenings and giving free legal advice. Soon, however, it expanded its activities. Inspired by the success of a farewell concert it organized for Father Huddleston and helped by the funds raised, the union organized a series of Township Jazz concerts, in which 'isolated concert groups . . . travelling about giving one-night stands at dances or weddings, thereafter combined to give large and varied programmes'.

When the trade unionist Dr Guy Routh left, his place was taken by Ian Bernhardt, the advertising consultant with an interest in drama. By 1958 the trade union had changed character substantially. It had become a promoting body in its own right, a commercial enterprise. The union had shifted the emphasis from protecting the interests of black artists to providing them with employment by acting as both agent and employer. Its promotions were almost exclusively directed towards the white market.

The union attracted considerable support for its activities from English-speaking whites. Writing of *Nongogo*, which the union produced, Nkosi called them 'do-gooders', who 'came out in large numbers from their well-furnished, velvet crannies in the Johannesburg suburbs to help mount' the play (1968, p.3). Some gave financial assistance in the form of donations, loans, guarantees, sponsorship, advertising or free services, others served on its various fund-raising, organizational and administrative committees, or assisted in various ways on the productions the union presented. As a writer in the 'black' newspaper, *Elethu*, boasted in 1962: 'Union Artists is run by leading South African business, legal and literary personalities who work *just for the fun of it*' (my italics).

Of these we have selected four to discuss — Robert Loder, Clive Menell, Edward Joseph and Ian Bernhardt. Behind these individuals, were the established structures of English-speaking capital — the mining companies, international trusts and monopolies, financial houses, the civic authorities and liberal bodies such as the Institute of Race Relations. Of all these Anglo-American Corporation, the mining giant, was the most powerful. It also played a most important role in the development and direction of the union's activities.

According to Scrape Ntshona, who was a member of the board of trustees of the union and knew Loder well, Robert Loder was on the board of Anglo-American.[51] Shortly after his arrival in South Africa from England he made the acquaintance of Jim Bailey, the proprietor of *Drum* and *Post*, and began to move in *Drum* circles, visiting the 'townships' with black journalists like Todd Matshikiza, who later wrote the music for *King Kong*. Loder then recognized that there was need for assistance in the artistic and cultural areas of black life, and so he began working with the union. He was particularly active in organizing *King Kong*. He was a member of the organizing committee, where he 'evolved into the chief administrator on the committee and devoted hours to the budgets which controlled the show and the documents and contracts which were needed for every phase of the operation' (Glasser, p.49).

He continued to play an important part in the union until he left for Zambia in 1962. Ntshona noted the personal friendship between Loder and the chairman of Anglo-American, H. F. Oppenheimer. Whenever there was a shortfall in the union's budget, Loder would undertake to meet it. Ntshona believed that this shortfall was met by Anglo-American.

Another important figure in mining circles, Clive Menell of Anglo-Transvaal Consolidated Investment Company, played an intimate part in the process of creating the *King Kong* script, as well as in supportive, administrative and financial ways. 'In the romantic atmosphere of a lovely studio-room [Menell's] with its striped woven curtains, easel and paints, records and piano, they would visualise (and act out) many of the separate scenes [of *King Kong*].' When the *King Kong* scriptwriter, Harry Bloom, had to return to Cape Town prematurely, Menell took over temporarily and wrote an outline which became the basic framework for the play's action, i.e. a day in the life of Sophiatown (Glasser, pp.11–12).

We have already had occasion to refer to the connection between *Drum* and the Chamber of Mines. Now we discover that the Union of Southern African Artists and the mining companies were similarly connected, as were the activities of the two cultural structures, *Drum* and the union, both multi-racial ventures and similar in many respects. The support the mining companies gave the union was not confined to the contribution of individuals associated with or employed by them. They provided the union with financial assistance in various forms. For instance, together with the Central New Agency, the bottlers of Coca-Cola and President Giant cigarettes, Anglo-American underwrote *King Kong* to the tune of £4,000. With Coca-Cola, President Giant and Anglo-Transvaal, it sponsored the union's next big production, Eugene O'Neill's *Emperor Jones*. Pages in the *Emperor Jones* programme were sponsored by, among other companies, Johannesburg Consolidated Investment Company (Barnato) Group of Mines and Goldfields of South Africa. They and other companies, General Mining and Finance Corporation, for instance, paid for advertisements in the programmes of various of the union's productions. Anglo-American continued to support the union for many years, rescuing it from bankruptcy in 1966, for instance, by granting it a 'loan'.

Edward Joseph, a stockbroker, was a particularly loyal supporter of the union. He worked on the organizing committee of *King Kong*. 'His hospitality extended to almost daily lunch-time meetings at his office, and numerous all-night sessions at his home. His wide range of contacts did a lot to rope in the enthusiastic assistance of many people.' On his death a few months later, an Edward Joseph Memorial Fund was set up. £2,500 was raised and used to found AMDA, the training wing of the union.

What fired his imagination in this work [i.e. *King Kong*] appeared to be the challenge to show the world the talent of the townships, which otherwise would long have remained unrecognized, as well as the conviction that here was a tremendously exciting inter-racial enterprise which, if it succeeded, might yet transcend the political stresses and strains that lie so near the surface in South Africa. [*King Kong* programme]

Though Dave Marais, the Mayor of Johannesburg at the time of the departure of *King Kong* for London, was not himself directly involved in the activity of the union, his short message, printed in the London programme, merits quoting here. It expressed an attitude to the work of the union, and to *King Kong* in particular, which was representative of the English-speaking establishment in the Transvaal. As mayor, Marais was the head of the United Party in the Johannesburg City Council:

King Kong died unrecognized in sport; by the same token, in providing opportunities to foster theatre and stimulate culture and music amongst non-Europeans, it may well be that the African Music and Drama Association will rescue and promote to fame some gifted individual who might otherwise, like King Kong, stray from the accepted path to end his life without fulfilling his talents.

That 'straying from the accepted path' might imply 'into African nationalist politics', as well as 'into crime', is suggested by the following assessment of King Kong's life by Mona Glasser, the play's historian:

This was the story of the real King Kong, of a man torn violently from one society and thrown into another . . . an unbalanced symbol of those contemporary Africans who have come to believe that might is right. [pp.4–5]

In both Dave Marais's and Mona Glasser's words we see again what we noted in the chapter on *No-Good Friday*, an implicit association in the minds of English-speaking whites between black crime and African nationalist politics. Mona Glasser's assessment includes another characteristic belief — that 'anti-social' behaviour amongst urban blacks, criminal or political, resulted from the imbalance caused by a too rapid transition from a traditional African society to an industrialized urban one.

Ian Bernhardt, the advertising consultant who took over from Dr Routh in the early 1950s as the chairman of the union, has been active for a long time in black and multi-racial cultural activity. Before he became a founder member of the union in 1952–53 he was an amateur actor in the East Rand, acting in many productions including one directed by Leon Gluckman, the future director of *King Kong*. He gave up acting when he became involved in raising funds for charities. His successful production of the Bareti Players'

The Comedy of Errors 'led to his appointment as Chairman of the Union of Southern African Artists'.[52] He organized the series of Township Jazz concerts that culminated in *King Kong*. His part in the growth and success of Union Artists was described by Harry Bloom:

> Bernhardt's work in the union has been remarkable. He not only built it into a powerful force in the South African entertainment field (one achievement, for example, was to persuade the British Actors and Musicians Union to insist on their members playing to audiences of all races when touring South Africa); but he brought African music and musicians out of obscurity, and through *King Kong*, into the view of the whole world. [Bloom, p.10]

Bernhardt himself described the work of the union as being an attempt 'to develop a form of theatrical expression which is true to the life of the urban African' (Maine).

Leon Gluckman's role in the *King Kong* production team will be discussed later. However, his expression of what he conceived to be the basic objectives of the union offers a useful and revealing example of the kind of idealism which appeared to motivate those English-speaking whites who actively supported and worked for the Union:

> . . . the first [—] to protect against exploitation artists who were becoming involved with fledgling and often impecunious impresarios, recording companies, and other persons and groups who were beginning to appreciate that the talent and potential talent of the African meant big business.
>
> The second [—] to explore, artistically exploit and, above all, organize the considerable talent which was exhausting and often wasting itself all over the country through lack of a basic unit to control and organize it for its own good.[53]

At this stage we might just note the implicit contradiction between these two objectives and how, given the second of them, the first seems to suggest that it was not so much the protection of black artists from exploitation that was intended, as much as the monopoly of the commercial and artistic development of their talent.

We have described some of the key figures involved in the union's activities and the ideals they themselves offered as the reason for their involvement. We shall, however, have to go beyond ideals and intentions to an examination of the actual objective interests of the individuals and groups who supported the union, and of those for whose alleged benefit the activities were organized.

As the most powerful and influential organization of what Ntshona called 'the liberal establishment', to which Loder, Menell and Joseph belonged, the ideological assumptions of the Anglo-American Corporation can be said to be an important and representative expression of its collective interests.

Fortunately, H. F. Oppenheimer, then joint deputy chairman and managing director of the corporation, has given us a frank and realistic assessment of its interests at that time in the development of South African society in a speech he delivered to the Oxford Union in 1956.[54] It was a carefully enunciated argument for what he called 'multi-racialism'. This meant the firm rejection of apartheid for the reason that it was bad for the economy of the country and an equally firm rejection of a fully integrated, egalitarian society.

'It is quite plain,' he said, 'that the separation of Black and White into areas of their own, what in South Africa we call "apartheid", if carried out to any significant extent, would destroy the economy of the country with disastrous results for all the races in it.' As the kind of economic progress he envisaged, based on mining and industrial expansion, could not possibly be built 'within the framework of the primitive social, economic and political system of the Africans . . . advancement of the Africans can take place only if the African way of life and *thought* [my italics], however picturesque it may be in some respects, is abandoned in favour of a state and society built on European foundations'. He continued:

> In the long run, however, African society must disintegrate and the Africans must become an integral part of an entirely different sort of society. Until they are able on the whole to do that — and it will take many years — it will not be possible to avoid — and, indeed, it will be essential to maintain not necessarily by law but by custom — a substantial measure of social and residential separation of the races. This separation, however, while in practice it will correspond broadly with the racial division and must inevitably, I am afraid, be reinforced by racial prejudice, is in its essence not a question of race but of culture, or, if you like, of class . . . the remedy for prejudice and intolerance lies, to my mind, in better education for both Black and White, and certainly not in an enforced proximity of communities whose ways of life differ profoundly from each other.

He pointed out that the situation in South Africa is fundamentally an economic problem 'obscured by questions of race':

> The fear of the European workers that African labourers, working for lower wages, may break down their high standard of life . . . is at the base of the so-called 'economic colour bar', by which African labour is confined, either by law or by pressure from the white trade unions, or by custom, to unskilled work. Such a limitation is obviously unjust and runs directly counter to our objective of helping the Africans to realize their full economic potential.

He advocated a 'multi-racial' society and strongly rejected the African nationalist movement in Southern Africa, 'whose objective is not a fair participation of Africans into a multi-racial society, but [its] transformation

. . . into an exclusively African country'.

Oppenheimer's position vis-à-vis blacks is very clear here, as is the extent to which his thinking was able to accommodate the aspirations of the black intermediate classes and the greater utilization of the labour of the black working class. Oppenheimer's vision entailed the full but gradual integration of blacks into a capitalist economy and a 'multi-racial' society which, however, would not be egalitarian, nor need in fact be even fully integrated, as long as it provided the most efficient structure for the continued generation of profit and exercise of power in the interests of his own class, both in South Africa and abroad. Within this structure cultural hegemony would operate as it does in other advanced capitalist countries, in the way described by Gramsci and others. Until then, any cultural activity which assisted the slow progress in the direction of such a society would be encouraged and supported. Such activity should necessarily, when involving blacks, be 'multi-racial', culturally European in form, and capitalist in function.

Of course, Oppenheimer's support for such cultural or educational activity and 'multi-racialism' benefited him in another important respect. It afforded him and his organization a progressive image, not only with some blacks in South Africa but also in Europe and America, the source of much of his investment capital.

There is enough in this speech to explain why the mining companies, or at least why Anglo-American, supported the activities of the Union of South African Artists. For here was 'multi-racial', cultural and educational activity, under white direction, in European cultural and artistic forms within a capitalist format. The earlier trade union image had rapidly given way, as the union became more and more an employer, to that of a commercial management – and, with the export of *King Kong* to London in 1960, Union Artists provided the companies with a West End showcase in which to exhibit to the best possible advantage their achievements and those of blacks under their patronage and tutelage. For instance, Anglo-American's advertisement in the supplement which accompanied the official programme of the London run of *King Kong* showed a photograph of black schoolchildren in a mine school with the following text:

> In the development of Southern Africa human advancement is closely associated with economic progress. The needs and aspirations and the cultural growth of the peoples who live and work in Southern Africa are receiving constant attention from the mining companies operating there. The picture shows children of African mine-workers at a school in one of the mines of the Anglo-American Corporation Group.

De Beers Consolidated Mines accompanied a photograph of traditional dancing with the text: 'In the hostels on the diamond mines of the De Beers Group, traditional dancing is a popular form of relaxation. In these hostels a wide range of social services is provided for African miners.'

To what extent though did the activities of the union benefit black artists or blacks generally, who had actually called for its establishment in the first place?

The desirability of action aimed at promoting certain individuals to fame and fortune in a situation where the majority continues to be neglected and poor is debatable. However, for such action to be successful – in the case of the union – it would have to be accompanied by structures which would ensure that the artists had adequate work opportunities *after* they had been brought to the notice of the 'outside world'. This the union did not, and could not, do. Instead artists were given a taste of fame and a relatively decent wage for a short period at home or exported to London or New York, only to find that when the show was over they were neglected and poor again.[55] White artists and administrators, on the other hand, were less vulnerable, and their careers were often conspicuously assisted by their work in the union.[56] Naturally, black artists noted this with some cynicism. It appeared to them that the activity of the union launched white artists into fame and employment with greater regularity than it launched black artists, and that the ambition of the union to become a 'powerful force' in South African 'show business' seemed to be more zealously pursued than either their interests or the cause of 'African theatre'.

The white writers of that time stressed the wretchedness of the conditions suffered by black musicians in the urban areas and their desperate struggle to eke out the meagrest of livings. Yet in the hall when the union was founded, the artists did not ask for a promoting body. In fact even the trade union, because it was administered by whites, aroused suspicions that it was actually a camouflage for yet another essay in the exploitation of black talent by whites. What the artists wanted was protection from, not more, white commercial involvement in their activities.[57]

A fact which emerges from the available records is that there was in existence at that time a genuine, independent, popular musical culture which was widespread and relevant to the everyday experiences of the people, including their political experience. Music *functioned in* the life of the community and made reference to and judgements about situations such as bus boycotts, riots, rail disasters and political trials, and such music was played at celebrations, political rallies and funerals. Performance, too, was not limited to a small group of talented specialists, but 'singing groups seemed to spring up in every shack and back alley of the townships'. In short, it was an independent culture which functioned *in* the community at all levels.

By promoting packages such as Township Jazz or large-scale musicals such as *King Kong* in white areas, and by providing rehearsal and practice facilities in the city centre of Johannesburg, the union diverted much energy and talent away from this culture. The popular life and culture of the black urban areas were for some time, at least, impoverished and their independence and functionality weakened by the growth of commercial motivation towards and dependence on the white-controlled organizations. The 'act' or sketch, which was included in musical programmes before and during the 'fabulous fifties', virtually disappeared at this time, and only with the resurgence in the

1970s of popular music forms such as *umbhaqanga* did it reappear substantially. The rise of the union coincided, too, with the virtual extinction of black close-harmony and concert groups.

Because it operated commercially in a society the very structure of which required the exploitation of cheap labour, it was unlikely that the union would be able to operate any differently from other South African commercial ventures. Its main function rapidly came to be that of a body which discovered black talent and purveyed it to white audiences in South Africa and abroad, and which did not hesitate even to call on the forces of the white state to settle its disputes with its labour force and contractors. In September 1966, for instance, *The World* reported that the cast members of *Sikalo* were unhappy with the way in which, whenever there was a disagreement between the artists and the officials, many of whom, incidentally, were black, the police were called in.

The ideal intentions and the promises made were the product of romantic optimism, at best, and the union was in no position to fulfil them. The result was a disastrous waste of talent and human lives, a weakening of the black group's own organic culture, a dependence on the 'big break' in white 'show business' and a further deepening of the cynicism with which blacks regarded relations with whites.[58]

It has not been our intention to reprove or condemn those whose work in the union, though often undertaken for the best of motives, had the consequences described above. Rather we have attempted to show that the ideals they professed were, first, contradicted by more influential, more pragmatic considerations and, second, that in the objective circumstances their ideal objectives were neither practicable nor desirable.

But predominantly it is hoped that this section has brought into focus the conjuncture of political, cultural and economic factors that characterized the relations of liberal English-speaking capital and urban blacks in South Africa at that time. Politically, the ideology of the former consisted of various non-egalitarian forms of 'multi-racialism'. Culturally, they demonstrated contempt for black traditional culture and a patronization of the evolving black urban culture. Having no confidence in the constitutive capacity of this culture, liberal capital and its associated intellectuals conceived of their relations with urban blacks as being tutelary. However, their political and cultural relations were based in the crucial facts of capitalist economic relations. The urban blacks constituted capital's cheap semi-skilled labour force. Thus multi-racialism in the context of cultural disparity and economic exploitation characterized their relations. We hope to demonstrate how this characteristic manifested itself in the process of making *King Kong* and in the final product itself.

The *King Kong* Production Team

No-Good Friday was produced by Athol Fugard and a small group of educated black amateurs who wished to perform 'serious' theatre in English. To some extent Fugard collaborated with the actors to create the script. In the case of *King Kong*, the union hired a *company* of professional musicians for the performance of a commercial musical with a script written by Harry Bloom, with the assistance of Ruth Williams, Clive Menell, Arthur Goldreich and Leon Gluckman. The production team included only one black member, the late Todd Matshikiza, once a journalist on *Drum*, at that time a razor-blade salesman; Matshikiza wrote the music. With this single exception black artists were excluded from the making, as opposed to the performing, of the play.

King Kong was therefore a 'collaboration' between members of the white group and members of the black group of a different kind, with a clear division between those who determined the play's ideological plan and content and its aesthetic form, and those who were hired and trained to execute it.

The two most influential members of the creative production team were Harry Bloom, the scriptwriter, and Leon Gluckman, the director. Gluckman had long been involved in white theatre in South Africa. He was, we are told, 'one of the foremost men of South Africa's developing theatre'.[59] He returned from a period in English repertory theatre, where he worked as assistant director at the Nottingham Playhouse, determined to continue working for 'the improvement of South African theatre'. He saw *King Kong* as an opportunity to explore his theatrical ideas freely, as 'there were no precedents for such an exercise'. 'To be born in South Africa is a boon,' he said, 'because to work here is to be in a position to express whatever talent you have – however big or small – to the fullest.' Of course, he was talking about being born white. Later, after *King Kong* had already been staged and he had already directed another play for Union Artists, *Emperor Jones*, he was to describe his work with black casts as 'the basic justification for being here', i.e. in South Africa. He saw his work with black casts as an educating process and he hoped it would promote mutual respect between the races. He wrote:

> This [*King Kong*] was a show by Black artists, with a white nucleus training, organizing and producing. As time goes on the African will learn to do more and more of this work for himself . . . I see the theatre as a civilizing force – one of the last channels open in a country that is violently political and ferociously materialistic. The theatre recognizes and accepts the basic spirituality of man. On those terms everyone can meet.

Harry Bloom expressed similar beliefs about the function of *King Kong*. The exercise of making it was 'a truce in the grim war of race relations'. The play demonstrated the necessity of collaboration between white and black, he felt, and – here he saw no contradiction – showed that Africans were capable of cultural achievements. Its very existence was a blow to racial discrimination and it opened up possibilities of advancement and success for black artists (Bloom, pp.19-20).

The characteristic relations of the white liberals with black South Africans emerge quite clearly here. There is the commitment to 'multi-racialism' and a tutelary relationship with 'the African' in the context of a commercial relationship. The educative role of the English-speaking whites, seen as a separate, technologically and culturally advanced group, is taken for granted, along with a vision of the gradual progress of the black group towards being able to do things the white way 'for themselves'. Bloom and Gluckman did not see themselves and the blacks with whom they worked as part of one nation in the development of whose culture they desired to participate. Their function was to work as 'agents' who would teach blacks aspects of their own European culture or, in other words, as 'agents' of the cultural hegemony of their group. They did not realize that such 'collaboration' could not prove that blacks were capable of their own cultural achievements. It could only show that blacks could be taught to participate on a simple level in theirs.

This is implicit in the following extract from a review of *King Kong* which appeared in the theatre pages of a Johannesburg white newspaper: 'This abounding vitality from the other side of the tracks would have meant nothing without the glitter and polish of Leon Gluckman's direction.' Nowhere did Gluckman, Bloom and the others attempt to correct this impression. In fact, they encouraged it. Only an independent black enterprise could prove this point – if indeed the point needed proving – as the cultural activists of the Black Consciousness movement of the 1970s realized.

Bloom and Gluckman were attracted to the story of *King Kong* and a play about urban life for reasons somewhat similar to those which inspired Fugard to do *No-Good Friday*. There was no doubting the enthusiasm of these men for that section of life they were able to observe in the black urban 'townships', Sophiatown in particular. It was this life that Bloom and Gluckman were trying to portray in *King Kong*, or as Bloom put it: 'the drama, colour and effervescence, as well as poignancy and sadness that is the peculiar flavour of township life.' Bloom saw in it an optimism despite the suffering, an 'indestructibility'. It was a world which, like Elizabethan England (a comparison made by Sampson, Nkosi, Modisane, Mona Glasser and many others), seemed so much more vital, energetic and interesting than their own.[60]

Another reason Bloom was attracted to the story of King Kong was the personality of the man himself. Bloom found Ezekiel Dhlamini, the original King Kong, a representative figure. Dhlamini had come from rural Natal to Johannesburg ('in this respect [he] was like most urbanized Africans'). The ambience of the boxing world gathered together precisely those elements in Sophiatown which fascinated Bloom – glamour, danger, beautiful passionate women, gangsters, the shebeen. For him, King Kong was a man who 'made his own rules' and got where he wanted by force. His glamorous life was an object of envy to the bulk of the urban black population. What is more, Bloom saw him as an example of the waste of black talent and ability caused by the apartheid system. In the end, too, he comes to personify Sophiatown itself, and his fall is the fall of Sophiatown, for by 1960 Sophiatown had been all but demolished.

Bloom would appear to have chosen a strong and meaningful content for his play. His apparent determination to stress the buoyancy and strength of the urban black culture, rather than its evil and degeneration as in, say, Alan Paton's *Cry the Beloved Country* or its passivity and cowardice as in *No-Good Friday*, and his sensitivity to the meaning of King Kong's destruction, promised an authentic and trenchant play.

Concerning the play's form, Bloom, Gluckman and Mona Glasser are all agreed on the difficulty of the problems that faced the production team. In addition to many serious practical problems, such as rudimentary rehearsal facilities, lack of transport, police harassment and muggings, the two most important artistic problems were reckoned to be the language problem and the inexperience and the lack of technique of the actors and dancers, or as Gluckman reportedly put it when he addressed the cast at the first rehearsal, 'Tradition – acting is alien to most of you.'

The actors in *King Kong* were not in the main recruited from the ranks of journalists, teachers and the educated intermediate classes, as was the case with *No-Good Friday* and in the productions of other organizations such as Mphahlele's Syndicate of African Artists. The actors in *King Kong* were, with very few exceptions, relatively uneducated professional singers and musicians. *King Kong* absorbed the Manhattan Brothers, Miriam Makeba's Skylarks, the Jazz Dazzlers and the Woody Woodpeckers. 'Other professional groups with colourful names abounded, and Leon Gluckman chose the members of the cast from such groups as the Chord Sisters, the Saints, the Swanky Spots, the Queen's Pageboys, the Katzenjammer Kids and the Crazy Folks.' Few of the cast could speak English 'well enough for dramatic purposes'. With the exception of three, none had ever acted in a play before. 'It would be true to say that the great majority of the cast of *King Kong* had never seen a play or been inside a proper theatre in their lives' (Glasser, pp.29–30).

The acting problems determined the form of the play. It was commercial and it had to be a musical, as it was aimed principally, says Bloom, at providing opportunities for the musicians and singers. In any case, he argued, township life is lived in the idiom of the musical. 'Musicals are an old tradition of the European and American stage, but really they properly belong to the African.' It was decided that the plot should be kept simple and the acting and speaking parts restricted to a very few. The structure was to be a story illustrated in a series of 'big pictures', or, as Mona Glasser put it, 'a thin line which would reach a number of theatrical "moments" which Leon knew would work'. It was to be story rather than characterization, visual not verbal, and the actors were to be 'free to dance and sing with their natural exuberance, and without the inhibitions imposed by acting roles'! Those who were called upon to act were type-cast. Finally, the style was to be flamboyant and exaggerated (Glasser, Bloom).

The form they chose resembled in many respects that of African traditional theatre and some of the later experiments in traditional form by West African playwrights, such as J. P. Clark's *Ozidi*. An emphasis on episodic narrative, unified and carried forward by song and dance, and a more pronounced use of physical and visual expression than dialogue, made for a form that was rooted in the oral traditions of Africa, as well as being more than adequate to contain the content of black urban culture.

Thus Bloom and Gluckman would seem to have provided themselves with a solid base in both form and content. This base, however, is flawed, as should already have become apparent. First, the *King Kong* production team romanticized Sophiatown life and, second, they underestimated the creative capabilities of their cast and its culture. The underestimation of the cast's real abilities was shared by Arnold Dover, the choreographer, Spike Glasser, the musical director, and Mona Glasser, the play's historian, as the following quotations reveal: 'they *fell back* on the simplest stage convention of all, the reminiscences of a "narrator" ' (Mona Glasser); 'few could speak English well enough for dramatic purposes, and even the best spoke it with the characteristic African accent' (Bloom); 'free to dance and sing with their natural exuberance, and without the inhibitions imposed by acting roles' (Bloom), 'the actors were not so much acting, as living out their normal lives on the stage' (Bloom); 'one of the difficulties, of course, is that they are used to *ex tempore* expression . . . the idea of "daintiness" in women is a bit alien' (Dover); 'as it turned out the new ideas, cleverly timed entrances and patternings with *no real dancing*, were most successful' (Mona Glasser); 'there were enormous problems in teaching [the African actor] to control his movements and to speak' (Gluckman). (Italics have been added.[61])

It should not be necessary to expose the errors contained in these assessments of the black actor and his art. Most of them are obvious. Why, for instance, should English 'with the characteristic African accent' be a problem? The white South African, after all, has his own 'characteristic accent'. It is a common racialist error to assert that when a black actor acts so well as to appear natural, he is not in fact acting but just 'being himself' or 'living out his normal life'. The dancers, we are told, were too bad to learn 'real dancing', the black actor found it difficult 'to control his movements and to speak', etc.! The only way to make sense of this is to assume that by 'real dancing' was meant European or white American dancing — Dover was a classical ballet instructor — and that the traditional and urban dances of South Africa were not 'real', and that the style in which the actors were required to move and speak was so foreign to them that, like children, they had to learn the simplest of human functions from scratch. Gluckman is, of course, right to insist on the necessity of technical training for inexperienced actors, and this applies to any section of any social group. His error lies in assuming that the techniques and forms and critical criteria of his own culture are the only appropriate ones.

In comparison with those of the rabid racialists, the ideological and cultural assumptions of Bloom, Gluckman, Glasser and the rest may have seemed progressive. The enthusiasm of the liberals for the vitality of black life and their recognition of the potential of black people to create (albeit under their guidance) may be refreshing and commendable by comparison. However, one must not ignore their essential underestimation of the integrity and validity of popular black culture as it really was, i.e. unromanticized. To them the actors in *King Kong* and their culture were willing but raw material which required a strenuous process of refinement before it could be poured into even the simplest of European moulds. Because they both romanticized the culture in which the play was situated and underestimated the performers who were to perform it, they simplified, trivialized, even distorted, its content and failed to exploit the real strengths of its form.

King Kong — The Play

Plot Synopsis

King Kong is the story of a well-known Johannesburg boxer, whose real name was Ezekiel Dhlamini. At the start of the play we see him at the height of his career. In the world of black boxing in South Africa he has no rival. Now a fight is being lined up for him in White City, London. After yet another spectacular victory in the ring, he and his party go to a famous shebeen, the Back of the Moon, where he meets its glamorous proprietress, Joyce, initially played by Miriam Makeba. They fall in love, much to the chagrin of Joyce's boyfriend, the gangster Lucky, who vows vengeance. In a fight with Lucky's gang, King Kong kills a man with his fists and is sent to prison to await trial for murder. This is the turning-point in his life. Although he is acquitted, he becomes embittered and, above all, loses the chance of fighting in London.

Lucky and his gang intimidate all future opponents and King Kong, unable to fight, becomes increasingly frustrated, even at one stage turning to crime. Ultimately, he is ignominiously knocked out by a lighter boxer, 'Little Greb', and becomes the laughing-stock of Sophiatown. He loses Joyce to Lucky and in his bitter, jealous rage King Kong murders her. Despite his plea for the death sentence, he gets life imprisonment with hard labour. However, he takes for himself what the judge would not give him, and drowns himself in the prison dam.

Culture

Though Harry Bloom expressed admiration for the buoyancy and vitality of Sophiatown life, in the script of *King Kong* he emphasized the sensational, especially the negative or 'imposed' elements of the culture, such as drinking, stabbing, crime, gangsterism, sexual infidelity and promiscuity, etc. In addition to the ideological reasons already noted, there were three important reasons for this. First, it was the fast, 'Elizabethan' sub-culture of the shebeen that whites who travelled to Sophiatown, Western Native Township and Orlando usually experienced. There was thus a natural tendency for them to mistake this sub-culture for the whole. Second, it was these aspects of the culture which the press had 'popularized', especially *Drum* and *Post*. Third,

King Kong, as a commercial enterprise, had to be popular with its predominantly white audience, and with them it was these elements that went down well.

Politics

The political function of the play springs from the contradiction between the liberals' opposition to apartheid and the economic relations determined by their class position in a capitalist society, in the case of the union, as employer of cheap black labour and producer for the white market. Whereas the first suggests critical comment, protest or satire, the second implies the distortion or romanticization of reality, an emphasis on entertainment and a suppression of the critical elements.

Despite this, the play's political significance went some way further than *No-Good Friday*. Its authors at least accepted the play's political context — unlike Fugard, who we are told had a 'distrust for politics', and his collaborators, many of whom were disillusioned with politics. *King Kong* embodies a blanket disapproval of government policy and racial discrimination, and does not by and large attribute the sufferings it causes to the sufferers themselves. Yet it shares the unwillingness evidenced in *No-Good Friday* to upset its white audiences. It never allows the culpability of the whites to obtrude.[62]

For instance, in scene one, the three women who begin the play are described as 'sitting outside the doors of their houses, at work already, sewing or doing the wash they have collected from white folk who live elsewhere' (p.29). Here 'folk' softens the connotations suggested by the more common South African phrases, such as 'whites', and 'live elsewhere' makes the legally enforced separation of the races for the purposes of efficient exploitation of black by white appear to be benign or accidental. As in *No-Good Friday* the real nature of the police is obscured. Here the policeman is a benign, unreal figure who drops in for a drink at the Back of the Moon with a prisoner (p.47) and shows lost 'country cousins' the way to the wedding (p.87).

Particularly revealing is the way in which the play presents the arrest of King Kong:

A minute later King's hands rise above the crowd. KING walks out, staggering. Stands for a moment, then the POLICEMAN emerges from the crowd, gently places his hand on King's shoulder, and leads him off. [p.91]

Yet Nat Nakasa tells us that the police shot King Kong repeatedly but he refused to fall.[63] But while the violence of the police is omitted, that of the gangsters is sensationalized, as in this extract:

Fellow: . . . Hey, let's run! It's the Prowlers!
(They exit in panic just ahead of Lucky and his Gang.) POP runs too, but the Prowlers block his way, and they start KNIFE DANCE. This is a gloating,

gleeful, sadistic dance in which they torment Pop. [p.52]

Lucky and his gang, like Shark and his, are projected as the real terror of the 'townships', not apartheid, and the police instead of being its instruments are seen as the people's protectors.

   The play does contain political criticism. In scene one, for instance, the discussion of Dan and the washerwoman turns around the unreasonableness of their white employers, the indignity of their job and the hardships it entails. Truffina says: 'I worked in one place for four solid years and they kicked me out because I took a bottle of milk to my room.' About her 'madam' Mabel snorts: 'And untidy. Leaves her petticoats all over the flat and I got to walk after her picking them up' (pp.29-30).[64] Then Jack, Kong's trainer, is unable to marry his Miriam because of the impossibility of finding accommodation. Sophiatown is being demolished. 'They pulling this place down so fast, we got to take turns to go to bed nowadays. We got our name down for a house in that new Township they're building out there in the veld. But it's going to take a long time' (p.36). The play comes back to this at the end, when Dan announces that his house is to be demolished and he and his family moved to alternative accommodation in the mockingly-named Sunshine Gardens.

   But the most explicitly critical passage is Jack's comments on the frustrations of being 'a non-white' champ, addressed to Popcorn, a camp-follower:

Jack: King was Champ — you remember? Yes — not so long ago. Heavyweight Champ, and there wasn't a fighter in this whole country — black or white — who could stand up six rounds with him. But what did it mean? Nothing. Oh, he was a big shot around the township, all right, but did you ever see a white reporter at one of his fights? No. Did you ever see his name when they made up the ratings?
Pop: No.
Jack: No — he was a non-European Champ, fighting for peanuts — and who pays attention to that? Champ. *(Laughs bitterly.)* Here, it's 'push my car — boy.' It's 'shut up, Jim.' 'Take your hat off when you talk to me', 'Where's your pass?' Champ or no Champ. Well, going to England was his chance to shake free from all this — a chance to be a proper Champ. [p.77]

   This accorded with the symbolic meaning attached to King Kong's life by Bloom and others of the production team. Bloom put it like this: 'His stubborn refusal to compromise became an inspiration to Africans struggling for emancipation, and many saw him as a symbol of the wasted powers of the African people.'

   This is a meaning the play could have communicated much more power-fully had it not been so anxious to avoid offence. The play does not provide an antagonist, a real figure that we can identify as being King Kong's *political* enemy, i.e. one who bears the responsibility for 'the wasted powers of the African people' and who makes the struggle for emancipation necessary in the first place. It thus emasculates and distorts the 'intended' meaning, i.e. that identified by Bloom. Instead of such an antagonist, we have Lucky, the gangster. King Kong's enemies, it appears, are the gangsters and himself. Thus again the radical analysis is subverted.

This is illustrated quite clearly in one potentially effective scene — the building-gang scene. Here the realism that becomes an increasing element in the second half of the play is well represented:

A building-gang at work. The men barefoot and poor with ragged clothes. Sweat, toil and poverty, are the notes set by their clothing. They swing picks and shovels, carry bags of cement, hurl bricks in a line across the stage, push wheel-barrows. A man walks among them carrying a pail of water — water is drunk from a ladle. [p.72]

Then they are paid. This is the moment of choice. Instead of making the political connection between their pay packet and their labour and rags, i.e. the inadequacy of their wages and the degree of their exploitation, Bloom brings on Lucky and his gang, 'brandishing knives'. A Zulu-speaking worker protests and, like Tobias, is knifed 'with deadly efficiency'. The political enemy — the white exploiter of black labour, in this case — is let off the hook and Lucky, the black gangster, hung there in his stead.

Bloom, attempting to answer criticism of the lack of political protest in the play, wrote:

> Many people have expressed disappointment that *King Kong* does not contain much more positive and outright criticism of apartheid. The feeling of those of us who worked on the play is that its existence, not to mention its success in South Africa and London, is the strongest possible criticism of all forms of race discrimination. [Bloom, p.13]

That this belief was widely held by others not directly connected with the making of *King Kong* is expressed in the following comment by Nkosi himself:

> . . . the resounding welcome accorded the musical at the University Great Hall that night [the opening night] was not so much for the jazz opera as a finished artistic product as it was applause for an Idea which had been achieved by pooling together resources from both black and white artists in the face of impossible odds. [Nkosi, 1965, p.24]

Nkosi's assessment of the meaning of *King Kong* is probably an accurate one. When, however, a political meaning is attached to it, as by Bloom, it is inaccurate because derived from the mistaken assumption that apartheid was purely a system based on the racial belief that blacks are inferior and not capable of participation in European social and cultural structures. It was the characteristic belief of the liberal whites and educated blacks that all that was required to change the system was to prove that some blacks could attain 'white standards' — or, as Ian Smith later put it, 'civilized standards'. But Wolpe has pointed out that the South African government itself was at that time already in the process of altering its official ideology from one based on the assumption of racial inferiority to one expressed in the phrase 'separate but equal'. Thus if the existence of *King Kong* did indeed make the point Bloom claimed it did (and this is more than doubtful), such a point was of little real *political* significance.

The political function of the play thus appears to have been determined partly by the ideology of the structures and individuals which created it and partly by its commercial function. It would seem that though the stated political position of Anglo-American Corporation, the union and the *King Kong* production team involved an opposition to apartheid and the government — if not to white rule and privilege — its economic relations, in this case, the commercial necessity of attracting a wider audience drawn from as many sections of the white groups as possible, meant that *King Kong* was less critical of the racial aspects of the system than the comments of its producers might at first have led us to expect. It was much less critical than, say, *Drum*, which was marketed in the black as opposed to the white groups.

Language

Language defines the relations of the groups and sections involved in this play. It is both the product and the expression of these relations. It is particularly revealing of the cultural aspects of its creators' ideology and it also has significant political uses.

The same problems of language that faced the makers of *No-Good Friday* faced those of *King Kong*. In fact, in the case of *King Kong* they were exacerbated by two extra ones. First, the artists in *King Kong* were relatively less educated and did not speak English with the fluency and clarity of those in *No-Good Friday*. Second, whereas the dialogue in *No-Good Friday* emerged from a collaborative process between Fugard and the actors, in *King Kong* such a process did not take place, and in fact contributions from the actors were frowned on — as we see from the following report of the director's reaction to some ad-libbing during rehearsals:

> The play itself had not remained static. When King Kong returns to the township unrecognized after his ten months' absence, one couple is supposed to walk past him muttering a crowd-scene mumble, but they had evolved the following noticeably audible dialogue for themselves:
> He: 'How about a date tonight, honey?'
> She (with loving arms around him): 'Oh, go jump in a lake!'
> 'I am sure', said Leon [Gluckman], 'that Harry Bloom would be most grateful to you for the improvement on his dialogue, but perhaps in this instance you could keep it to yourselves.' [Glasser, p.65]

The script of *King Kong* was not, in fact, all Harry Bloom's work. It had been evolved by an all-white team of writers in Clive Menell's studio. This they did without apparently consulting black writers, though Nkosi, Modisane, Nakasa, Themba, Motsisi and others were working in Johannesburg at the time. The only improvisation that was tolerated, apparently, was that of the designer, Arthur Goldreich, who during the writing of the play 'would rush about playing everyone's part. He would arrive on an imaginary bicycle, leap off and be the character who had been waiting for him, return to his bicycle and ride off again only to reappear as a bootlegger, shebeen queen or whatever was called for at that moment' (Glasser, p.11).

The cast was expected to perform the script, not help to create it — despite the fact that it was they who had an intimate knowledge of the authentic culture of Sophiatown, and despite the recognition by Dover, Spike Glasser and others that improvisation was precisely the area in which the special talent of the inexperienced actors and musicians of the cast lay. In the previous chapter it was suggested that the method begun in *No-Good Friday* of collaboration between writer and actors, including the use of improvisation, would make for more authentic dialogue as well as characterization and situations. It certainly proved the case with Fugard, whose later collaborations with Kani and Ntshona, *Sizwe Banzi* and *The Island*, are his best work. The necessity for an alternative form of making the play when whites are involved and the subject-matter is drawn from black culture is related to what Nkosi wrote about Fugard's inability to understand the mind and feelings of a black prostitute in *Nongogo*, and what a black critic wrote of Harry Bloom's novel, *Episode:*

> Perhaps if the author had lived among his characters and seen their conduct with his own eyes, he would have been able to portray them more powerfully . . . This is the cause of the failing of our white writer in general.[65]

The results of this 'failing' in the case of *King Kong* included dialogue which, though in certain important ways it constituted an advance on that of *No-Good Friday*, often produced impossibilities, inaccuracies and insulting parody, the inauthentic use of the 'd' (instead of the authentic 'the') in the language of the gangsters being the most obtrusive — as in 'de divident in de boot of de car, and dey sight us on de main road. Dey whine us' (p.46).

In at least three respects the language of *King Kong* is an improvement. First, it makes use of some of the genuine vocabulary of the urban culture, especially that of the gangsters. Second, it does not on the whole import artificial grammatical errors but settles for a more neutral, more universal language, as in the following example:

Truffina: I worked in one place for four solid years and they kicked me out because I took a bottle of milk to my room.
Mabel: And untidy. Leaves her petticoat and stockings all over the flat and I got to walk after her picking them up.
Dan: Mabel?

Mabel: Yes, Dan?
Dan: I think you are ready for another change.
Mabel: Me? Leave my Madam? You're crazy. She is just a little bit impossible that's all. Oh, I'll have to fly. She'll kill me if I come late. [pp.29-30]

Third, the decision to make the visual elements and music and dance, rather than words, express the main thrust of the action, makes for a greater use of the theatre's varied expressive resources and leaves a rather spare and in places effective dialogue.

We have seen that the above characteristics originate to some extent in cultural patronization and belittlement, but this does not entirely rob them of their effectiveness. Let us take as an example Bloom's use of the language of the urban gangsters and other sections — including, incidentally, many of the cast:

Harry: We pull away. Den — POW.
Gangsters: Pow!
Harry: Day twa us.
Lucky: Hit you?
Harry: No, miss! We swung de Buick. [pp.46-7]

These gangsters are almost certainly talking *tsotsitaal* not American — the use of the authentic *tsotsitaal* word *twa* for 'shoot' or 'gun' suggests this. This is Bloom's translation, then. 'Pow' is a mistake, it is an English ideophone. The ideophone is a developed linguistic characteristic of so-called 'Bantu' languages and it is used precisely. *Twaa!* would have been more authentic. *Den* is not authentic, nor is *dey*. But *de* is from the *tsotsitaal 'die'*, meaning 'the'. The original phrase might have been 'Ons swing (?) die Buick'. However, when placed in an English context it takes on other connotations, shared with *den* and *dey*, i.e. the American Sambo stereotype, a connotation which Bloom's white audiences might have relished, but which was nevertheless a distinct distortion. Still, the urban language was given place on stage, possibly for the first time. Phrases like '(d)ey twa us' were a step in the right direction — and would have been even better had Bloom written 'they' and avoided the inaccurate and stereotypical 'dey'.

The use of visual elements and music and dance instead of dialogue is illustrated particularly clearly in Act One, Scene Six, when to illustrate what King Kong's circle of friends is doing while he is in jail, there is a series of 'vignettes' with very little dialogue, in which the momentum and even meanings are maintained by the accompanying music. For instance, Joyce is shown being photographed with her friends to 'a jazzed-up piano version of Back of the Moon song' — i.e. for her, life is as exciting as ever and Kong seems to have been forgotten (pp.56-7). The second, showing a new boxer, Jack, training in Kong's place, is acted out to 'a ragged version of Oh Those Marvellous Muscles' — i.e. Kong's place has been taken by a tyro (pp.57-8). The entire scene is given cohesion within the structure of the narrative by the comments and conversation of the gossips.

The dialogue within the vignettes is brief and functional:

Joyce poses. She is all preening, and while her mind is on the talk, she's putting an awful lot into the posing. She drops something from her bag. Two men rush to pick it up.
Two men: Joyce!
Joyce: Thanks, boys. Jordan, how come we don't see you around the Back of the Moon any more?
Jordan: My wife.
Joyce: Well, bring her along.
Jordan: Oh, it'll spoil the fun, Joyce.
(Jordan offers her a cigarette. Two men rush forward to light it.)
Men: Joyce, Joyce.
Joyce: Thanks, boys. [pp.56–7]

We know that the reason for the emphasis on the visual and music and dance was the alleged inability of the actors to act and talk. This attitude, and the cultural underestimation it involved, determined the content of the 'vignettes' — the trivial and clichéd topics of conversation and humour and the unfaithful preening of Joyce, the stereotypical shebeen queen. Later we shall compare her with a character in Kente's *Too Late* who penetrates this stereotype. But the dramatic principle itself is not invalidated. *In this case* the principle was adhered to in order to make it easier for the actors. Others might adhere to it because it is in itself dramatically sound.

Essentially, the language problem in *King Kong*, as in *No-Good Friday*, concerned writing plays in English about the non-English-speaking people of Sophiatown to be acted by them for an English-speaking white audience. Fugard attempted to solve the problem by collaborating on the script with his actors — and this was positive. But he and his cast were educated intellectuals and they neither respected nor quarried the rich mine of Sophiatown's uses of language. Bloom and the others did not collaborate with the actors, but because they did, to some extent, respect these uses of languages, they attempted to produce a dialogue which, though disfigured by cultural distortion and ignorance, reflected these uses — and this too was a positive step towards finding an effective dialogue for popular black theatre in English.

Aesthetics

The play is a 'musical' in the American tradition, with a foundation in realism which becomes more pronounced as the action progresses, especially in Act Two. Structurally, it is characterized by the siting of the musical within a 'realistic' narrative framework. It is divided into two Acts, the first of which is 'happy' and celebratory, the second of which is 'tragic'. It is also cyclical. The curtain call resurrects King Kong and returns to the scene in which he first makes his appearance.

The main action is 'tragedy' in perhaps the most elemental sense. A big man falls from happiness and success to misery and death. Though reasons are advanced for his fall — his imprisonment, the role of Lucky, the collapse of his plans to go to England, racial discrimination — the energy of the play is concentrated in the narrative, in the episodes and events and not in motivation, moral issues or human psychology. However, King Kong's fall is all the more moving because of two symbolic extensions the play makes. King Kong is clearly not only a great individual but also a representative figure. He is larger than life because he comes to be the personification of the energy, strength, ability and aspirations of urban blacks themselves. He is no intellectual, like Willie. He is uneducated and his roots are proletarian. This is not all. In addition to embodying the vital energy of the people, he comes to embody the very physical environment in which that energy was active — Sophiatown. When King Kong goes, so does Sophiatown — 'this town is coming down fast now', says Pauline at the end of the play, *with a sigh* (my italics) (p.92).

Thus although the action concentrates on the fate of an individual, his social meaning is retained. He is a representative figure, an embodiment, even, of his community. The narrative emphasis of the action binds it firmly to the artistic traditions of the majority, but its tragic ending raises problems — a point we shall be discussing. The play appears to be sited in popular black culture. It is popular rather than 'serious' theatre. The function of the choric commentary is actually given to the representatives of the working men and women of Sophiatown, yet there is the contrast between King Kong's energy and Pauline's sigh.

One central contradiction stands out. This is the contradiction between the realism suggested by the theme's political and symbolic context and the artificiality of its American 'musical' form. The narrative framework in which the main action is set is provided by the activities and reminiscences of the three washerwomen, Pauline, Lena and Truffina, and 'an old gossip', Dan Kuzwayo, which takes place in a Sophiatown backyard. It is in their conversations, stretching over the period of a working day, that the various episodes of King Kong's story are evoked. Though this well-worn device is used crudely, it is nonetheless effective. Their yard appears on the forestage four times during the course of the play. In Scene One it is early dawn. The characters are 'at work already, sewing and doing the wash'. Dan is smoking his pipe. The three washerwomen are busy discussing their white 'madams'. A little kid plays 'The Little King Kong Theme' on the penny whistle and this provides the opportunity for Dan to begin telling the others about King Kong himself.

Later, in Act One, Scene Six, 'Dan Kuzwayo is having his hair cut by Lena. Truffina is sitting on the ground sewing'. Nearby dawdle a couple of school kids. Pauline enters scouring a pot. They talk of jail, of jail as a common experience for blacks, of jail as an embittering and changing experience. In the last scene of the play, Act Two, Scene Six, they sit round braziers and talk of Dan's notice of demolition and removal to Sunshine Gardens, and the unromantic realities of the marriage of King Kong's trainer and Miriam, who have had to kick out their mother to make room in their tiny house for a new baby.

The yard in which they talk and work appears far removed, not only from the world of King Kong in the play, i.e. the legend, but also from the glamorous life of boxers, big-time crooks and high-class shebeens in real-life Sophiatown. Dan, it is true, claims to have been in King Kong's corner in his fighting days. Pauline bumps into him at the celebration after his release from prison. But the others, though they have heard of him, never knew him.

The forestage area, which remains their yard throughout the action, repeatedly distances the main action and contrasts it with the everyday world of the working majority. The main action takes place in the world of legend, in which the central figure is heroic, epic. In comparison with the narrative framework, the main action is unreal. The musical form of the play emphasizes this. It also, however, 'justifies' it. Because we accept the form's conventions, we accept the romanticism, the exaggeration, the emphasis on the exotic, the novel, the 'zoot' and the 'jazzy', which in real terms are a distortion of the culture of Sophiatown. King Kong is a legendary figure. The form is the American musical. All is explained — except of course the initial decision to deal with the legend of King Kong in this way at all, i.e. as an American musical.

Of all the South African papers, characteristically only an Afrikaans daily, *Die Burger*, questioned this decision. The critic of this paper 'found it a scandal to have twisted the real tragedies of the African people for the making of "show business".' Why did the union decide to handle material, which on the admission of Bloom and others was deeply connected to 'the real tragedies of the African people', in this way?

Bloom writes that it was 'not merely because we wanted to give new opportunities to our concert artists, but because township people live in the idiom of musicals'. Mona Glasser, defending the play against *Die Burger*'s criticism, writes that Bloom believed the African 'does not consider himself defeated. Something tells him that the future is coming his way, and he therefore buoys himself up against the miseries of the present day with a healthy raw spirit'. She continues: 'To use the "real tragedies" of the African people for the making of show business was to affirm the optimism of the African people.'

Both these answers are transparently inadequate. Bloom's represents yet another statement of his romanticization, his mistaking aspects of black urban culture for the whole. As for Glasser's, an analysis of the operation of the 'musical' form of *King Kong* and the effects of 'show business' on the play's political meanings, for example, makes it clear that the form distorts and obscures 'the real tragedies of the African people' rather than affirming their optimism.

The real answer is surely to be found in the function and ideology of the Union of Southern African Artists and the *King Kong* production team itself. The play was a commercial undertaking, for all its idealism. It was 'show business'. The form of the play was dictated as much by this characteristic as by the artistic factors cited by members of the production team and, as Bloom's words quoted above make clear, the romanticization of Sophiatown culture entailed in the use of the form actually coincided with the conception they had of black urban culture.

Not only did the form 'justify' cultural distortions, but it significantly transformed the relation of the everyday world of the narrative framework and the legendary world of King Kong, Joyce and Lucky, a world which was as much fantasy as legend – fantasy into which the likes of Truffina, Pauline and Lena might often escape in their dreams, but which they were never likely to experience. The relation between the musical legend of King Kong and their everyday struggle is neatly illustrated when, in Act One, Scene Seven, King Kong takes Pauline's washing bundle from her head, hurls it away and sweeps her into the dance (p.62). The effect of distancing King Kong's world not only helps to endow it with a legendary quality, but also generates by the end of the play a powerful feeling of loss. In real life there was a complex symbiotic relationship between the world of Truffina and the others and that of King Kong. King Kong, like Ezekiel Dhlamini, was once an ordinary person like them. The ordinary world of Truffina thus produced the hero King Kong. The hero, King Kong, also once inhabited physically this ordinary world – Sophiatown – and like the other inhabitants wished to transcend it – in his case by winning money overseas and starting a transport business. He failed because, like the other inhabitants of Sophiatown, he was discriminated against. He was thrown back into it, became frustrated and was destroyed, like many others in Sophiatown, by the criminal elements that segregation and poverty in the black urban areas produced. Then, distanced by death and time, he became a legend. He was thus at the same time close and removed from the ordinary inhabitants of the backyards. At the end of the play, when King Kong's attempt to transcend his condition has failed, the ordinary world of the yard remains. Real life continues – the reality of life without legend.

In actuality this was a bleak reality, out of which the memories of King Kong had momentarily transported Truffina and company. There is no doubt that Bloom recognized much about the relationship of the real King Kong and the lives of real working men and women. But in his play the relationship is modified. The harshness is not there. There is a feeling of loss but its tone is almost mellow. There is a prevailing nostalgia. Pauline captures the effect of it when she says: 'This town is coming down fast now' and *sighs*. Or again:

Pauline: Old times . . .
Lena: And things that we dream of . . .
Pauline: And sadness . . .
Dan: And disappointment.
Pauline: All jumbled up. [p.94]

Then right at the end:

Truffina: Tch.
Lena: Ayee, that was sad.
Dan: There'll never be another Champ like King Kong. That boy was great.
  [p.96]

The sigh and the sad shake of the head are what *King Kong* evokes. The
heart is touched, but the head and its workings are carefully avoided. Harsh
realities are softened by sentimentality. At the end of the play Dan, the old
man, gets a letter:

Dan: I been invited to travel, all expenses paid. Listen to this.
(pulls out a letter, reads it, tilting it to catch the light of the brazier)
'Greetings, We notify you that as your house has been set down for
  demolition, you must make arrangements to vacate same by 30th instant.
  On day aforesaid a truck will be put at your disposal to transport your
  possessions and family to alternative accommodation in Sunshine Gardens.'
Truffina: Sunshine Gardens? Oh, I know the place. Plenny sunshine, all right,
  but not much else. [p.92]

Mona Glasser assures us that official letters did indeed begin like this —
'Greetings' — in order to avoid dignifying their black recipients with other
more respectable titles, like Sir and Madam. Her somewhat dubious
explanation was not, however, available to the audience and, particularly
given the tone of the rest of the letter, its opening sounds implausibly
'chummy'. It then goes on to announce amiably that Dan will have to leave
his house (which will be demolished in order to clear the area for white
habitation — a perspective which is scrupulously avoided) and go to Sunshine
Gardens (a euphemism for a euphemism — Meadowlands, the raw stretch of
veldt a good ten miles further from the city, to which the inhabitants of
Sophiatown were largely sent). The fates of Sophiatown and King Kong were
linked. How Dan, and we, respond to the forced removals and demolition
is how we respond to the waste and destruction of human richness and
ability personified by King Kong — a meaning Bloom himself has called our
attention to. Now, the authentic wording of such letters in real life might
evoke a sense of anger and possibly a determination to resist. Instead this
letter is friendly ('a truck will be put at your disposal'!) and Dan is gently,
humorously stoical. The play intends us to sigh and lament, not rage and
revolt — an intention which the play's cyclical structure reinforces.

In our discussion of *No-Good Friday* we noted its 'suspended' ending. A
suspended ending can, if it follows the effective statement of a problem or
suggests a genuine debate, be functionally positive and forward-looking. A
cyclical ending has the effect of putting the action beyond our intervention
as an audience. What we have seen is beginning again. Though it moves, it is
static. Thus when King Kong reappears, we are comforted — it is a surrogate
'happy ending' — or at least persuaded that the tragic cycle is a natural or
universal law which cannot be halted or altered. Neither of these effects

suggests the possibility of human action against forces that are responsible for the catastrophe — which in any case remain in this play either obscured or muted.

Function

The play was chiefly directed at white audiences. Its function in that case may have been to prod gently their consciences and touch their hearts, but essentially there was the reassurance that nothing which threatened them would result from King Kong's fall or the demolition of Sophiatown or from the other consequences of their domination. At the same time there was an opportunity for condescension and some self-congratulation. They were not, after all, racialist or oppressive because there they were, watching and applauding a musical in which black actors were performing, seemed happy and above all levelled no accusations at them — a recipe, one would have thought, for considerable commercial success.

Though the play was directed at the white groups, many blacks saw it. We have little record of their reactions, except the following:

> The reaction to *King Kong* from the less sophisticated among the African audiences at times reflected the lack of theatrical tradition, the difficulty of understanding the stage and the concept of a play. Many people knew the Manhattan Brothers, the Woody Woodpeckers, the Saints and others as variety groups.
> 'What is this King Kong?' they asked.
> 'I don't understand,' one complained. 'We heard the guy was dead. How can he come back?'
> Some members of the audience were disappointed. 'Why don't we get the real guy?' they wondered. 'There's not enough music', was a frequent complaint. 'Why does everybody talk all the time?' [Glasser, p.56]

We can compare this with Bob Leshoai's account of audience reactions to the union's plays in the early 1960s in the black urban areas. There was 'only slight acceptance to wholesale rejection', which he put down to the influence of close-harmony groups and variety concerts. On one occasion the union took 'a very elaborate and expensive show' to Bloemfontein and was greeted by shouts such as: 'Pull down those corrugated irons! To hell with your lights! To hell with speaking, give us music!' (Leshoai, 1965, p.45ff).

King Kong and the union's 'elaborate and expensive shows' did not speak to them. Only one voice in *King Kong* did. That was the voice of Todd Matshikiza.

Todd Matshikiza

Matshikiza composed the music for the musical and wrote two lyrics — 'Ityala lala madoda' and 'Hambani, madoda'. These were in the urban conglomerate language, Nguni, and therefore only the black audience could understand. Though the lyrics of most of the songs were provided by Ruth

Williams, both the music and the lyrics of these two songs were by Matshikiza himself.

Matshikiza was born in the small Eastern Cape town of Queenstown (eQonce). He had worked as 'bookseller, messenger, waiter and journalist [on *Drum* and *Post*] and was currently a salesman for a firm selling razor-blades'. Anthony Sampson, who was his editor on *Drum*, wrote that 'he moved easily among Europeans. Yet, unlike most urban Africans, he had never rejected his tribal roots, and took pride in them'. He had once proudly and sympathetically told Sampson of the initiation rites he took part in when he became a man. 'He felt and showed no strain between his Xhosa tribal background and his European way of life,' wrote Sampson (p.88).

In other words, Matshikiza, as a journalist and salesman, was a member of the urban intermediate classes, but his attitude to his traditional, rural background indicated that he did not share the characteristic attitudes of his class. This is apparent in his music for *King Kong*, which is both eclectic, urban and international, and at the same time nurtured by the rhythms and melodies of traditional Xhosa music.

'Ityala lala madoda' is sung when, in the first scene, early morning in Sophiatown is evoked on the upstage area. 'The people of the township are going to work.' A preacher, 'a crowd of urchins', African nuns, a policeman, Lucky and his gang cross the stage.

> *Ityala lalamadoda*
> *nguAndazi noAsindim'*
> *Ityala lalamadoda*
> *Alaziwa mntu.*

In the text this is translated as:

> The fault of these men
> lies in their ignorance. [p.27]

This is not, however, the words' real meaning. In Xhosa oral tradition the three folk personifications, uAndazi (Mr I-don't-know), uAsindim (Mr It's-not-me) and uAlaziwa-mntu (Mr Nobody-knows), have a self-explanatory didactic function. Matshikiza is here looking with some understanding but also with criticism at the people of the community of which he is a part, and he admonishes them by referring to the three figures of Xhosa didactic literature. The majority in Sophiatown suffer, he implies, because they refuse to accept the responsibility of alleviating that suffering by taking action.

The effect of Matshikiza's admonishment to his people is not the same as that of Father Higgens to Willie in *No-Good Friday*. Whereas Father Higgens made it clear that by taking action he meant no more than reporting to the police, Matshikiza addressed himself explicitly to blacks, all blacks (i.e. those who could understand the words), and did not predicate what he meant by action. This was in the best tradition of Xhosa satirical literature, in which trenchancy is cloaked in an imprecision only an 'outsider' would find imprecise, as the following stanza from a well-known poem by J. J. R. Jolobe illustrates:

> I saw him hungry with toil and sweat,
> Eyes all tears, spirit crushed,
> No longer able to resist. He was tame.
> Hope lies in action aimed at freedom.
> *I have seen the making of a servant*
> *In the young yoke-ox.* [Qanguie, p.9]

'Hambani madoda', or the Bus Queue Song, is sung in the more sombre second act. Again it is very early in the morning, still dark, and bitterly cold. King Kong had been defeated by 'Little Greb' the night before, but the song transcends the individual fate of King Kong:

Hambani madoda	Keep moving, men
Siy' emsebenzini	we are going to work
Sizani, bafazi	stand with us, women
Siyahlupheka	we are suffering
Amakhaza nemvula	cold and rain
Ibhas' igcwele	the bus is packed
Sihlutshwa ngootsotsi	the *tsotsis* prey on us
Basikhuthuza	robbing us of what we have
Siyaphela yindlala	half-dead with hunger
Nemali ayikho	no money
Hambani madoda	keep moving, men
Isikhathi asikho	it's getting late
Hambani madoda	keep moving, men
Isikhathi asikho	it's getting late. [pp.82–3] [66]

The reason for the song's strength is that it seems to swell from a thousand throats. The words conjure up, not the pain of one man, who no matter how grand in stature or representative in function remains one man, but that of an entire community. Here the romanticism and commercialism of the 'musical' and its 'theatrical' plot are swept away by the work of the one man in the creative team of *King Kong* who fully understood because he had experienced and above all accepted the culture of the people of Sophiatown and was equipped to express it. He was not excited by its novelty, attracted by its vitality, sentimental or patronizing about its capabilities. He was a part of it.

'Hambani, madoda' is choral and written in one of the authentic languages of Sophiatown, in this case Zulu modified by Xhosa (Nguni), as spoken in the urban areas of the Witwatersrand. This roots it firmly in both the popular urban and traditional cultures. Because of his knowledge of and sympathy for these cultures, Matshikiza was able to do what Fugard, Bloom, Gluckman and even Fugard's black collaborators were not able to do. 'Hambani, madoda' seems to demand a dramatic vehicle of quite another stature. What follows the song in the play, however moving it may be on another level, seems trivial in comparison:

Jordan: Anyone go to the fight last night?
Man: King against Little Greb? What for?
Jordan: Nobody go?
Crowd: No.
Jordan: I wonder what the result was. [p.83]

Above all, 'Hambani, madoda' not only expresses the pain and the suffering but combines this static element with a dynamic one, absent in the rest of the play. 'Hambani, madoda' — 'keep moving, men' — invokes a determination to go on, to struggle and to survive.

The political meaning of these songs is liberatory, they spring from the fullness of the majority's traditional and urban contemporary cultures and languages, and they ignore the paying audience in favour of those who did not 'understand . . . the concept of a play' but could hear Matshikiza's music.

7. 'A Deep Insight into the Loves and Hates of Our People'

In this chapter we shall be looking at a work by the black playwright, Gibson Kente, whose 'independent' theatre company was the most popular in the country during most of the period after its establishment in 1966-67 up to Kente's detention in 1976.

Too Late, which was written and produced in 1974-75, was a commercial musical play and lay therefore in the tradition initiated by the Union's *King Kong* rather than that established by *No-Good Friday*. *Too Late*, however, was not, like *No-Good Friday* and *King Kong*, written by a white writer. No whites were involved in its staging and administration at all. Furthermore, it was not primarily created for a white audience. Instead it was created for a black one — and then not even for an audience of the educated intermediate classes. Some understanding of how this alters the perspectives can be gained from considering, for instance, that in a sense King Kong, whose struggles and frustrations were only the *subject* of *King Kong*, becomes in *Too Late* the author himself — for the system that destroyed King Kong was the same as that against which Kente had to strive.

It is as if Todd Matshikiza were to have stepped out of *King Kong* and his subservient role in it and struggled for and won the liberty to write and direct the whole play himself. In fact, Kente and Matshikiza were from similar backgrounds. Both were born in the Eastern Cape and spoke Xhosa. Xhosa traditional music and culture and the Christian church were major influences on their music. The choral harmonies of 'Hambani, madoda' are there in the song 'Ngabayini?' in *Too Late*. They were both influenced by American jazz and 'township' rhythms. In important cultural senses, Kente was Matshikiza's heir.

The Making of an 'Independent' Entrepreneur

Between 1959 and 1976 Gibson Kente's career went through three phases. From 1959 to 1966 his theatrical work was largely conducted under the aegis and influence of Union Artists. From 1967 to 1973 he achieved economic independence and consolidated this with the production of three successful musical plays, *Sikalo, Lifa* and *Zwi*. From 1973 to 1976 he came to be identified with the black political struggle and at the same time immensely improved the profitability of his theatre activity. In 1976 he was arrested while working on the filming of his play *How Long*. On his release the following year he returned to the making of uncontentious musicals, but more recently a political content has re-entered his work.

In 1972, Kente described his early career in an interview:

> I suppose then I'll have to give you an insight into my background and how I got to be involved with songs and writing scripts. I started this at school in Loveday. Then I left for East London and formed a very popular group, the Symphonic Five. All the songs were completely new. In '55 I came over here [i.e. the Transvaal], to Hofmeyr. I was doing social work. I formed up a group by the name of the Kente Choristers. *Ngcwele ngcwele* was one of the products of that group. I was set off, man. Then after that I left for the studios. I was a talent scout with Gallo. I did some writing for Miriam Makeba, the Manhattan Brothers, Letta Mbuli, and many others, like Thoko Shikuma. I spent another two years talent-scouting. Then I got bored with that. I wanted something more creative. I was tired of writing three chord sequences. I wanted to write songs that had weight. My first problem was to get hold of a script. Well, I ran from pillar to post, trying to get township people to write a script. Casey Motsisi was one of them. He just made promises but they never materialised. I decided just to sketch something on my own. That was the birth of *Manana, the Jazz-Prophet*. By then I had not done any studies on stage work. I felt now before tackling *Sikalo* I had to have a bit of knowhow, about the stage and all that entails. I started buying books, mainly Stanislavsky, let us say Russian, French, English and American. When I tackled *Sikalo* I had some knowledge. At least I could make out stage right from stage left, downstage from upstage. Well, I'm still very busy with that. [*S'ketsh'*, Summer 1972, p.8]

Thus Kente's early career had been in music, like most of the artists who worked with the union either in *King Kong* or later plays. In the Transkei he had been at Bethel College, a school run by the Seventh Day Adventists. 'Every Sunday,' Kente later recalled, 'was like the typical revival meet in the States. We yelled with piety. We yelled till we had to speak in whispers the following day. Man, we yelled' (*The World*, 4 April 1966).

Four years after Kente arrived in Johannesburg, *King Kong* was created. Kente must have been as taken up by this event as everyone else. Although he does not seem himself to have been directly involved, many of the top vocal groups for whom he wrote were. Later, in 1967, when asked for the reason for the 'boom' in black theatre that was taking place at the time, Kente said:

> The death of variety concerts made artists and writers look for a new medium and after the spectacular success of *King Kong* everybody in non-white showbiz switched to the musical and this is the climax of the switchover. [*Drum*, 9 May 1967]

King Kong was then the immediate model and inspiration for Kente, which together with his own desire to write more 'weighty' music and 'do something creative', prompted him to search for a script. It is significant that Kente, unlike others at the time, did not go to a white writer for his script. Instead he tried to get 'township people' to write one for him and, when they failed, wrote one himself. Thus he avoided some of the problems referred to previously which result from a white writer writing about black society.

There is little record of his first play, *Manana, the Jazz-Prophet*, and, unlike his other plays, it was never revived. According to Vinah Bendile, who acted in *Manana*, *Sikalo* was a re-write of the earlier play. The first performance of *Sikalo* was in December 1965. Though it is possible that Union Artists provided assistance of some kind, *Sikalo* was at first performed independently of Union Artists. Presumably after Union Artists had seen the play, an announcement was made to the effect that Union Artists would present *Sikalo* early in 1966. This follows the normal pattern and seems to indicate that at this stage Kente was not sufficiently strong to contemplate independent theatrical activity, but was on the contrary relying on Union Artists to repeat their *King Kong* success with *Sikalo*, which they presented at the University of the Witwatersrand Great Hall in July 1966.

When *Sikalo* was taken over by Union Artists, they not only appointed their own company manager and administration, but insisted on their own director, Meshak Mosia, becoming co-director with Kente. Kente objected to this but was overruled. In September 1966 cast members were complaining about the management's tendency to call in the police to settle disputes. Kente had been deposed as director and he retaliated by threatening to withdraw the rights of the play. Richard Exley, the director of Union Artists at the time, when asked to comment on the disaffection in the company said: 'he was not aware of any complaints among the members of Union Artists'. One week later the entire cast of *Sikalo* walked out after rejecting the terms offered them for their forthcoming national tour. The cast demanded a R20 a week minimum plus R1.50 per day touring allowance, instead of the R17.50 offered. Kente apparently did not take part in the negotiations. Union Artists then announced that *Sikalo* would be performed, with a new cast, at the Lesotho Independence Day celebrations and claimed a 30-month control of the rights. Kente had the support of the original cast and went ahead with rehearsals, announcing at the same time plans for a new production, *Lifa*. In October Kente's *Sikalo* was 'on the road' again. By this time Union Artists was experiencing a crisis and could do nothing to stop Kente. There followed a wrangle over 'reparations'. Kente had already paid Union Artists 'between R500 and R700' but Exley was demanding R1,000 more. This prompted Kente to announce in December that he was severing all connections with

Union Artists as long as Richard Exley was 'still boss'. Kente returned all the costumes.

In October 1967 Kente was able to register his company under the Companies Act, with the aim of 'uplifting the standards of musicals and plays by means of lectures and helping would-be producers and directors'. 'At first,' Kente stated, 'I will concentrate on my own productions.'

Whatever feelings Kente might have had for music and theatre, it was clear that he was a professional, determined to make a living and preferably a profit in the commercial theatre or, as it is commonly called in South Africa, 'showbiz'. He was in an identical position to that of other members of his group who attempted to make a living, not by selling their labour to (white) employers but by establishing their own independent businesses in the black urban areas.

Previously we included in the commercial intermediate class the big traders, businessmen, gangsters and theatre and entertainment entrepreneurs. As this class owned property and equipment and hired labour, it was relatively closely identified in function with the (white) bourgeoisie proper. This identification evidenced itself not only in a cultural affiliation with that class and its agents, but also in a relatively conservative, sometimes even reactionary, attitude on political matters. For instance, W. J. P. Carr of the Johannesburg Non-European Affairs Department wrote of this class of 1957:

> Now being men of prosperity and business standing, their whole attitude and approach to important issues affecting Natives generally is characterized by a real sense of responsibility, with a much clearer appreciation of the economic and financial issues involved in public affairs. There is no attraction for the best class of these men in the wiles of the political agitator, nor do their children figure among the ranks of the delinquents. Respectable men of substance, with a real stake in the community, they exert an influence that extends far beyond their numbers, and they constitute a very important — perhaps the most important — element in preserving stability in urban Native society.[67]

Significantly this article was published in *Optima*, the magazine of mining capital in South Africa.

Though Carr's opinion on this was partly wishful thinking, and overestimated the 'reality' of this class's stake in the community while underestimating their impatience with the restrictions they faced, as blacks, on their ability to amass and consume wealth, it does point to a real tendency to political conservatism, a fact which has been noted by many commentators, as in the following remark by H. J. and R. E. Simons: 'Few businessmen played a leading role in the African National Congress' (p.621).

The attitude of this class to segregation and multi-racialism was characterized by ambivalence. For if segregation restricted their ability to expand their commercial activity, multi-racialism would expose them to vigorous competition from white capital in their own preserve, the black urban areas.

In the case of Kente, the nature of the live entertainment industry proved to be particularly advantageous. Black trade and commercial activity was susceptible to the competition of white business which, because of its control of capital and because of the support of the government, was able to a large degree to circumvent the monopoly that black traders were officially entitled to in their own areas. The entertainment industry, however, differs from other commercial and productive industries in that it packages and markets not material products but human and cultural ones. Apartheid as a racial system, though it is more or less indifferent to material products, classifies and segregates people and therefore human products. While the market for the material products of white-owned industry is not greatly inhibited by segregation, the marketing of live entertainment is.

For instance, tinned jam is produced in South Africa by white-owned industry. Though there are no supermarkets in black urban areas, tinned jam is bought by black and white alike at supermarkets in the white areas. As the small shops which sell it in black areas sell it at a higher price than it is sold in white areas, the black consumer obviously prefers to buy it at the super-market nearest to his workplace in the white areas, or in town on a Saturday morning. In any case, many of the small shops in the black areas are reduced to being mere agents of white-owned wholesalers. Thus separate development only slightly inhibits white control of the marketing of tinned jam.

Live entertainment is another matter. It is offered in the consumer's leisure time, i.e. when the black consumer is compelled by law to be in the black areas. The product marketed must be to the black consumer's taste, which in the case of drama and music, for instance, is a cultural matter and difficult for those who do not belong to the culture to ensure. Attendance depends to a large extent on coverage afforded by black journalists in the so-called 'black press'. In these and other ways, separate development does inhibit the marketing of live entertainment by white companies or entrepreneurs. A black entrepreneur, despite lack of capital (for which he can to some extent compensate by obtaining sponsorship from white companies), and the restrictions placed on his activities by government legislation, is therefore in a stronger position to compete in black urban areas in the live entertainment industry.[68]

Kente's career until 1973 was thus a struggle to establish himself as a successful businessman and artist in the field of black entertainment in competition with other companies, some of which were white-controlled and others black-controlled.

By the 1970s Kente had largely succeeded in doing this. His theatrical organization at times employed three large companies of actors, actresses and musicians, an administrative and technical staff, drivers, public-relations and advertising personnel and others. His organization owned transport adequate to take his employees all over South Africa. He himself owned a modest but (by Soweto standards) 'posh' house in Dube and indulged in

considerable patronage and conspicuous consumption. In 1971, when his
fortunes were at a comparatively low ebb, he was able to offer his wife a
managerial position in his organization with a salary of R500 a month. In
1974 Kente was paying his average regular actor R50 a week, while 'old
hands' in important roles were receiving R100 a week or more. By way of
comparison, the average wage in the better-paid manufacturing section for
black workers in 1971 was less than R57 per *month*. Mary Twala was a
despatch clerk in Swaziland before joining Kente in 1967. Her salary with
Kente was three times what she had earned as a clerk.

One performance of a popular play such as *How Long*, with tickets selling
at R1.50 each and an average attendance of 500, might gross R750. At some
venues with large halls, such as Kwa Thema, Springs, takings might be more
than R1,500. A play might be performed between three and six times a week
– sometimes, though exceptionally, even more. *How Long* has been known to
be performed three times in one night. In the period 1973–76 Kente
invariably had at least two productions on the road. It is thus possible that
in an average week, with four performances of each play, his organization
grossed about R6,000.

Kente was thus an established member of the commercial intermediate
class. He made numerous statements which indicated that as a commercial
entrepreneur he thought predominantly in economic terms and not in racial/
national terms. He made it clear that he hoped to expand beyond the limits
placed on him as a black entrepreneur whose activities were confined to the
black areas, into the more lucrative markets in the white areas. After all, if
Kente's average weekly gross from two plays was R6,000, the weekly gross
after paying the cast of the white-produced 'tribal musical' *Ipi Tombi*, at the
Brooke Theatre at about the same time, was estimated to be R17,780.[69] Of
course, Kente expressed the hope to expand his operations in terms suggested
by the capitalist ideology of multi-racialism. For example, in 1971 he said:
'Of course, my greatest wish is to see *Zwi* playing before a white audience
here at home.' In 1972 he was asked whether it was true that he once said he
performed his plays in Soweto to perfect them for white audiences in town.
He replied: 'I think this sort of art is meant for people, be they black, maroon
or mustard.'

Kente was by no means insensible to the injustices of the political system
during the early period. In a volume presented to Robert Loder on the
occasion of his leaving Union Artists and South Africa in August 1962,
Kente wrote: 'It's not only sunny South Africa but also a South Africa which
has dark corners.' But this was before he had become a successful entrepreneur.
His later public statements, though sometimes revealing a consciousness of
the restrictions of the system, were, like those of others of his class, never critical
of it. As he told an interviewer in 1972:

> Of course, I find myself confined to certain themes and trends. Should I
> say sociological trends? There is a lot of material that has not been tapped,
> some very funny, some very touching, but, well, we have to respect the law

In the final period there is a distinct change in the content and tone of his plays. By 1973 Kente found his position, as the most successful commercial theatre entrepreneur in black areas, threatened from a number of directions, including members of his own class, both white and black, the government, the black intellectuals and the black working class itself. This pressure compelled Kente to adopt a more politically committed stance.

Kente had made repeated efforts to expand his activities out of the black areas. In 1966 Union Artists had controlled access to white audiences in South Africa and abroad. Having experienced the price of their assistance, Kente was understandably against co-operating with established white managements in South Africa. In 1971 he was planning to film *Zwi* and take it on tour to Zambia and East Africa. In July 1972 he announced plans to take *Lifa* and *Sikalo* to London for a 'working holiday'. A performance of *Zwi* at the University of the Witwatersrand Great Hall was arranged. However, all these attempts to expand his activities failed. At the same time, ominously, white commercial managements (in South African Theatre Organization, for instance) and the state (the West Rand Bantu Board) began to encroach on his domain, threatening not only his virtual monopoly in the black areas but ultimately his very existence.

Thus at the same time as Kente was failing in his efforts to expand his activities out of black areas, he was being subjected to new pressures from white organizations and the government itself in the black areas. This had the effect of strengthening his sectional antagonisms, i.e. his frustration at the restrictions he faced as a black entrepreneur, at the expense of his class attitudes. In other words, his ideology became more nationalistic.

If Kente's efforts to enter the white market had so far failed, those of Welcome Msomi and two actors, John Kani and Winston Ntshona, had not. Kente realized he could learn little from Msomi's *uMabatha*, an adaptation of *Macbeth*.[71] It had no base in the black audience, being an article created exclusively for the local white audience and for export. It was acted in Zulu and sited in the traditional culture − thus quite removed from the tradition Kente (and his audiences) were used to. In addition neither *uMabatha* nor *Sizwe Banzi* were independent black ventures. Nevertheless there was a lesson for Kente in the success of Kani and Ntshona in *Sizwe Banzi*. The political nature of its contents was obviously a reason for its success, especially abroad. Another play that had been successful in black areas, for the short period before it was banned, was the People's Experimental Theatre's *Shanti*. This was even more outspokenly political. Audiences in black areas therefore were demonstrating that they responded to a more substantial and militant political commitment. The Black Consciousness movement had politicized the intellectuals and the youth, and because of rising unemployment, inflation and industrial unrest, the black working class itself was more politically conscious than before.

Another significant development was the shift in the social composition of Kente's cast and audience and in black theatre generally between the years 1966 and 1976. This shift was something Kente found profitable − and encouraged. At the same time, however, it was one of the factors which brought about the radicalization of his material and therefore ultimately his detention. Kente's casts were drawn from progressively lower strata of the society. He employed progressively less educated, less well known and younger artists, and trained them. By 1973–75 Kente was being praised for his ability to take young, inexperienced novices and turn them into accomplished professionals.[72] In his first two productions he had worked with his peers. In later productions, such as *Lifa* and *Zwi*, he was still employing people from the musical and entertainment profession, such as Pinise Saul, Zakithi Dhlamini and Josh Makhene in *Zwi*. But in *How Long* and *I Believe* many of his actors and actresses were of school-going age, unemployed and only semi-educated. The trend continued in his next production, *Too Late*, and culminated in a cast of extraordinarily young, unknown performers for *Can You Take It*. In 1972 Kente was already complaining of the problems this caused him:

> . . . secondly, there is the question of their educational attainments, the difficulty of their conceiving the script, giving it proper interpreta-tion. You find that I have to spend a lot of time having to explain the meaning of a word so that an actor should be able to know what he is saying . . . This will only be rectified when we get people of higher calibre educationally, and who have got aims in life. You get one or two occasionally with Matrics, or someone who had attempted nursing. But on the whole they are of very low educational standard.[73]

Kente interestingly pays deference here to the hegemonic notion that a person needs to be educated, i.e. speak fluent English, to be a good actor. Not only is this notion disproved in Kente's own casts by cases such as Ndaba Mhlongo and Kenny Majozi, but Kente himself went on to employ less educated artists.

A similar trend is discernible in the audience Kente attracted. The premieres of *Sikalo* and *Lifa* were glittering social occasions, and for *Lifa* Doc Bikitsha, the journalist on *Post*, nominated Kente 'impresario of the year'. A letter to *Post* called Kente 'another Shakespeare or Shaw'. However, Joe Tlholoe of *Drum* sounded a note of caution. Though he considered *Sikalo* to be the best of 'the present crop' of musicals, he wrote that 'a really original musical on township life has still to be written. The present crop . . . are just good for a family evening out. Lack of depth seems to be their major failure.' By 1972 this criticism of Kente's work had become established among the educated intermediate classes. *S'ketsh'* magazine sounded out the opinions of an actress/ journalist, a lecturer in African languages, a playwright, a librarian and the Organizing Secretary of the YWCA in the Transvaal for their views on Kente's work. All praised his ability to entertain, but complained of superficiality and lack of provocation, intellectual stimulation, deeper meaning or message (Summer 1972, p.15).

Kente's later political plays went some way towards meeting this criticism and he regained the patronage of sections of the educated strata. Nevetheless

Kente himself made it clear that the educated intermediate classes were not the audience he had in mind when making a play. In October 1974 Kente closed *I Believe* after seven months. 'I have come to realize,' he explained, 'that the production only goes down well with the élite whereas I write for the man in the street.' Others of the intermediate classes recognized this. A journalist, commenting on the fact that *Lifa* was to play in Durban at 11.30 pm after the popular *umbhaqanga* singer Mahlathini, wrote: 'And the people who go to see Mahlathini are usually the same people who like to see Gibson Kente's shows.' In other words, the proletariat patronized both Mahlathini and Kente — though in actual fact it was the lower strata of the working class, migrants and domestic workers who tended to patronize *umbhaqanga.*

It is hardly necessary to point out the economic realities that were an important element in the trends discussed above. They constitute the characteristic efforts of the capitalist employer to employ cheaper and less protected labour and to exploit the most profitable market available. Thus by the time he wrote *Too Late*, Kente could in economic terms be described as a black businessman entertainer who employed cheap unskilled labour and sold his product to the black working classes and youth. He wished to expand his commercial activities beyond the limits imposed on him by government restrictions and the competition of the white sections of his class. At the same time he wished to preserve and expand his dominance of the market within those limits, i.e. in black areas throughout South Africa.

These aims and activities embodied a number of contradictions. The desire to expand beyond the limits imposed by separate development conflicted with the official policy, yet the need to preserve and expand dominance in the black areas depended to a large extent on that policy. Then, too, his mass audience became more and more politically defiant of the official policy and urgent in its desire for change — and his material, to remain successful, had to cater for this. Yet as a successful businessman, defying the state, or civil disorder in the black areas — let alone a popular uprising — constituted a considerable threat to his financial interests.

As it turned out, the radicalization of his later plays brought Kente into direct conflict with the already encroaching Afrikaner nationalist authorities, who were pursuing their aim to consolidate their hegemony in the black group at the expense of both the English-speaking white group and black nationalism. In February 1974, only three months after the premiere of *How Long*, Kente had been banned by the township superintendents of the East Rand and the Vaal Triangle from performing it in halls under their jurisdiction. Kente interviewed Jannie Kruger, the chairman of the Publications Control Board, who assured him that the board would take no action against his play. The superintendent at Natalspruit nevertheless insisted on a letter from the censorship board. The Department of Bantu Education banned him from performing *How Long* at the Wilberforce Institute, a black teachers' training college under its jurisdiction. *I Believe*, Kente's next play, encountered similar problems, and in May Kente saw an official at the

Department of Sport and Recreation. By June *How Long* was being banned in the Cape as well.

Initially, the action of the local authorities and the state did not seriously affect Kente's ability to function commercially. Though it seriously reduced the areas and venues available to him, the publicity the banning of his plays received ensured that where they *were* performed, and they were performed to capacity audiences. It was noted in *The World*, for instance, that people were travelling in large numbers from the East Rand and the Vaal Triangle to see *How Long* in Soweto, where it was not banned. Ultimately, however, this resulted in his arrest, a serious disruption of his commercial activities and the dispersal of his companies.

Too Late — the Play

Plot Synopsis

Saduva, who lives in the northern Transvaal, loses his parents and comes to live with his maternal aunt, Madinto, in Soweto. Madinto, who runs a shebeen, has a crippled daughter, Ntanana. Saduva meets Totozi, Ntanana's friend, and they fall in love.

Troubles begin to multiply as Saduva struggles to get the necessary stamp in his pass or reference book permitting him to seek work in Johannesburg — though he is aided by a priest, Mfundisi. An over-zealous and vengeful police-man, Pelepele, not only hounds Saduva over his pass but arrests Madinto for selling liquor illicitly.

With Madinto in prison, Saduva and Ntanana are destitute. Then Saduva himself is arrested and imprisoned for a pass offence. Ntanana is murdered by Pelepele as she tries to prevent the arrest. Saduva emerges embittered from prison and in one version of the play almost kills Pelepele. He is prevented by Offside, the local gossip, a layabout and friend of Saduva's. At the end Saduva, Madinto and Totozi are re-united.

Culture

King Kong is the model on which Kente originally based his musical plays. *Sikalo* was clearly modelled on it closely. Like *King Kong*, it was a musical set in the culture of the black urban areas and it highlighted the same 'sensational' areas, such as gangsters, shebeens and jazz. *No-Good Friday*, it is true, was also based in this milieu, but it was *King Kong* and not Fugard's play that inspired Kente. Similar though it was to *King Kong*, *Sikalo* already incorporated certain modifications. The hero in *King Kong* is an isolated, elevated figure. Sikalo is a 'typical' township youth. In *King Kong* the world of the hero and his peers is likewise an elevated one, structurally and chronologically separated from that of the working-class characters in the narrative framework. In *Sikalo*, and in all Kente's other plays, we are presented with an integrated community. In the early plays his central characters are neither taken from the wealthy nor from the very poor. In all his plays the (extended) family, not as in *King Kong* the individual, is at the centre, and there is a powerful sense of an integrated community.

In *Too Late*,[74] first performed in Soweto in February 1975, the story — of less importance in *Too Late* than in *Sikalo*, as we shall see later — centres once again on the family, not the nuclear but the extended family. Saduva comes to live with his maternal aunt, Madinto, after his parents die. To Ntanana, Madinto's daughter, Saduva is strictly speaking a 'cousin brother' but she calls him 'brother', or *buti*, and to all intents and purposes their relationship is that of brother and sister. Madinto and Ntanana have Saduva come to live with them, despite their own straitened circumstances — Ntanana is crippled and Madinto is forced to keep a shebeen. This generosity within the extended family spreads beyond the family into the community. When Madinto is in jail and Saduva is on the run from the police, Ntanana is reduced to eating 'peels' she picks up in the street. When Saduva rushes in, she shares her 'peels' with him. On seeing this, their friend Totozi immediately offers to spend all she has (20c) on bread and cool drink for them. While she is out, Offside, the unemployed layabout, enters with some *pap en vleis* (meat and porridge). This he shares with them automatically (p.112). Saduva is not left to struggle with his problems alone. Offside, Dr Phuza, Mfundisi and the others do the best they can to help him.

Now it was noted that both *No-Good Friday* and *King Kong* tended to emphasize the negative aspects of black urban culture, to accentuate its failings. *Too Late* presents a more balanced picture. The positive elements, exemplified here by the strong sense of community, the sense that the family extends into the community, are traditional cultural elements which have, to an extraordinary degree, survived the process of urbanization and racial and economic exploitation. These are reflected in this and others of Kente's plays. An image of this goodness in the midst of filth and evil is the toy and the rubbish bin (p.115). Madinto has just been released from prison. She does not know it yet but her daughter, Ntanana, has been killed by Pelepele, the policeman:

Madinto looks worn out and worried. Slowly walking, she keeps looking around as if asking 'Where now, my Lord?' Her eyes suddenly land on a toy next to a dustbin. Her face opens into a glare of joy. She goes to pick it up. Like a little baby she hugs it and admires it.
Madinto: At least something for Ntanana.

Later we shall see the importance of Offside in this regard.

The same cultural sympathy is present in Kente's treatment of the people who inhabit his community. Here he is able to penetrate stereotypes. That of the *tsotsi* is one — which we shall see later when we come to look at the *majitas*. Another example is Madinto. The shebeen queen is a stock character in plays set in the black urban culture. We have already noted Joyce in *King Kong*. Another is Queeny in *Nongogo* by Fugard. Madinto is not a stage stereotype; she is not the glamorous romanticization of Bloom's imagination.

123

She is first a woman and a mother, and only secondly a shebeen queen. The reason for her being a shebeen queen emerges clearly when she is jailed. As Mfundisi says:

> Amongst us today, we have two kids who are a sad example of destitution. A girl who can't even work for herself to be deprived of the only armament to enable her to meet and face the demands of life, the means to advance herself at school is a sad thought. She has a strong and courageous brother. A sweet and humble boy. But what they eat, how they survive and where they stay and sleep, is a mystery to me. [pp.107–8]

Madinto is not sophisticated and 'immoral', as stage shebeen queens are 'meant' to be. She is a generous and loving woman who in order to maintain herself and her daughter is compelled to sell liquor. Compare Kente's stage directions for Madinto's shebeen with Back-of-the-Moon:

Madinto's home. Warm, very tidy, nice yet not expensive furniture. Two chairs, a bench, a table, a bed and a small armchair for Ntanana. There are two small cooking pots and one huge one. This very big one is never used for cooking but as a camouflage to hide drinks. It has a big hole underneath. [p.97]

The black policeman, Pelepele, is a member of the family who has put himself beyond the pale by not respecting the conventions of his community. His 'outsider' status is associated with rural overtones in his characterization and language.

Kente's play thus presents an affirmative image of Soweto society. There is the sense of an integrated community observed whole from inside rather than selectively from outside, as in *No-Good Friday* and *King Kong*. The dialectic referred to earlier of constitutive and imposed, positive and negative elements in the society, is much more faithfully represented. Though the ugliness and degradation are not hidden, the supportive strengths and human affections which sometimes transfigure them are shown. There is beauty amidst evil — a balance lacking in the other two plays. The play also penetrates stereotypes. In fact, there is the cultural understanding we last experienced in Matshikiza's two songs.

Kente's shift of emphasis from individual to communal action introduces two other important points, namely the tendency to stress the integrated nature of the community by negating or avoiding ethnic and class divisions within the community.

Saduva is from Tsaneen in the northern Transvaal, a Shangana-speaking area, and his name is Shangana. In terms of vulgar prejudice Shanganas are a relatively despised group, being traditional and conservative. Yet Kente makes his hero a Shangana. He did the same thing in *I Believe*, which is a plea for ethnic unity. The problems encountered by Zwelitsha, the young hero, mostly stem from ethnic prejudice. His love for Kurula, a Shangana-speaking girl, which incurs his mother's displeasure — she is of Xhosa origin — is an example. The absence of ethnic prejudice in Kente's work is very positive and a sign too of the strong tendency towards the disappearance of consciousness based on ethnic chauvinism in the urban industrial areas of the Transvaal (see above, pp.39-40, and note 17).

In *No-Good Friday* and *King Kong* we were concerned largely with the fates of relatively gifted or special people. In *How Long* the class of the central characters was unequivocally proletarian. Asinamali Twala (literally translated, 'We-have-no-money Carry-a-burden') was a municipal dustman. In *Too Late* the class of the central characters, though generally proletarian, is not as distinct — largely because they are so young. Madinto runs a shebeen, but Saduva is unemployed, Ntanana was at school before her mother was jailed and Totozi is a worker of an unspecified kind. In addition to these characters, there are the police, a doctor, a priest, a layabout and the *majitas* (petty criminals).[75] They will be discussed more fully in the section on politics.

However, it is clear that what is emphasized in *Too Late* is not the factors that divide class from class in the black community, but those that obscure such divisions. If Saduva suffers because of pass laws, and Madinto because of liquor laws, which they are compelled to infringe in the circumstances that they as black people experience, so Dr Phuza's drunkenness stems from frustration at the limits to advancement placed on professionals like himself because they are black. The way in which the system, like the skeleton in the medieval Dance of Death, is no respecter of persons or rank (if they are black) is illustrated in the queue at the pass office. Offside, the layabout, Phuza, the doctor, Mfundisi, the priest, and Saduva all stand awaiting the pleasure of the pink gloves and the disembodied voice which is the white official (p.108).

It is these humiliations that the upper strata of the black community constantly jib at. In May of the previous year, for instance, Soweto traders called for the removal of the requirement that they have their passes signed monthly. They did not call for the abolition of passes.

It is not that class distinctions are not *reflected* in the play. They are. For instance, Dr Phuza and Mfundisi clearly belong to the intermediate classes. This is expressed not only in the deference shown them by the other characters in the play, but in concrete situations such as the bus rank at the beginning of the play. Here buses and taxis are caught to work, i.e. to town, or to other parts of Soweto. The doctor and Mfundisi catch taxis not buses, which provide the transport for 'the working class' which 'flows into the rank', for the 'office girls, ordinary workers', etc. When Offside tries to engage the doctor in conversation, he 'gives him a dirty look and steps away from him'. 'I'm not interested,' he says, and like the upper-class tailor's dummy in Trevor Griffiths' *The Comedians*, calls for a taxi (p.95).

Class distinctions are implicit in the society Kente depicts, but Kente's own class vision results in an avoidance, possibly quite unconscious, of episodes and facts which would highlight the contradictions expressed by them. For instance, Mfundisi is a very 'democratic' sort of *mfundisi*. It is difficult to determine whether he is a minister of an established 'white' church (e.g. Anglican, Wesleyan, etc.) or an independent 'African' church. In the same scene at the bus rank he leads everyone in a Zionist hymn, 'Kwela-kwela Nantsi nqwelo-Mzalwana', in order to fool the police into believing a Zionist service is in progress (p.96). Yet his ability to act as an intermediary for Saduva at the pass office implies he belongs to an established 'white' church. An authentic priest of the 'white' churches would have introduced a greater social contrast, as would one of Soweto's successful doctors rather than the relatively shabby Dr Phuza. They would almost certainly have travelled to town in their own cars rather than joining battle at the taxi rank, for example. In the 1970s even the wives of certain doctors were driving expensive cars.

By depicting such a doctor and such a priest and avoiding more obviously 'élite' ones, Kente effectively softens the real class distinctions and contradictions in Soweto society. Mfundisi and Dr Phuza evidence virtually none of their social group's characteristic snobbery, and 'hobnob' with the proletarian characters (except for Offside) as if social status hardly existed. They are also neither of them conspicuously well-off. Dr Phuza confesses in church: 'I find myself too much with patients who haven't got the means . . . I am getting poorer by the day.' Thus the rich/poor dichotomy is also softened. This is not to say that doctors like Phuza did not exist in Soweto, or that social distinction was not to some extent blurred by conditions. The point is that the effect of depicting a Phuza and an Mfundisi, rather than some of the more celebrated, wealthier members of Soweto's élite, suggests a more homogeneous society than exists in reality.

This integrated community is held together by a shared Christian ideology. Whereas many of the plays written by the younger Soweto-born playwrights reflect a more cynical urban morality, like the *moegoe/clever* morality referred to in the discussion of *No-Good Friday*, Kente's moral norms are Christian. When secular cynicism is expressed Kente relies on the audience to disapprove of it. For instance, the morality of the *majitas*, i.e. *clevergeid*, illustrated by their rejection of education in favour of crime, is expressed by *tsotsi*-type characters who end up hardened criminals indulging in sodomy in jail, and is calculated to shock the bulk of the audience. When Saduva 'questions the usefulness of God' it is intended to indicate his desperation and the iniquity of the pass laws rather than constitute a serious attack on Christianity as such. The most powerful element in Kente's plays, his music, is religious to the core. The words and the harmony, and the depth of feeling with which the singing invests them, indicate an unquestionable bedrock of faith in the Christian God's existence and in his righteousness and his will to help those that believe in him. Of the 13 songs with lyrics in *Too Late*, five are straightforwardly religious and another two are quasi-religious in that they include references to 'God' or 'the Lord' — e.g.

I'm in the street without a place to stay
nothing to eat I seek a job each day
I am always told: 'Sorry, there's none for you.'
Lord, I'm slaving, starving all day.
[*Too Late*, II, p.17]

Among the religious songs is a setting of Psalm 21, 'I will lift up mine eyes', sung by Mfundisi at the pass office after Saduva has been forced to make a dash for it or be locked up and endorsed out of Johannesburg. The Mfundisi's later attack on the church is not an attack on God or Christianity as such, but on the abuses thereof.

A measure of the Christian morality with which Kente binds his community together is the regular expression of 'sentiment' at moments of intimacy or comradeship:

Ntanana (on being introduced to Saduva for the first time): Oh, Mama. The very thought of having a brother and companion is both warm and wonderful. [p.98]

or again:

Saduva (to Totozi when she offers to buy food for Ntanana and him): Toza your heart is a treasured gift from God. [p.112]

Another is the importance in the play of the character Mfundisi and of the church itself. The symbolic importance of the latter will be gone into later. With regard to Mfundisi, it is sufficient simply to point to the particular functions accorded him in the play. We see him as the intermediary between the system and the ordinary man. It is he who battles tirelessly to help Saduva avoid imprisonment, he who finally succeeds in securing his release. Mfundisi voices criticism of the harshness and injustice of the laws that persecute Saduva and, in the second version of the play — in which, incidentally, he plays a much more important and outspoken part — he delivers the final speeches. In a real sense, therefore, Mfundisi is the voice of Kente's Christian community.

Now, it has historically been the educated intermediate classes in the black group who have ascribed to and propagated the ideology of Christianity, in its established, i.e. its European, forms. Christian teachings have traditionally played an important part in the ideological struggle of the ruling groups and classes in South Africa to maintain their dominance, especially by 'legitimizing' a non-violent morality. As we shall see in the chapter on *Shanti*, the Christian taboo against the use of violence for revolutionary purposes is one of the important ideological barriers the play attempted to break through. Kente's play affirms it.[76]

In Kente's plays, Christianity is a source of concepts about social justice, human goodness and love which provide a yardstick showing that the oppression of blacks is wrong. Yet at the same time it is the only source of salvation which the plays project. The appeal is not to 'action aimed at freedom', but to God's justice and to God's power to intervene. Take, for example, the celebrated song from *How Long*, 'Black Child':

> Just hold on, one prayer
> lending a light to that poor black child
> with education, my Lord.
> Just one prayer, just one wish,
> lending a light to that poor black child
> with education.
> Help the black child in the street
> that his days are[−]
> make him read and write
> make his future bright, O Lord
> help that black mother and the father
> help them get that child [−]
> This is all I ask for, O Lord.
> Please listen, Lord.[77]

The culture, therefore, that Kente's plays depicted was that of a closely-knit and supportive community, held together by family and racial ties and by its Christian morality and faith. It is a community which is socially integrated. It suffers under a racially oppressive system which affects all its inhabitants, poor and better-off, educated and uneducated, alike. Those who prosecute or serve the system are either outside the community, in both the literal and the racial and spiritual senses, or are 'sell-outs' — members of the community who have betrayed it — like the policeman Pelepele. However, such a vision is an idealization and its depiction, as we have seen, involved obscuring and idealizing certain factors.

Thus Kente in *Too Late* takes us way beyond *No-Good Friday* and *King Kong* in terms of cultural authenticity. His intimate knowledge of the culture of Soweto, and his need to portray the lives of ordinary people, results in a cultural picture which is in many ways true to life. Yet Kente, though black, was also a member of the intermediate classes. Thus though his racial/national identity informs his work with authenticity, his class identity propels him towards idealization.

Politics

Whereas *King Kong* (and, of course, *No-Good Friday*) raised social and even political issues, none of Kente's four early plays did. Instead the plots exploited what is called 'human interest'. Kente created characters and set them in a social milieu which the audience could identify with. He then placed them in situations which either amused or moved the audience to pity or terror. His music was the principal instrument for developing the emotional potential of these situations. If the plays had a message at all, it was that 'every cloud has a silver lining' or 'that's life'. As Sikalo's mother put it to her son, in one of the songs from *Sikalo*:

> Cheer up, my darling, you can't go on like this
> consider, darling, that life is not all bliss
> solve your troubles if you can
> don't drive yourself insane
> just stand up like a man
> look ahead! lift your head from the pain.

It was this formula which made Kente's plays economically successful and popular with black audiences in the 1960s. In *How Long, I Believe* and *Too Late* the human interest and the message of hope in times of trouble remain. Kente merely 'places' the human interest and the message in context, i.e. in the context of apartheid South Africa, a step that he had indicated in 1972 he would like to take but, as he said, 'we have to respect the law'. Now in these later plays it is not 'life' that is to blame for troubles, but a racially discriminatory system. The message of hope is embodied in *Too Late* in the repeated catchphrase 'Courage!' with which the characters sustain each other.[78] The change can be seen clearly if we compare *Too Late* with *Sikalo*.

Both Sikalo and Saduva struggle to survive in a terrorized environment, that depicted in *King Kong* and *No-Good Friday*. Both are arrested and imprisoned. In *Sikalo*, *King Kong* and *No-Good Friday* it is the gangs, the *tsotsis*, who terrorize. In *Too Late* it is the officers of the law. Sikalo is sent to jail for a criminal offence after being framed by gangsters. Saduva is arrested by the police for infringement of the pass laws. In *Too Late* Kente is concerned to demonstrate the workings and effects of racial discrimination in South Africa, a concern which is quite absent from his earlier plays. This meant a structural change. The episodic form is retained, but here it is no longer exclusively or even mainly a narrative form. The form is now didactic and demonstrative. Kente intends us to see apartheid and its instruments, the pass officials and the police, in action. He intends us to see the pass laws at work, the effects of unemployment, the brutalization in prisons, etc. This is now at least as important as Saduva's adventures and human relationships.

Thus the tendency observed in *No-Good Friday* and *King Kong*, and among English-speaking whites generally, to attribute the sufferings of black people to social evils for which they carry a considerable share of the responsibility, though still present (but not explicit) in *Sikalo*, is absent in *Too Late*. Instead, though the black policeman, Pelepele, is a brutal bully, we are shown the system and the man in pink gloves for whom Pelepele is but a tool. In fact, Kente suggests, even the man in pink gloves is ultimately not responsible: 'Did I make the damn laws?' he snaps in frustration as Mfundisi challenges his handling of Saduva's case (p.111). The finger points beyond him to the legislators and architects of the entire apartheid system.

Basically, there are two political attitudes expressed in the play, determined in this case by generation and to some extent by class. The youth, i.e. the *majitas*, and Saduva, express a more radical rejection of the apartheid system. The older generation, i.e. Dr Phuza and Mfundisi, express a reformist one. In the opening scene of the play the *majitas*, Sguqa and Matric, ex-students now living by crime, demonstrate to their school friend Diza that the traditional method of trying to find a job in order to pay for one's university education is an expensive charade. Diza has lost money using public transport while looking for a job. The *majitas*, in contrast, have profited handsomely from crime. In other words, in the present system at the present time crime pays a school-leaver better than looking for a job. The social and political implications of this need little explanation. Rising inflation and unemployment, constant disturbances and mass expulsions at the 'black' universities and a second-rate education at black schools are some of the reasons. However, the important critical point here is that no longer are *tsotsis* simply terrifying or glamorous thugs, feared but unexplained. Here Kente with admirable economy demonstrates their social and political roots, penetrating, as he does with Madinto, the stage stereotype of which Shark and Lucky are variant examples. He also, incidentally, explains the growth of theatre activity at schools and among school-leavers and the increase in the numbers of school-leavers in his own casts.

After the interchange between the *majitas* and Diza, Dr Phuza enters and attempts to take up the argument where Diza left off:

Dr Phuza (spots Matric): Matric, for God's sake, come here. *(he pulls him over to one side)* Molimo, Matric, why upset and disappoint your parents as well as your principal? The most brilliant student at school just decides to destroy his future.
Matric: My parents don't understand, Doc.
Dr Phuza: Bosh! That's hot capital bosh. Now tell me something sensible because your parents have asked me to talk with you.
Matric: The question is — what to study, Doc. To be a lawyer, a doctor or a teacher?
Dr Phuza: All of them if you like. What's the difference?
Matric: But the streets are overflowing with doctors, lawyers and teachers who to me are second-grade professionals.
Dr Phuza (offended): Are you suggesting that I'm a second-grade doctor?
Matric: As long as you are still getting a black wage at hospitals. So it is with lawyers who can never rise to the status of being judges.
Diza: But there are opportunities in the homelands.
Matric: Am I in the homelands?
Police whistles. [p.92]

Matric is easily able to refute the doctor's arguments. He shows that he understands how racial discrimination has made a mockery of the doctor's ambitions and achievements and caused him, like many others, to collapse into disillusionment and drunkenness. The final question: 'Am I in the homelands?' is answered unequivocally by the police. At this early stage in the play it is the *majitas'* radical rejection of the system that prevails.

After demonstrating the corruption of the policeman Shunqu, whose name means 'bribe', and the viciousness of Pelepele, Kente presents us with a church scene in which the priest sermonizes:

> The church is corrupt. The church is now a tabernacle of evil . . . It has ceased to foster the love of God. Man has reduced it to a platform for his own evil ideas and ideologies. People hate in the name of the church . . . Suppressive laws are made and these are backed by some churches. [p.106]

Thus the tone of militant criticism of the 'system' continues. Not only, we are told, does the 'system' render education and the pursuit of professional qualifications a mockery, but it corrupts and abuses the Christian religion. We should at this point reiterate that it is not Christianity itself that is being censured, but rather its abuse.

Now, this position is one that we might have expected Kente as a black businessman to support. Like black professionals, black businessmen were thwarted in their ambition to advance themselves. We have seen how Kente's own efforts to expand failed in the face of racial restrictions. Like King Kong, Kente had reached the top in the community to which his activities are by law restricted. His dream of *Sikalo* on Broadway is the equivalent of King Kong's title fight at White City Stadium.

The pass office, the most visible expression in the eyes of urban blacks of the apartheid system, follows, with its inevitable corollary, jail, where Saduva is forced into homosexual relations by, significantly, Matric, the radical critic of the 'system', now a hardened criminal. The political statement embodied in these scenes is one Kente still seems prepared to associate himself with – i.e. that job reservation and unemployment have made of the educated Matric and Sguqa hardened criminals, and the innocent Saduva is in danger of going the same way.

Our fears are confirmed when we next meet him. He has become an '*induna* on a prison road gang. Totozi is shocked at the transformation.'

Saduva (to other prisoner): Fuck you! Wenzani? What do you think you're doing?
Totozi (not believing her ears): Saduva! Must I believe?
Saduva: I'm sorry.
Totozi: You've changed.
Saduva: You don't expect to be dumped in the wilderness with lizards and snakes and still come out the same.
Totozi: Can you yield so soon? Can you lose faith so easily? Where's your God?
Saduva: They did not arrest him with me. I wonder what he would have done if those hooligans *(pointing to other prisoners)* did to him what they did to me?
Totozi: Sadu!

Saduva: Totozi, just leave me alone. *(He pushes her away.)* By what crime am
    I here? What's my sin? I hate the whole system.
(Band intro. Song – 'You're a man now')
Totozi (singing to him): Lord, no courage. [p.118]

Here again then is the radical rejection of 'the *whole* system', also
expressed by a young person. As the rejection expressed by the *majitas*
implied not just a rejection of the worst abuses of racial discrimination but
also of Bantu education, job reservation, 'Bantu' professionals and the upper
strata, the traditional values of the older generation, etc., so Saduva seems to
reject the prison system and the society's religion as well as racial discrimination. But now Kente is preparing to check the anarchic or radical energy of
the play together with its political position.

The ideas expressed earlier in the play by the *majitas* have now by
implication been discredited. After all, the audience is entitled to ask, what is
to be made of ideas that lead one into crime, jail and sodomy? Similarly, in
the case of Saduva's outburst, the context makes it clear that the audience
should not regard it as an insight into the system's evil, authenticated by his
suffering at its hands, but, as Totozi does, only as evidence of Saduva's
brutalization and corruption in prison. He has lost courage, as Totozi says,
and given in to the cardinal Christian sin of despair.

The process gathers momentum and by the end of the play the radical
discontent of its earlier scenes has been transformed into a message of
moderation. This emerges in both versions of the play. In the first, Pelepele
has just attempted to rearrest Saduva for manhandling Dr Phuza. The doctor
is given the last words of the play:

Pelepele: What's wrong, doc?
Offside: Saduva roughed him up a little.
Pelepele: Mas'hambe, mfana. [Let's go, my boy.] Back where you come
    from.
Dr Phuza: Listen, Pelepele, if I want to open up a case, I know where the
    police station is. Now just leave that boy alone.
Pelepele: So you encourage these boys to attack people in the street?
Mfundisi: Pelepele, do you realize that youth is now losing respect for the
    law?
Pelepele: Yes, abasiboni. [they don't pay any attention to us.]
Dr Phuza: Do you ever ask yourself why?
Pelepele: I don't know why. They are silly [i.e. naughty].
Mfundisi: Don't you think some of you policemen get unnecessarily harsh?
    And fail to help and be considerate, like in this boy's case *(pointing to
    Saduva).*
Pelepele: Mfundisi, we are doing our duty.
Dr Phuza: Still, your duty does not warrant to enjoy chasing these boys –
    even those who come pleading to you for help – like beasts.
Mfundisi: Again like the case of this boy.
Dr Phuza: Leaving the law, for now I am afraid unless something is done about
    this pettiness, the law is going to end up with a hot potato in its hands.

Can't something be done to curb the bitterness in both young and old
before it's TOO LATE?

[*Too Late*, I, p.22]

In the published version of the play, it is the priest who is given the major
statements. Of Saduva, who in this version has almost stabbed Pelepele to
death, he says:

> We all know that this young man was God loving, peace loving and law
> abiding. What's changed him? What's put hatred in him? From school
> children to the teachers, from the poor to the rich, the illiterate to the
> enlightened, the tsotsi to the law abiding, this hatred and resentment
> is rife. Tomorrow that poor young boy will be labelled dangerous and
> against the laws of the country. Forgetting that politics were forced
> on him. It's like being thrown into the rain and expected not to get
> wet, or food put into your hungry mouth yet still prohibited to eat.

In his last speech he sums up the play's meaning, placing it in a wider, national
context:

> Let us ask ourselves these burning questions? Can any force stop the
> prevalent bitterness in youth like Saduva? When even ordinary workers
> and labourers can organize massive strikes without influence nor
> leadership? Are these not clear and vivid signs of saturation. That boy
> will never be the same again. Can't the powers that be do something?
> *Doctor:* Before it's too late? [p.123]

In the first version, the doctor and the priest do not call on Pelepele to
desert the police force. They make no radical criticism of the 'harsh' laws the
policeman is expected to enforce, laws which even if enforced humanely
would still be 'harsh'. Instead the doctor actually believes that the problems
are only 'pettiness'. His statement amounts to this: 'It is not the laws that
need to (or can) be changed. It is the officers of the law who should curb
their excesses because these excesses are driving both young and old (but
especially the young) to a radical rejection of the law (and the system itself).'
The doctor implies that he finds the status quo, if enforced with more
humanity, preferable to the radical and militant alternatives that might
result from the anger of the youth.

In the second version while the priest protests against the system that
creates 'hatred and resentment', he implies that 'politics' is an evil which
must be prevented — a hegemonic notion derived from the ideology of the
intermediate classes of the English-speaking white group, as we have seen.
Especially revealing, however, is the alarm with which Mfundisi regards the
signs, particularly visible in the strikes of the early 1970s, that the black
proletariat was capable of taking organized mass action by itself, without
turning to the traditional intermediate class leadership. In such a situation,

Mfundisi and the doctor address a combined appeal to the state to do something to stop the process.

If we accept the statements expressed here by the doctor and the priest as the playwright's final statement, it is clear that we are in the presence of a contradiction. The radical analysis, which is expressed by the younger characters, though consistently upheld by the objective facts of their experience as revealed in the play, is gradually discredited. We see the *majitas* degenerate. Saduva's criticism is seen as only shocking evidence of his own corruption. Finally, the doctor, discredited in his debate with the *majitas* and by his own hopeless drunkenness, and the priest are thrust forward to cap a radical play with a reformist conclusion.

I believe that the analysis of Kente provided in the earlier sections of this chapter prepares us for this. As a black businessman entertainer for whom the black majority constituted his most profitable available market, it was essential for Kente, unlike other black writers of the educated intermediate classes, or Fugard and Bloom for that matter, to project in his plays a popular culture in which class divisions are played down in favour of racial cohesion. This accounts for the more authentic cultural content of the play. As his efforts to expand his commercial activities were frustrated by white competition and government restriction, his political position was likely to include a black nationalist tendency. This, together with the play's popular nature, accounts for the radical current generated in the play by the younger characters. However, as a member of a vulnerable section of an intermediate class whose existing economic interests were partly identified with those of the (white) bourgeoisie and antagonistic to those of the (black) working class, it was important for Kente to call for a solution which palliated rather than mobilized the frustrations of the black worker and the youth. The radical statement is hence subverted by Mfundisi and Dr Phuza's plea for moderation.

However, in order to determine the political function of a play it is necessary to go beyond a consideration of the play as written or conceived by its author(s). It was Engels who wrote: 'The many individual wills active in history for the most part produce results quite other than those intended — often quite the opposite' (*Selected Works*, p.613). Kente's political plays, as performed, functioned in ways that Kente, judging from an analysis of his plays as written, did not intend. This phenomenon is reflected in the fact that those in authority to whom Kente was able to defend *Too Late* as a *script*, e.g. the Publications Control Board and the Department of Sport and Recreation, did not insist on the political volatility of the play. Those who had to deal with its effects at the level of public performance in the black urban areas, e.g. the township superintendents, did — even when the play had been cleared by the higher authorities. There were two main reasons for this: first, the function of music in Kente's theatre, which will be looked at later; second, that the radical elements in the audience simply disregarded Kente's moderate pleas in favour of the more radical sentiments expressed by the characters they identified with, such as Zwelitsha in *I Believe* and the *majitas* and Saduva in *Too Late*. The fact that in the context of the plays themselves these sentiments were discredited was irrelevant to them. Hence *Too Late*'s function as a political play was probably more radical than an analysis of the script suggests or than Kente intended it to be.

Of course, it is theoretically possible that Kente was able to anticipate this phenomenon and under a smokescreen of 'moderate' and Christian noises, intended his plays to mobilize the revolutionary energies of the black working class and youth. However, Kente's class position does not prepare us for such a hypothesis.

Aesthetics

During the period in which Kente was struggling to establish himself he developed in response to the cultural demands of his market away from the *King Kong* model to a more individual genre.

King Kong dies tragically, a broken and defeated man. *No-Good Friday*, which like *Sikalo* is about the struggle between an innocent man and gangsters, ends with the struggle not resolved. However, it is implicit that Willie will perish at the hands of Shark and his gang. *Sikalo*, on the other hand, ends with the gang arrested and Sikalo freed from prison. All Kente's plays, with the exception of *I Believe*, have 'happy endings'. The reason for this was partly commercial, partly ideological. A happy ending was part of the Kente formula of giving the audience a ray of hope, comfort in adversity, etc. It was, however, also the result of Kente's being a black playwright, who viewed the sufferings of his people not as inevitable and eternal, but rather as temporary. He avoids the melancholy passivity of the *King Kong* ending and the artificial suspense of *No-Good Friday*'s.

The development in Kente's work related to structure has already been referred to briefly. The episodic plot, which Bloom and Gluckman had resorted to because of the 'limitations' of their actors, remained in all Kente's plays (until *How Long*) a vehicle for narrating the 'story' of the hero or heroine. By *Too Late* Kente had partially transformed it from a purely narrative structure into a didactic one, in which episodes served to provide the audience with information and demonstrate social forces and their effects on human beings. In *Too Late* Kente establishes the social environment before introducing Saduva and his story. In the following scenes, although the story of Saduva is being advanced and our interest in Madinto, Ntanana and Totozi as human beings is being developed, this is not done independently of the play's demonstrative purpose. We see the corruption of the police, religion, the inhumanity and indignity of the pass office, the prison cell and the road-gang. Only then, when the social realities of Saduva's 'story' have been clearly demonstrated, do we witness the resolution at a personal level.

No scene demonstrates the development of Kente's art as clearly as that of the church scene, a traditional scene not only in the work of Kente but in black theatre in general. This is so not only because it provides ample scope for two of the main ingredients of popular theatre — music and comedy — but also because church services, along with weddings, funerals and wakes, are a central social and cultural element in urban black life. In the closely-knit Christian community depicted in *Too Late* this is especially so. Mfundisi plays a central part in the play, as we have seen, and his church stands at the centre of the community. The church scene is the one scene in which virtually all the inhabitants of this community — i.e. virtually the entire cast — are assembled. In a world that scatters and breaks up, in *Too Late* the church pulls together and unites.

The characters that come together in this scene are quintessentially Kentian. Saduva, Totozi and Ntanana are 'straight' characters. It is around their lives and relationships that the human interest of the play revolves. The congregation is already seated when a drunk Dr Phuza enters, 'fighting very hard to keep an even walk'. (The doctor's surname literally means 'Drink'.) He belches, sits on Totozi's lap by accident and finally manages to get seated. Offside is 'too composed and looking very innocent and Holy'. His comic opportunity comes later when he is able to berate Pelepele and his police officers soundly in front of the whole congregation, and then, 'cashing in' on Mfundisi's eloquent evocation of Saduva and Ntanana's plight, he begins a 'collection', claiming to be 'Treasurer for the Poor Society'. Mfundisi himself enters 'highly spirited', which in this context means possessed in the religious sense, though in others it could mean drunk. He calls out 'Halleluya' 'even before reaching the pulpit'. Later the *majitas* rush in, followed by Pelepele, the policeman, whose name means '[hot] pepper or chili', and other policemen.

This congregation of vivid, familiar and comically-drawn characters is characteristic of all Kente's plays. He had the actors — or was able to train them — to play these parts. In *No-Good Friday* the individuality of the other characters was subordinated to that of the central character, Willie. In *King Kong*, although the same process of subordination took place to some extent, other lesser characters were allowed a certain amount of independent existence — Popcorn, Jack, Miriam and Dan, for instance. In *Too Late* characters develop a profuse existence which is dependent less on their role in the play than on their being a well-known part of Kente's community. These characters almost always have developed comic traits but, at least in *Too Late*, the comedy is informed and intermingled with seriousness.

Take Offside, for instance, who, as his name implies, exists outside conventional society and its exigencies. He has no pass book — never had one — has never worked, never paid tax, has no family, no apparent home, etc. There are similar characters in others of Kente's plays — Manyanyatha in *Zwi*, for instance. Offside's comic function is profound. Because he exists beyond the constraints that bind other members of the community, Offside is free to do or say what he wishes. His role is similar to that of the medieval court fool, or certain *imbongi* in the traditional African society. His irreverence and 'madness' are both amusing and deeply satisfying to an audience who in their daily lives have to cope with the irksome realities which Offside deliciously ignores.

The ease with which he bites the law by the nose and makes fun of the

pass system at the same time, in the following extract, is but one example.
Here Offside has just bought a hat and a jacket from Dupla, a very cheap
store in town. Both are far too small for him but, as he explains, it is cheaper
that way. The receipt in question is for the goods he bought:

Matric (teases him): Dupla? Couldn't you buy from a better shop than Dupla?
*(Enter Shunqu, Pelepele and other constables, demanding passes. Offside
quickly takes receipt from Matric, and moves away.)*
Pelepele: Heyi wena! [Hey, you!] Where you to? Produce.
*(Sergeant Shunqu is busy making a deal with the Majitas. They give him
money.)*
Offside (giving constable the receipt): Duplicate.
Pelepele: But this is a receipt. *(He is not well read.)*
Offside: Correct. Receipt for the Duplicate.
Pelepele: What is the Dupla?
Offside: Short form for Duplicate [i.e. application for a duplicate pass book].
Pelepele: But there's a price here. R12.25. R twelve twenty-five.
Offside: R stands for Reference book, twelve stands for month December,
    and twenty-five the day. So I'll get my reference book on the twenty-fifth
    of December.
Pelepele (not satisfied but fearing to expose his ignorance): O, I see.
*(Shunqu after pocketing the bribe, is watching nonchalantly. He is aware his
man is being fooled.)*
Shunqu: Constable, is he alright?
Pelepele: Yes, Sajini, he's o-right.
Shunqu (smiling): Let's move then, gentlemen. [p.104]

On another occasion Offside escapes arrest by slipping out of his jacket.
'If they miss me,' he grumbles later, 'why arrest my jacket. I mean it's no
accomplice' (p.114).

Offside is not only a comic and cathartically anarchic character, he is also
the embodiment of *ubuntu* – the characteristic the African communalists
picked out as summing up the humanism of 'black' as opposed to 'white'
culture (see p.155ff.). *Ubuntu* literally means 'the quality of being human'.
Though Offside possesses little, what he has belongs to anyone who needs
it. He shares his *pap en vleis* (meat and porridge) with Saduva and Ntanana,
and gives his meat to Saduva in prison. He is a force for goodness in the play
in many other ways, and at a crucial moment he is prepared to risk his own
life to save Saduva from killing Pelepele, though Pelepele is his scourge and
elsewhere Offside is a coward.

Ideologically, Offside is the missing factor in *No-Good Friday* and *King
Kong*. He is the spirit of comedy – but an affirmative spirit who embodies
the society's strength and *ubuntu* in the midst of poverty and misery. He is
the counterpoise to Shark, Lucky and Pelepele. Though seeming to be outside
the society, he is the embodiment of its will and capacity to *constitute* its
own personality and to survive.

In other skilful ways Kente has implied the serious meanings of his play
in the apparently comic business of the church scene. The comedy suggests

seriousness at the same time as it undercuts and deflates it. For instance, the entrance of the policemen, headed by Pelepele, the man who will murder Ntanana, into the 'house of God' in pursuit of the *majitas* is presented comically. We laugh to see their impotence, their hypocritical deference to religion as they are 'ashamed to arrest the *majitas*'. But Kente gives their entrance its full symbolic meaning:

Pelepele: We are lost.
Mfundisi: No, you are welcome. [p.107]

The church is the emblem of Kente's integrated Christian family from which Pelepele has temporarily excluded himself. He is lost but, like the sheep in the parable, he may be found again.

At the same time there is a sharper, satirical element, which again Offside capitalizes on. In church the police are powerless and Pelepele, soon to be murderer, and Shunqu, the taker of bribes, 'take off their helmets, they crawl to their seats' and there they are compelled to listen, while Offside, the hobo and joker, taunts them in front of the community and in front of their prey, the *majitas*: 'Mfundisi, I am tired of playing hide and seek. I want to lead a normal life but how can I with people like PP?'

Mfundisi then takes Offside's lead and delivers his evocation of the unjust situation in which Saduva and Ntanana find themselves as a result of the law and police persecution. As so often happens in Kente's theatre, the emotions generated by his speech and the situation are expressed in a song, in this case, sung by Saduva:

> I'm in the street
> without a place to stay
> nothing to eat
> I seek a job each day
> I'm always told sorry none for you
>
> Early in the morn
> I have to run and hide
> without a pass
> I'm always scared and wild
> I strive — I starve
> Lord, each day.

The function of music in Kente's theatre is a topic deserving separate treatment. All we can do here is to reiterate that the impact of his 'political plays' on black audiences was far greater than a study of the play's script would suggest. One reason, already cited, was that the radical sections in the audience responded to the radical elements in the plays and disregarded Kente's moderate overall meaning. Another was that Kente's theatre was especially effective in non-intellectual, unarticulated areas of communication. The total message of these plays was far more powerful than that which is contained in the script, because important elements of the play's impact remained unarticulated. Now, while continuing the uses made of music in *King Kong*, e.g. connecting episodes, creating atmosphere, substituting for dialogue, Kente makes it much more central to his work than it was even in *King Kong*. It becomes in fact the most powerful vehicle for the expression of the emotional or spiritual elements of the plays. In this respect it operated on essentially racial/national lines and was similar to the achievements of Todd Matshikiza in *King Kong*. A writer in the *Black Review 1972*, when talking of music in the context of Black Consciousness, observed that black music 'is now being used effectively as a means of communication, often running deeper than words' (p.47). It is this ability of Kente's to communicate with the black audience 'deeper than words', through his music, which makes his political plays more powerful than the script suggests. Our own first-hand experience revealed how the music of these plays was able to fuse an audience of separate and divided individuals in an experience of intense cultural identity. It is significant that the songs which achieved this were invariably in an African language, like the short hymn which follows Mfundisi's sermon and translates the words and meanings of the sermon into an experience which far transcends them:

Ngabayini	*lisono sam'*	(What could it be − my sin?
andilazi	*lityala lam'*	I do not know − my fault.
intoni le	*libadi lam'*	what is it − my misfortune
ububi bam'	*nobomi bam'*	my evil − and my life.
kunzim' ukondl' isisu sam'		Hard to fill my stomach
nempahla yabantwana bam'		clothes for my children
kunzima nomsebenzi kum'		hard my toil
ngabayini	*lityala lam'*	what could it be − my fault?)

Language

The words, the script, of *Too Late*, are a totally inadequate measure of the impact of the play in performance before the audience it was written for. Kente was never a 'writer'. That he looked for a 'writer' when he wished to produce his first musical indicates this. Kente was a playmaker, a director, a choreographer, a musician, but not a 'writer'. Had he found a 'writer' for that first play, white or black, it is possible that his work would have been more lucid, more impressive − on *paper*. It is doubtful, however, whether its effect on an audience would have been more powerful. A performance of a play by Kente is an exciting experience, which a study of this kind cannot adequately communicate. But it is a fact which has to be borne in mind as we analyse and particularly as we make assessments based on Kente's *written* script.

Kente's literary weakness was one of the reasons why the educated did not hold him in higher esteem. Though Kente's expressive theatrical technique was advanced by the time he wrote the play, they mistook the unsophisticated literary elements for a general superficiality of content and form. They criticized him for lack of 'depth'. They were blind to the 'depth' of the play's structure, and impervious, as others in the audience were not, to the play's ability to communicate in non-verbal areas. The murder, for instance, of Ntanana by Pelepele was a piece of theatre they might well have taken for crude buffoonery, but which Kente's audience found painful and immediate:

Saduva: Whilst waiting for Toza, rest too, Ntana.
(He puts her head on his lap. He takes out the mouth-organ and plays a very sad hymn. He is deep in thought. Voices wailing sweetly off stage. Ntanana falls asleep, too. Saduva plays as if saying to his God, 'Why forsake me?'
He is now reaching dizzy heights of emotion. Then Pelepele and three others enter. Pelepele tips his men to be silent. They creep up behind Saduva, Ntanana and Offside. Pelepele grabs Saduva by the collar, the others grab Offside. Offside plays drunk. Saduva sighs from shock. Orchestra takes over. Voices to climax. Ntanana wakes up and screams. At first she's confused. But when she sees what is happening she goes for Pelepele. Pelepele, holding Saduva firmly with one hand, claps Ntanana twice. Both times she falls and gets up and goes for him. The third time Pelepele shoves her hard with his foot. Offside slips out of his jacket and runs for dear life. Ntanana falls again. This time she goes headlong for Pelepele's stomach. She clings on to his balls like an octopus. Pelepele, after punching and pushing her, groans with pain. Second policeman tries to pull her as well but then decides to hold Saduva.)
Pelepele (screaming for help): Leave that boy! Leave him!
Second policeman: Why? No-no-no pass.
Pelepele: Can't you see. I am dying. Yoo! Yoo!
Then Pelepele gets a deadly idea. Aims and strikes with all his might on Ntanana's head — the blow that ends her life. Ntanana sinks slowly down Pelepele's legs and knocks the ground with a thud. Tenor sax and voices die, synchronizing with her sinking.)
Pelepele: Ifil' inja. [The dog is dead.]
(He massages himself above the balls. Saduva frantically calls as he is being pulled away.)
Saduva (crying like a baby): Ntanana!
Exit police with Saduva. From a distance his voice still echoes 'Ntanana'.)
[pp.112–3]

Ntanana is a cripple. This is no doubt an advantage to any playwright bent on sentimental dividends. However, the immediacy and pain are derived from the way in which Kente transforms her disability from an emotional or conceptual fact to a physical one, by exposing her condition to Pelepele's brutality, in conjunction with the physical, psychological and symbolic effects of *her* attack on the policeman's balls.

The question of the literary weakness of Kente's script raises an important linguistic matter — for in essence it only poses problems to those readers or viewers who are habitually English-speaking. *Too Late* was based in a non-English-speaking culture, performed by non-English-speaking actors, to non-English-speaking audiences, and written in English. Kente expressed his reasons for not writing in African languages thus:

> You mean Zulu, Xhosa, Sotho and all that? That's out of the question.
> It would mean I would have to have about four plays running at the
> same time. One running in the Free State for the Sothos, one in the
> Cape for the Xhosas, another in the northern Transvaal for the Pedis.
> It's almost impossible. Well, I think we're all aware that English is quite
> a medium for all of us. I won't write in Xhosa.[79]

There are two points we have to bear in mind when assessing the language
of plays such as *Too Late*. The first is that the language is only part of the
play's expressive vocabulary. The experience of the play is communicated
in music, dance, comedy, mime, gesture and other visual devices as well as
language. The second is that how the dialogue sounds to a native English-
speaker or the educated black English-speaker is not relevant in this case.
It is how the dialogue sounds to the audience for whom Kente intended the
play that is relevant — and their response indicates that they were more than
content with it.

The first thing we note about the language of *Too Late* is the complete
absence of *imported* or artificial grammatical errors. Instead, we have English
as it is spoken in the black urban areas, modified by Kente's own writing.
Though it is partly an invented language — after all Saduva, Madinto, Ntanana
and the rest would not in real life speak English in the first place — it is based
on an English that has developed organically in the culture of the community
in which the play is set.

Take Act II, Scene I, in the *Too Late* (I) script, in which Ntanana, Totozi
and Saduva meet up. Madinto is in prison and Saduva on the run:

Ntanana: Totozi.
Totozi: Hallo, Ntana.
Ntanana: Did you get the job?
Totozi: Only a promise for next month. *(She spots the peels in Ntanana's
hands)* What are you eating? Amaxolo? Hayi, sisi, lahla! [Peels? No,
sister, throw them away!] . . . How did Sadu fare at the Pass Office?
Ntanana: He is not back yet. I am worried.
Totozi: What could have happened?
(Enter Saduva running blindly.)
Totozi: Saduva!
Ntanana: Buti. *(Helping him as he falls, to protect him.)*
Totozi: You don't have to tell us what happened.
Saduva: God, I'm hungry.
(Ntanana takes out some peels and gives him.)
Saduva: Thank you, Ntana.
Totozi: I've got at least twenty cents. Let me see what I can get.
Saduva: Totozi, your heart is a treasured gift from God.
Totozi: Thank you, Sadu. I'll be back soon. [p.20]

The opening exchange between Ntanana and Totozi is a relaxed equivalent of what they might have said in Zulu/Xhosa. The shock at seeing Totozi eating peels pushes Ntanana out of English into the vernacular — 'Amaxolo?' etc. Her next question, however, contains the bookish expression 'How did Sadu fare?' In reality she would probably have said: *'uSadu uhambenjani ePass Office?'* Colloquial 'Soweto English' reflects this: 'How did Sadu go at the Pass Office?' 'Fare' would appear to be Kente's more 'educated' modification.

From there the dialogue continues in standard 'Soweto English', including the touching 'Buti' (brother). It is noticeable that when intimacy, warmth or agitation are to be expressed, Kente sensitively and authentically uses the vernacular. The next of Kente's modifications of standard 'Soweto English' is Sadu's 'sentiment' — 'Totozi, your heart is a treasured gift from God'. The modification does not consist in the use of 'sentiment'. The tendency to 'praise' (*ukubonga*) someone who shows generosity is an aspect of traditional culture which has survived strongly in urban areas. It is the transposition into the language of another culture which distorts it. 'Praise' of this kind is culturally inseparable from the vernacular. Anything but an extraordinarily skilful rendition into English will sound awkward because such sentiments are no longer the usage in English-speaking culture.

This extract therefore indicates a basic organic form of English, i.e. 'Soweto English', which shows a tendency to move towards African languages at certain points and towards the more literary English of the educated black intermediate classes at others.

What Kente came to do increasingly after *Sikalo* was to incorporate words and phrases from the vernacular languages. Educated reviewers who have found his English dialogue puerile have praised this. Sipho Sepamla, the poet and playwright, wrote in a review of *How Long*: 'I recall the opening 15 minutes or so of the play when my heart warmed up to a scene which had every conceivable tongue of the townships, English toyed with as is done in our world.' Aggrey Klaaste wrote of *Too Late*: 'Gibson Kente has the deft ability of putting such apt township phrases into his characters' mouths that they often happen to be what stays with us longest after we've seen his plays.' An interviewer put this to him in 1972: 'Do you realize that in your plays you get very good laughs from people like Kenny Majozi when he uses a word in Zulu? . . .' Kente replied:

> I seem to disagree with you. Because if you remember in *Sikalo* Kenny never used any Zulu, but he was very popular. Even now (in *Lifa*) he's got a lot of laugh lines in English. I wouldn't say it's because he's using Zulu lines. It's the part as such. It's a comedy part.[80]

In addition to using the vernacular to express warmth or agitation or in songs, Kente uses it for characterization and as an indicator of status. By and large the central characters such as Saduva, his family, peers and associates speak 'Soweto English'. As one goes 'higher' than this group into the upper strata, the language becomes more 'English'. The following utterances of Dr Phuza are examples:

> Bosh! That's hot capital bosh! Now tell me something sensible, because your parents have asked me to talk with you. [p.92]

and:

> Damn it! Are we bound to wait here until the cows come home? [p.109]

Nevertheless, in keeping with the doctor's integration in the community, he is quite capable of saying things like the following:

> Don't worry, boys. That pick-up van is so bloody full I don't know how those people moves their eyes, never mind their asses. [p.92]

As one goes 'lower' into the uneducated or rural strata, the languages become denser with pidgin English and the vernacular. Pelepele is the most notable example, but Shunqu, the jail warder, the road-gang policeman and Saduva as *induna* all do the same. Pelepele, for instance, says to Madinto: 'Voetsek kimi! Isifebe lesi! [Voetsek to me! You whore!] Madinto, I'll show you you are a nutting' (p.94); to Shunqu: 'Yes, Sajini, he's o-right' (p.104); when he murders Ntanana: 'Ifil' inja [The dog is dead]' (p.113); and to Saduva, when he is told that Saduva has manhandled the doctor: 'As'hambe, mfana [Let's go, boy]. Back where you come from' (*Too Late* (I), p.22).

Thus it would be true to say that Kente as an educated man who writes in English shares in this respect the attitude of Fugard and company in *No-Good Friday*, and Bloom and company in *King Kong*, to the uneducated or non-English-speaking and migrant or rural sections. However, in important respects the study of Kente's art and his use of language reveals a much greater authenticity and accuracy, together with a greater sympathy in the depiction of urban black culture.

In his tendency to depict an integrated black community, Kente is greatly assisted by his use of English. An accurate rendering of language as it is used in Soweto would reveal a far greater stratification than *Too Late* and its English dialogue suggests. With everyone more or less speaking the same language, the stratification is obscured.

★   ★   ★

Fundamentally, Kente aimed to produce plays which the popular black audience in the towns would like. This he did with great skill and success. That he was able to do it can in the main be attributed to his own cultural affinity with his audience. Together with Kente's personal skills, this cultural affinity produced in *Too Late* (and other plays) possibly the fullest and most humanly rich picture of the culture of ordinary black South Africans in South African theatre to date. Or, as the black actor Sam Williams put it in a letter to *The World*, after long being cynical of Kente's achievement:

> Man, say what you like about the guy, but hell, the man has got a deep
> insight into the loves and hates of our people, both petty and genuine.
> He has made it his business to know what the people want and he goes
> out and gets it for them. That is why he is in business. [*The World*,
> 3 January 1974]

Yet we are concerned to explore how the advances our playwrights have
achieved can be built on and carried forward towards a true democratic
theatre. Kente's class position, as we have seen, had serious consequences,
especially in the political meanings of his plays. Next we examine a work of
the Black Consciousness movement, which drew attention to many of the
factors of cultural domination which we have identified in *No-Good Friday*
and *King Kong*, and possessed a political ideology which appeared more
radical than that of Gibson Kente, in order to ascertain to what extent the
search for a genuine theatre of the majority is carried forward in their work.

8. 'A Dialogue of Confrontation'

Shanti, written by Mthuli Shezi, was, like *No-Good Friday* and *King Kong*, an inter-racial collaborative effort, but of a different kind, for in the case of *Shanti* no whites were involved; instead, members of different black groups collaborated.

Though both Kente and Shezi were black, their circumstances differed in a number of respects. Shezi was personally involved in a political movement, the Black Consciousness movement, and wished to make a specifically political use of theatre. *No-Good Friday, King Kong* and *Too Late* were created by artists for artistic and/or commercial reasons and with no conscious reference to an aesthetic or ideological framework which took into consideration the nature of cultural domination and the function of art in a society such as South Africa. Though Nkosi, Bloom, Kente, etc. were conscious of certain political dimensions and imagined that their work might have some political function, they were primarily concerned with other, non-political, objectives. Similarly, what political function they had in mind was conceived within the ideological framework of multi-racialism. Though Kente's *Too Late* pictures a tightly knit black community, there is nothing in it which challenges the multi-racialism he publicly supported on a number of occasions.

Shanti, on the other hand, was written within the parameters of a movement which was particularly conscious of cultural domination and specifically rejected multi-racialism. This was the Black Consciousness movement.

Black Consciousness

The Black Consciousness movement, though it developed in the nationalist tradition of black political struggle in South Africa, gave decisive emphasis to racial/cultural factors and to the common interests of all blacks, i.e. black Africans, 'Coloureds' and 'Indians'. The movement attempted to use its theory to explain and expose to blacks all areas where their racial/cultural interests were threatened or damaged by the activities of the dominant white groups and their 'agents' among blacks. This led to the first systematic delineation of 'black' viewpoints and 'correct' black attitudes to the entire gamut of black-white relations and black affairs — to the white government, to the white liberals, to religion, to Bantu education, to bantustans and bantu-stan leaders, to the press, the radio, music, art and literature.

For the first time, a black politico-cultural movement issued its own guidelines in the name of South African blacks as to what blacks should approve or condemn, what they should support or resist. Black Consciousness, the ideology that inspired these interventions, was disseminated through influential publications, such as the *South African Students Organization Newsletter* and the *Black Review*, and through minor newsletters, through conferences, press statements, leadership training seminars, community work, art festivals and theatre.

In a letter to other South African student bodies and organizations Stephen Bantu Biko, president of the South African Students Organization (SASO), related the origins of the Black Consciousness movement.[81] He began his account with the implementation of the Fort Hare Transfer Act of 1959, 'which brought Fort Hare under direct government control', and the establishment of 'tribal' universities in the same year. Two attempts at the establishment of black student organizations — the African Students' Organization of 1960 and the African Students' Union of South Africa of 1961 — foundered, and for a long period the only existing student organizations in which black students could take part were the National Union of South African Students (NUSAS) and the University Christian Movement (UCM), founded in 1967. There was soon a black majority in the latter body, and the dialogue between black students which began there eventually culminated in a conference in December 1968 at which the Student Representative Councils from the black campuses decided to set up a black student organization. The South African Students Organization (SASO) was duly founded in July 1969.

The feeling that gave rise to its foundation was, according to Biko, 'that a time had come when blacks had to formulate their own thinking, unpolluted by ideas emanating from a group with lots at stake in the *status quo*'. Both NUSAS and UCM were considered 'white-dominated' and they 'paid very little attention to problems peculiar to the black community'. 'Some people began to question the very competence of pluralistic groups to examine without bias problems affecting one group especially if the unaffected group is from the oppressor camp.'

The following is a part of SASO's manifesto:

SASO believes that:
3. (a) South Africa is a country in which both black and white live and shall continue to live together;

(b) that the white man must be made aware one is either part of the solution or part of the problem;

(c) that, in this context, because of the privileges accorded them by legislation and because of their continual maintenance of an oppressive regime, whites have defined themselves as part of the problem;

(d) that, therefore, we believe that in all matters relating to the struggle towards realizing our aspirations, whites must be excluded;

(e) that this attitude must not be interpreted by blacks to imply 'anti-whitism' but merely a more positive way of attaining a normal situation in South Africa;

(f) that in pursuit of this direction, therefore, personal contact with whites, though it should not be legislated against, must be discouraged, especially where it tends to militate against the beliefs we hold dear.

4. (a) SASO upholds the concept of Black Consciousness and the drive towards black awareness as the most logical and significant means of ridding ourselves of the shackles that bind us to perpetual servitude.

(b) SASO defines Black Consciousness as follows:

(i) Black Consciousness is an attitude of mind, a way of life.

(ii) The basic tenet of Black Consciousness is that the black man must reject all value systems that seek to make him a foreigner in the country of his birth and reduce his basic human dignity.

(iii) The black man must build up his own value systems, see himself as self-defined and not defined by others.

(iv) The concept of Black Consciousness implies the awareness by the black people of the power they wield as a group, both economically and politically, and hence group cohesion and solidarity are important facets of Black Consciousness.

(v) Black Consciousness will always be enhanced by the totality of involvement of the oppressed people, hence the message of Black Consciousness has to be spread to reach all sections of the black community.

(c) SASO accepts the premise that before the black people should join the open society, they should first close their ranks, to form themselves into a solid group to oppose the definite racism that is meted out by the white society, to work out their direction clearly and bargain from a position of strength. SASO believes that a truly open society can only be achieved by blacks.

5. SASO believes that the concept of integration cannot be realized in an atmosphere of suspicion and mistrust. Integration does not mean assimilation of blacks into an already established set of norms drawn up and motivated by white society. Integration implies free participation by individuals in a given society and proportionate contribution to the joint culture of the society by all constituent groups. Following this definition therefore, SASO believes that integration does not need to be enforced or worked for. Integration follows automatically when the doors to prejudice are closed through the attainment of a just and free society.

6. SASO believes that all groups allegedly working for 'integration' in South Africa . . . and here we note in particular the Progressive Party and other liberal institutions . . . are not working for the kind of

integration that would be acceptable to the black man. Their attempts are directed merely at relaxing certain oppressive legislations and to allow blacks into a white-type society.

7. SASO, while upholding these beliefs, nevertheless wishes to state that Black Consciousness should not be associated with any particular political party or slogan. [*Black Review*, 1972, pp.40–2]

The other important body within the Black Consciousness movement was the Black People's Convention (BPC). 'In the 1960s,' wrote Biko, 'the African National Congress and the Pan-Africanist Congress had been banned so the main realities we were confronted with were the power of the police and leftist noises of the white liberals' (Woods, p.97). The participation of the black intelligentsia was crucial if the question of how to foster a new consciousness was to be solved. SASO was formed to bring about a 'change of consciousness among graduates' in order to get them to identify 'with the needs of the black community'. In order to extend the process into the wider community and to involve 'the masses . . . in the development of a new consciousness', BPC was formed as 'a political movement under the banner of Black Consciousness' (*Black Review*, 1972, p.10). The following are excerpts from a statement issued by the BPC Ad Hoc Committee to the press in January 1972:

> It is the inalienable birthright of any community to have a political voice to articulate and realize the aspirations of its members.
> In this our country, Africans, Coloureds and Indians comprise the Black Community which has been deprived of this inalienable right; and for too long there has been a political vacuum in the black community.
> False impressions have been created that it is illegal and unlawful for blacks to found political movements and to engage in political activity unless such activity has been created as prescribed and approved by white society and its government.
> The Ad Hoc committee is therefore working towards the formation of a Black People's political movement whose primary aim is to unite and solidify black people with a view to liberating and emancipating them from both psychological and physical oppression.
> Our interests therefore lie within the black community and our sole aim will be directed towards realizing its needs, which needs will coincide with those of all black people throughout the world.
> It is therefore essential and imperative that all black people, individuals and organizations, should pool their resources together in order to achieve their aspirations. Their future destiny and ultimate happiness is in their hands. [*Black Review*, 1972, p.12]

At the BPC's first conference in July 1972, at which Mthuli Shezi, the author of *Shanti*, was elected vice-president, the following aims were decided on:

- to liberate and emancipate blacks from psychological and physical oppression,
- to create a humanitarian society where justice is meted out equally to all,
- to co-operate with existing agencies with the same ideals,
- to re-orientate the theological system with a view of making religion relevant to the aspirations of the black people,
- to formulate, apply and implement the principles and philosophies of Black Consciousness and Black Communalism,
- to formulate and implement an education policy of blacks by blacks for blacks. [*Black Review*, 1972, p.12]

Other groups and activities which came to be associated with the Black Consciousness movement included ASSECA (Association for the Educational and Cultural Advancement of African People of South Africa), a national organization founded in 1967 which concentrated on assisting blacks in the education of their children; IDAMASA (Interdenominational African Ministers' Association), founded in 1965, which concentrated on education, scholarships, research into traditional culture, youth work, interdenominational activity and from 1972 the enunciation of Black Theology; BCP (Black Community Programmes), 'a co-ordinating and enabling agency' which produced the annual *Black Review*; the Black Press Conference, convened to work towards the establishment of an independent black press; the Union of Black Journalists; and the Black Workers' Project and the Black Allied Workers' Union (formerly Salesmen and Allied Workers' Association) with a concept of trade unionism that, unlike that of 'Western' unions, extended its activities 'beyond the factory' into the 'ghetto'. A number of youth organizations were formed in 1971–72 to inculcate Black Consciousness among young people and school students, e.g. SASM (South African Student Movement), the League of African Youth and the Junior African Students' Congress, though action by teachers and principals made this difficult.

In July 1972 the SASO conference realized that 'culture is tied up with the aspirations of a people' and formed a committee (Culcom) 'that would deal specifically with the awakening and heightening of cultural awareness and the involvement of the black people in their struggle for identity, self-respect and liberation'. A Theatre Council 'to cater for poetry, music, drama, fine arts and films' was projected. In the same month, the South African Black Theatre Union (SABTU) was formed in Durban after a national black drama festival organized by the Theatre Council of Natal (TECON), whose leading members, Strini Moodley and Saths Cooper, were active in the Black Consciousness movement.

The philosophy of the movement was still in the process of formulation when its most articulate spokespeople were silenced by banning, detention and criminal charges. Biko and seven other SASO leaders were banned in March 1973. Biko was detained in 1975 and again in 1977, dying in detention in September 1977. After a pro-Frelimo rally in Durban, in 1974, went ahead despite a government banning order, Black Consciousness leaders throughout the country were arrested. In 1975, 13 of those detained were charged under the Terrorism Act. Among those on trial were Strini Moodley and Saths Cooper of the Theatre Council of Natal (TECON) and Sadecque Variava and Solly Ismael of the People's Experimental Theatre (PET), the group which performed *Shanti*. They were found guilty and sentenced to prison sentences on Robben Island.

In the writings of Biko, Pityana and contributors to the SASO newsletters the philosophy enunciated was not absolutely coherent. There were substantial individual differences in interpretation. Even Biko's philosophy was at times confused, definitely eclectic, often contradictory. However, a definite nucleus of argument and vision is discernible in most of the serious writers of the BCM, and a definite continuity and development from the early years to, say, 1976, existed.

According to these writers, Black Consciousness, by analogy with class consciousness, which is an awareness of the objective realities of one's class position, is based on an awareness of one's position in South Africa as a black person. It is a consciousness of what being black means in that society, and therefore also a consciousness of self, of identity. This consciousness is something to be both accepted and resisted. The fact of blackness and being of the black races is to be accepted with pride and assertion. The oppression, both physical and spiritual — or as Biko put it, both outer and inner — that is the concomitant of blackness in South Africa, is to be resisted:

> SASO is a black student organization working for the liberation of the black man first from psychological oppression by themselves through inferiority complex and secondly from the physical one accruing out of living in a white racist society. [p.100]

The application of the twin principles of acceptance of blackness but rejection of oppression carried the exponents of the philosophy into a comprehensive process of re-evaluation.

The movement's appreciation of the importance of history and culture and the inward forms of oppression led it to make the comprehensive attempt to identify the mechanisms of cultural oppression. Only by exposing the mechanisms of cultural oppression would it be possible for the oppressed to begin the slow, painful process of clearing their minds and hearts of oppressive values and images upon which their condition of bondage so depended. In *Shanti*, when Thabo announces that he is thinking of resigning from the political movement, Shanti challenges him: 'You want us to wait, wait for the crumbs falling from the master's table?' (p.74). The BCM realized that there would be no real freedom so long as the nature of the 'table' was defined by 'white' cultural forms and values.

It is not the intention here to attempt a critique of Black Consciousness as a theory of liberation. Nor is there any need to trace in detail the ideological roots of the movement in the Pan-Africanist, Negritude and Black Power movements of Africa and the diaspora. However, at least a brief assessment of the movement's theory and practice as regards cultural domination needs to be made in order to indicate the theoretical progress, or lack of progress, made by the movement in this area.

The realization that conquest and colonization, together with Christian proselytization, had degraded, distorted and destroyed the history and culture of the indigenous peoples was not new amongst South African blacks. Many writers and politicians attempted to preserve or restore their history and culture, and the importance of this activity as part of the process of uplifting and strengthening the people had long been understood. However, as the political struggles of the period up to the emergence of the ANC Youth League in 1944 had been led by the educated Christian élite, and were conducted in the context of proving to the ruling whites the black man's ability to take his place in the world of white culture and 'civilization' alongside the whites, the historical and cultural heritage of pre-Christian, pre-'civilized' Africa was obviously not an appropriate weapon.

According to Biko and others, it was the evolution of Africanist and Pan-Africanist ideology and its advocacy of withdrawal from association in the same organization with those who were not of the nationalist culture — in this case, black African — that opened the way to the reinstatement of the political context of African history, traditional culture and especially language, and to the conversion of the struggle from an élitist activity directed at securing a 'place' in white society for the few, into a mass activity directed at the complete take-over of the state and the restructuring of the society according to what was perceived to be the needs and culture of blacks. 'Very few black organizations were not under white direction . . .,' Biko wrote. 'It was only at the end of the 50s that the blacks started demanding to be their own guardians' (p.20).

The origins of the BCM in SASO, however, and SASO's struggle to establish itself as a student movement in opposition to NUSAS, to a large extent determined that there should be differences between the BCM and the earlier traditions of political activity. Black Consciousness developed in an area where cultural hegemony was possibly at its most intense, amongst the people who were perhaps in the best position to recognize and resent it. It came from two sources. First, there were the white liberal students who dominated NUSAS, and then there was the Afrikaner Nationalist hierarchy which dominated the 'tribal' universities.

One of the important ideological measures taken by the Afrikaner Nationalist government had been to withdraw all black students, including 'Indians' and 'Coloureds', from English-speaking white universities and establish special government-controlled colleges for them. Now, the black intellectual had traditionally found the liberal hegemony of the English-speaking white group, with its apparently sympathetic ideology, persuasive and influential — far more so than the official ideology of separate development. Thus, freed from the former and firmly rejecting the latter, the black student of the late 1960s developed more independently than ever before. In

1959 black African students totalled 1,871. By 1964 they had hardly increased; there were 1,897. The following year their number had increased to 2,349, but in 1974 there were 7,845. The net result, therefore, was a large increase in educated blacks who no longer affiliated to the liberal ideology of the English-speaking white group as strongly as their parents had done, rejected separate development and were thus ready to develop the ideological basis for an alternative black hegemony.

That the 'tribal universities' were blatant instruments of cultural indoctrination was known to all. W. A. Maree, when Minister of Bantu Education, freely admitted this when he said:

> Where one has to deal with underdeveloped peoples, where the state has planned a process of development for those peoples, and where a university can play a decisive role in the process and direction of that development, it must surely be clear to everyone that the state alone is competent to exercise the powers of guardianship in this field. [UNESCO, p.92]

What had not been so evident to black intellectuals until the late 1960s was that the traditional intellectuals of the English-speaking white group, in the popular mind historically associated with the black groups in their political struggles, were actually the 'agents', in the Gramscian sense, of the general hegemony of the white groups:

> Their [the whites'] agents are ever amongst us, telling us that it is immoral to withdraw into a cocoon, that dialogue is the answer to our problem and that it is unfortunate that there is white racism in some quarters but you must understand things are changing. [Biko, p.50]

In his essay 'Black Souls in White Skins?' Biko concentrates his full attention on exposing what he calls the 'do-gooders', i.e. the white liberals. This was a characteristic emphasis in most Black Consciousness literature when it concerned itself with the question of 'white racism' and whites in general.

The movement believed that the traditional relationship with the white liberals was damaging in terms of political effectiveness. Moreover it believed that this relationship was in itself an aspect of the cultural domination of the white groups in the society as well. Whites constantly dominated organizations because they were able to dictate the cultural relations within them. They were, as Biko complained, always teachers while blacks were always students:

> In being forced to accept the Anglo-Boer culture, the blacks have allowed themselves to be at the mercy of the white man and to have him as their eternal supervisor. Only he can tell us how good our performance is and instinctively each of us is at pains to please this powerful, all-knowing master. This is what Black Consciousness seeks

to eradicate. [p.94]

The attack on white liberals in the field of student affairs and politics had soon to be extended to the English-language press, which was misrepresenting their activities, and to the established churches, another traditional 'supporter' of the black cause. Their developing ideology, together with the direct experience of operating within NUSAS and the UCM and having their actions and statements reported, interpreted or criticized by the English press, by liberal institutions such as the Institute of Race Relations and the Christian Institute and by various eminent liberal artists and intellectuals such as Alan Paton and Nadine Gordimer, helped them to understand the function of the liberal white intelligentsia with some clarity. They advocated a policy of total withdrawal from all unnecessary contact with them.[82]

The BCM was always much more effective in dealing with the problems posed by this, as opposed to other sections of the ruling white groups. Important as it was to expose its complicity in white hegemony and to take steps to neutralize it, such action did not essentially challenge the structures of power commanded by the white groups as a whole. The inability to evolve fresh methods in the vital area of opposing white political and economic might remained one of the movement's two abiding theoretical (and objective) weaknesses. The other, the related problem of its class affiliations, will be touched on later.[83]

The process of withdrawal from contact and collaboration with the liberal whites, and that of racial/cultural consolidation, provided the necessary base for the execution of the other important aspects of the struggle against cultural (and political) domination. Blacks were to withdraw wherever possible from complicity in their own domination. Having done this, they were to set about repairing the damage already done and constructing alternative cultural (in the broadest sense) structures with which to oppose white domination.

The damage that had to be repaired was considerable and can best be understood by reference to two great theorists of psychological and cultural despoliation in the Third World, Frantz Fanon and Paulo Freire. Compare the following accounts of the psychological and cultural states of the oppressed as offered by Fanon, Freire and Barney Pityana, a leading figure in the BCM:

> [In the colonial situation] the enslavement, in the strictest sense, of the native population is the prime necessity. For this its systems of reference have to be broken. Expropriation, spoliation, raids, objective murder, are matched by the sacking of cultural patterns, or at least condition such sacking. The social panorama is destructured; values are flaunted, crushed, emptied. The lines of force, having crumbled, no longer give direction. In their stead a new system of values is imposed, not proposed but affirmed, by the weight of cannons and sabers.
>
> —The setting up of the colonial system does not of itself bring about the death of the native culture. Historic observation reveals, on the

contrary, that the aim sought is rather a continued agony than a total disappearance of the pre-existing culture. This culture, once living and open to the future, becomes closed, fixed in the colonial stasis, caught in the yoke of oppression. Both present and mummified, it testifies against its members. It defines them in fact without appeal. The cultural mummification leads to a mummification of individual thinking. The apathy so universally noted among colonial peoples is but the logical consequence of this operation . . . As though it were possible for a man to evolve otherwise than within the framework of a culture that recognizes him and that he decides to assume . . .

Exploitation, tortures, raids, racism, collective liquidations, national oppression take turns at different levels in order literally to make of the native an object in the hands of the occupying nation.

This object man, without means of existing, without a *raison d'être*, is broken in the very depth of his substance.

[Fanon, 1967, pp.33–5]

Irresistibly attracted by the life style of the director society, alienated man is a nostalgic man, never truly committed to his world. To appear to be rather than to be is one of his alienated wishes. His thinking and the way he expresses the world are generally a reflection of the thought and expression of the director society. His alienated culture prevents him from understanding that his thinking and world-expression cannot find acceptance beyond his frontiers unless he is faithful to his particular world.

[Freire, *Cultural Action for Freedom*, p.14]

and

In cultural invasion . . . the invaders are the authors of, and actors in, the process; those they invade are the objects. The invaders mould; those they invade are moulded. The invaders choose; those they invade follow that choice — or are expected to follow it. The invaders act; those they invade have only the illusion of acting, through the action of the invaders.

[Freire, *Pedagogy of the Oppressed*, p.121]

. . . the black person has been 'uprooted, pursued, baffled, doomed to watch the dissolution of the truths he has always treasured'. As a result of this antinomy that co-exists with us Blacks, we can draw two conclusions: 'White men consider themselves superior to black men. Black men want to prove to white men at all costs, the richness of their thought, the equal value of their intellect.' This is true and is to be regretted. It is a negative way of expressing one's values. It creates the unfortunate impression that all values are white-oriented and all standards are white-determined. This I cannot accept. I believe that we have values and standards which are bound to be different from those of the Whites simply because the Whites enjoy the privileges Blacks are robbed of. There cannot be much in common between two peoples in that situation of imbalance. I am not aspiring to be equal to a White man but I am determined to establish my worth as a God-created being. I have to assert my BEING as a person.

[Pityana in van der Merwe, p.178]

A few lines later in the same essay, Pityana quotes Fanon at length:

'I am not a potentiality of something,' writes Fanon. 'I am wholly what I am. I do not have to look for the universal. No probability has any place inside me. My negro consciousness does not hold itself out as black. It IS. It is its own follower. This is all that we blacks are after, TO BE. We believe that we are quite efficient in handling our BEness and for this purpose we are self-sufficient.' The point I am trying to make here is that we shall never find our goals and aspirations as a people centred anywhere else but in US. This, therefore, necessitates a self-examination and a rediscovery of ourselves. Blacks can no longer afford to be led and dominated by non-Blacks.

[Pityana in van der Merwe, p.180]

According to the BCM, the best way to reconstitute the crushed and dominated personality of the black person was for one to do things for oneself. This was not intended in the 'white' individualistic way (cf. self-made man) but in the context of 'African communalism'. It meant, in other words, to achieve self-sufficiency within a community – a communal effort – without expecting assistance, guidance or leadership from outside the community. Hence the slogan: 'Black man [sic], you are on your own.'[84] Blacks should organize their own lives, struggle together to solve their own problems themselves and in so doing recover their confidence, their faith in their ability to organize, to be responsible, to lead, to take decisions (all activities traditionally monopolized by whites) – in short, to cope with freedom.

According to the movement, the process of withdrawing from all association with whites was the essential initial step in this programme. The establishment of all-black self-help community projects, cultural organizations, educational and artistic ventures, etc. was the next one. These were seen as important means of rebuilding morale and producing a creative, confident personality. However, as the black groups were subjected to constant cultural and psychological invasion by the dominant white groups, this in itself was not enough. Alternative cultural values and concepts had to be enunciated in order to ensure that what the black groups were building did not turn out to be the same white building blacks had evacuated in the first place. Similarly, if the struggle for eventual freedom was to be waged effectively, it would be necessary to evolve social and cultural concepts upon which a future 'open society' might be based. In other words, the foundations for an alternative hegemony had to be laid.

Biko and others, having rejected 'white' capitalist society, turned back to black history and the traditional culture of pre-colonial South Africa in order to re-establish the continuity interrupted by the European conquest and Christianity. They were acutely aware of the importance of history in their struggle, because they realized that an oppressed people has to rediscover the truth about its past, which has been distorted or suppressed by the oppressor, in order to achieve the pride in self and people which is a necessary pre-condition of effective resistance. 'Blacks want to know, and must know, more about who they were and who they are if they are seriously concerned about *whom* they intend to become' (*Black Review*, 1972, p.1).

Acceptance of one's people's history necessitates the acceptance of the traditional culture. This, too, needs to be revalued and 'liberated' from the misconceptions and degradations propagated by the oppressor. When this is done, the revivified culture not only becomes an inspiration, but it also provides the basis of the cultural critique of the oppressor's society and the defining characteristics of the new one that the oppressed people intends to build in its place. The traditional African culture provided the movement with a socio-cultural theory they called African or Black Communalism:

> Now we are advocating black communalism, which is, in many ways, similar to African socialism. We are expropriating an essentially tribal background to accommodate what is an expounded economic concept now. We have got to accommodate industry and politics. But there is a certain plasticity in this interpretation precisely because no one has yet made an ultimate definition of it.
>
> [Biko, in Woods, p.141]

They hoped to develop an African communalism which synthesized the virtues of 'black' traditional culture with 'private enterprise'. They stressed what they felt was the importance of man and human relationships — as opposed to profit and ownership — in black culture and that of the integrated community, as opposed to the individualistic materialistic society of the whites. African communalism would produce a community-based, man-centred society. Other characteristics such as the love of communication with other people, conversation and music and religiousness were mentioned. The new structures the movement hoped to evolve would be constructed in the light of these values.[85]

Whereas previous political organizations had conducted the struggle against apartheid either by professing a commitment to non-racial structures (the ANC, for example) or purely black African ones (the PAC), the BCM accepted the racial structures provided them by the apartheid state and organized their struggle within them. They thereby simplified the complexities of South Africa's race/class conjunctures by accepting the basic division of black and white. Blacks were literally all those who were, in whatever degree, discriminated against by the state for racial reasons. Therefore a characteristic feature of the BCM was its advocacy of black solidarity and the involvement of black Africans, 'Indians' and 'Coloureds' in the organization. However, their goal was control of the entire country and the creation of an 'open society' in which whites would be invited to participate, if they wished, but on black, not white, terms. This concept was summed up in the often-repeated image of the banquet table. The BCM pointed out that previously the black 'élite' had hoped to be favoured with a place at the white table:

> Their protests are directed at and appeal to white conscience. Everything they do is directed at finally convincing the white electorate that the black man is also a man and that at some future date he should be given a place at the white man's table.
>
> [Biko, p.21]

This then, in brief, was the philosophy and strategy of the BCM. Its effectiveness did not derive from the development of a sophisticated theory of political and cultural domination. It derived rather from the uncompromising application of a few clearly-grasped principles to the full gamut of social relations. The process by which the movement's philosophy was communicated and its strategy put into practice was what the movement (and Freire) called 'conscientization':

> The term 'conscientization' refers to learning to perceive social, political, and economic contradictions, and to take action against the oppressive elements of reality.
>
> [Freire, *Pedagogy*, p.16]

> Conscientization is a process whereby individuals or groups living within a given social and political setting are made aware of their situation. The operative attitude here is not so much awareness of the physical sense of their situation, but much more their ability to assess and improve their own influence over themselves and their environment . . . thus then conscientization implies a desire to engage people in an emancipatory process, in an attempt to free them from a situation of bondage.
>
> [Biko, in Woods, p.145]

By the creation of a political organization, the BPC, the movement was able to attract to itself a wider range of important and influential black leaders, especially drawn from the educated and professional classes — lecturers, educationalists, social workers and trade-unionists (white-collar). The movement failed to attract the commercial sections of the intermediate classes, despite its advocacy of 'free enterprise' and 'black capitalism'. The movement was aware that the support of sections of the black intermediate classes was not enough, and that steps had to be taken to win the support and participation of the workers. A Black Workers' Project was established and the Black Allied Workers, a white-collar union, was formed. Nevertheless, in the short period in which it was active before its banning, the BCM remained predominantly a movement of the intellectual and the non-commercial intermediate classes.[86]

Given the circumstances in which the movement operated, it could hardly be expected to have developed a coherent theory of cultural domination. Still, it made important progress in the business of understanding the complex mechanisms the dominant groups in South Africa employ to preserve their dominance over other groups. Biko, for one, approached the Gramscian concept of hegemony when he discussed what he called 'the system'. One should remember that the following statement was given verbally in court while testifying in the BPC/SASO trial on behalf of his comrades in the movement, and is thus hardly detailed or comprehensive:

> Our fundamental meaning of the term System is those operative forces in society, those institutionialized and uninstitutionalized operative forces in society that control your being, guide your behaviour, and generally are in authority over you. Now this is implying government certainly, thus implying the agents of the government, the police especially. There is the tendency in our ranks to regard the police as the System, but the System is also the entire process of oppression. [Woods, p.145]

Here, in an incipient form, we have the concept of direct, i.e. coercive, and indirect, i.e. cultural, educational, religious, forms of domination. The insistent and outspoken intervention of the movement and its related bodies on a wide range of cultural issues testifies to the extent of their understanding in practice, if not completely in theory, of aspects of the operation of cultural hegemony.

The BCM's ideas were varied and eclectic. Though it was the first black political movement in South Africa to base its ideology and programme on colour and was inspired by the writings of Fanon, Freire, Aimé Césaire, George Jackson and other black figures such as W. B. du Bois, Marcus Garvey and the Negritude school, it admired the achievements of Marxist liberation movements such as those in China, Guinea-Bissau, Mozambique and Angola. The net result of this eclecticism was that, though colour was of fundamental importance in the ideology of the movement, both the national and class factors are referred to from time to time — with that of class and class analysis becoming increasingly important.

That the BCM had not solved but rather shelved the race/nation problem is evidenced by the contradictions that sprang from the simultaneous adherence to the concept of black solidarity, in which black meant African, Asian and Coloured, and concepts such as African communalism. How, for instance, was it possible to reconcile African communalism as a system which derived from African traditional society with the different historical cultures of 'Indian' and 'Coloured' members of the movement? Much of the movement's momentum, too, derived, as it did in the earlier nationalist movements, from the historical facts of conquest. As 'Scene-watcher' wrote in the SASO newsletter: 'we know that our fore-fathers were robbed of their land and their wealth' (5.1, p.3). Indian and Coloured members could join the black Africans in claiming a history of depredation and exploitation but could not claim that *their* 'fore-fathers' had possessed the land in South Africa before the white conquest.

Class, and Marxist analysis, to the extent that it was known at all, was originally heatedly rejected as being nonsensical in an intensely racialist society. It was also associated with attempts by white 'leftist sympathizers' to define the black group's struggle for it and to inhibit its solidarity. Biko, for instance, wrote in 1971:

> To us it seems that their [the liberals'] role spells out the totality of the white power structure — the fact that though whites are our problem, it is still other whites who want to tell us how to deal with that problem. They do so by dragging all sorts of red herrings across our paths. They tell us that the situation is a class struggle rather than a racial one. Let them go to van Tonder in the Free State and tell him this. [p.89]

Elsewhere a class analysis is referred to as 'twisted logic'.[87]

This is not to say that the Black Consciousness theorists were totally unaware of the realities of class and economic relations. Capitalism was constantly evoked as an exploitative system which had to be restructured. It was recognized that, objectively speaking, economic factors linked the poor whites to the black group and Biko, at least, knew about the economic roots of racism (p.50). However, Black Consciousness was an ideology and it was principally concerned with fighting an ideological battle. Overwhelmingly the most potent, the obsessive, ideology operative in South African society was racial. Crucial Marxist concepts were not available to the movement's theorists — they might have profitably asked themselves why. There is evidence that there was at least partial ignorance of the Marxist concept of class, and the important base/superstructure model was unheard of. It was thus not Marxism that Biko and the others were rejecting, but whites who advocated dogmatic Marxist rejection of race and nationality as irrelevant concepts in favour of class, when all the empirical evidence *seemed* to prove that they were not only relevant but primary. The movement had identified 'white racism' as the principal enemy and it was believed to be so perniciously corrupting as to have subsumed all other perspectives. Thus capitalist exploitation was seen to be the characteristic racial/cultural behaviour of the white race. The culture of capitalism was simply 'white' culture. Class within the black groups was rejected as an alien concept, in conflict with the African communalist tenet of communal 'belonging'.

But, as has been the case with other militant racial ideologues in capitalist or colonial societies (du Bois, Fanon, George Jackson, Leroi Jones/Imamu Baraka, to name but a few), the experience of racial oppression under capitalism, particularly when seen not simply as an isolated or parochial

159

phenomenon but in conjunction with the experience of other black and Third World peoples throughout the world, led a section of the movement inevitably in the direction of Marxist and neo-Marxist positions. From an insular racial/national analysis, elements in the movement progressed steadily towards a class/international anti-imperialist one. This process was hastened by the victory in Mozambique in 1974 of Frelimo and the establishment, not of an African communalist or African socialist, but of a Marxist-Leninist state.

In 1975, for instance, in an article on 'Apartheid and the Anti-Imperialist Struggle' in the SASO newsletter, the writer stated that 'patterns of production can no longer be ignored' and that 'there will be no end to exploitation and under-development within the framework of the imperialist system'. He warned of the complicity of the 'Black élite' in this system, and how it was designed to stimulate the development of 'property consciousness' instead of 'communal commitments', i.e. instead of Black Consciousness and African Communalism (5.3, pp.5-7). Biko in his evidence at the SASO/BPC trial came as close as was possible in the circumstances to advocating a form of socialism in preference to capitalism, and at certain points seemed to attach greater importance to economic factors than racial ones as the cause of exploitation in South Africa, as in the following statement: 'Capitalistic exploitative tendencies, coupled with the overt arrogance of white racism, have conspired against us. Thus in South Africa now it is very expensive to be poor.'[88]

Even the word 'black' began to be redefined with greater flexibility to include '*all* those who are socially, economically, politically or otherwise discriminated against in South Africa on the basis of colour, race or creed'. This presumably was a flexible enough definition to include banned or imprisoned white Marxists or liberals. In other words, Black Consciousness showed distinct signs of evolving away from colour categories in the direction of the concept of the 'majority' as offered in the introduction to this book.

The fundamental weakness of the theoretical formulations of the BCM in its purely racial expressions is the acceptance of race or, more strictly, colour as the basis of the analysis of South African society in general and cultural domination in particular. Quite correctly, the movement set out to remove from the minds of the oppressed the values, images, ideas, etc. that the oppressor had planted there. Yet, as we have indicated earlier, we believe that national and economic factors are fundamental 'moving forces' in society, and that race is essentially ideological and largely emanates from national and economic conflicts, functioning predominantly to obscure the national and economic forces. The BCM, by couching its ideological opposition to oppression in racial terms, may have seized upon a potent tactical weapon and made great advances in the theory and practice of resistance, but ultimately it confirmed the impression in the minds of the oppressed that they are oppressed on account of the colour of their skin, which is precisely the analysis favoured by the liberal intelligentsia of the South African and Western bourgeoisie or, in the terminology of the movement, the 'white liberals' and 'do-gooders'. If the ideas of the oppressor are to be thoroughly rooted out from the minds of the oppressed, nothing short of the abandonment of this analysis will do.

The Theatre Activity of the Black Consciousness Movement

The ideology of Black Consciousness explains and describes much of what has been already discussed concerning earlier, and especially multi-racial, theatre activity. For instance, the élitist attitudes of the educated 'English-speaking' black intellectuals who traditionally collaborated with whites, exemplified especially in the cast of *No-Good Friday*, were roundly condemned in the literature of Black Consciousness. In fact education, traditionally a mark of status, became for some writers 'the quickest way of destroying the substance of African culture', and Biko at one point defends the contempt peasants entertained for educated black Christians (p.70). In order to appreciate this position we only have to recall the Bloke Modisane of *Blame Me On History*, with his contempt for 'African culture' and his refusal to commit himself to political struggle. His secret desire to be white was precisely the state of mind the BCM had identified within the black groups generally, and which they recognized had to be radically reformed:

> All in all the black man has become a shell, a shadow of a man, completely defeated, drowning in his own misery, a slave, an ox bearing the yoke of oppression with sheepish timidity.
>
> [Biko, p.29]

The writers of the movement afforded telling insights into the state of mind of the white liberals as well. 'How many white people fighting for their version of a change in South Africa are really motivated by genuine concern and not by guilt?' wrote Biko (p.65). Fugard himself admitted, on a number of occasions, that it was guilt that motivated him to work with blacks, including even the actual founding of Serpent Players.[89]

Other examples include the reversal of the connotations attached to 'black' and 'white' which were present in *No-Good Friday* (and *The Blood Knot*) and *King Kong*;[90] the recognition of the validity and dignity of the African traditional culture, which had been consistently ridiculed and disclaimed in theatre and literature written by educated blacks, as in all three plays examined so far; the recognition that, given existing relations, multi-racial collaboration with whites invariably resulted in white control and domination; a rejection of the tutelary role of whites, as exemplified in the function of Father Higgens in *No-Good Friday* and the condescension of Bloom, Gluckman and the rest; and the need to repair the psychological damage of oppression — which suggests an artistic content which encourages, gives hope or inspires people rather than confronting them with their degradation (i.e. Black Consciousness required that the dialectic between constitutive and imposed or positive and negative elements in the culture should be resolved by an emphasis on the former and the virtual exclusion of the latter, not as in *Too Late* the more 'balanced' view).[91]

In contrast, the movement's articulated theory of art and theatre was rudimentary. Numerous references were made to drama and its importance (not only to the spectators but also to performers and organizers) as an instrument of conscientization and liberation. Biko wrote:

> Black culture above all implies freedom on our part to innovate without recourse to white values. This innovation is part of the natural develop-ment of any culture. A culture is essentially the society's composite answer to the varied problems of life. We are experiencing new problems every day and whatever we do adds to the richness of our cultural heritage as long as it has man as its centre. The adoption of black theatre and drama is one such important innovation which we need to encourage and to develop. [p.96]

Yet the public statements of such bodies as SABTU (South African Black Theatre Union) in Natal and the Cape and Mdali (Music, Drama, Arts and Literature Institute) in the Transvaal seldom go much beyond clichés such as that black theatre ought to be 'revolutionary', embody 'black values' and conscientize. For example, Mdali adopted the following programme on the occasion of its founding in May 1972:

> We have come together, active Black men and women, contemporaries, to form a genuinely Black Theatre and art movement, for short known as Mdali.
> We aim to liberate ourselves mentally, to believe in ourselves, to forge our standards and to stop accepting standards dictated to us by other racial groups.
> We aim to expose pseudo-organizations and pseudo-representatives purporting to represent Black Theatre and art.[92]

As the last of Mdali's aims makes clear, the organizations which partici-pated in the Black Consciousness theatre movement made their attitudes to the work of the groups that operated outside the movement extremely clear. They also made quite clear what kinds of theatre and theatre activity they opposed and why. If these pronouncements are taken together with the general theory of culture propounded by the BCM and the principles actually embodied in the work of the theatre groups, it becomes possible to enunciate to some extent a theory of Black Consciousness theatre.

An essential element of the theory is that blacks should not collaborate with whites. The reasons advanced for this are that the whites in the group will dominate and as 'agents' of the white racialist establishment their direction will result in a work which politically and culturally does not operate in the interests of blacks but rather in those of whites. Similarly, those blacks who did collaborate with whites were criticized and urged to withdraw from the association. Biko called them 'a danger to the community':

> Instead of directing themselves at their black brothers and looking at their common problems from a common platform they choose to sing out their lamentations to an apparently sympathetic audience that has become proficient in saying the chorus of 'shame!'. These dull-witted, self-centred blacks are in the ultimate analysis as guilty of the arrest of progress as their white friends for it is from such groups that the theory of gradualism emanates and this is what keeps the blacks confused and always hoping that one day God will step down from heaven to solve their problems. [p.23] [93]

In the Mihloti newsletters, such blacks were called 'non-whites'. For instance, the cast of Workshop '71's play, *Crossroads*, were labelled 'non-whites', 'schizophrenics, guinea-pigs'. [94]

The movement's rejection of the non-political work of Kente was not less vigorous than its rejection of multi-racial collaboration. Though Kente was his own man and operated an independent black company which had long since severed ties with whites, the movement regarded him too as an 'agent' of the cultural invasion and subjugation of the black community. Kente had not undergone the inward process that Black Consciousness demanded. His earlier plays manifested this.

Nomsisi Kraai, one of the actors in *Shanti*, was probably thinking of Kente's work as well as that of other writers of popular musical drama when she expressed her contempt for 'comical dramas' (see below, p.170). Kente was possibly included in Mihloti's indictment of 'plays that tell you how unfaithful our women are . . . of our broken families, of how Black people fight and murder each other, or bewitch each other, pimp, mistrust, hate and despise each other', though the plays of Sam Mhangwani and others are more guilty of this than Kente. [95] Molefi Pheto, a founder of Mihloti and chairman of Mdali, gave as one of the main reasons for the formation of his theatre group, Mihloti, the kind of material that Mhangwani and Kente were producing and the fact that no one was protesting against it. [96]

A distinction came to be made between 'Black Theatre' and 'theatre presented by Blacks'. This paralleled another distinction between 'Blacks' and 'non-whites'. A member of the black group who still aspired to the values of the white society and resented his exclusion from it, was not 'Black' but 'non-white'. 'Black drama is not Black drama solely because it has Black actors, directors and depicts Black scenes. If the play does not place sufficient emphasis upon the creation of a revolutionary mood and does not see Black liberation as a priority then it is not Black drama but drama presented by Blacks' (*Black Review*, 1973, p.105). According to this definition, Kente in his non-political phase produced 'theatre presented by Blacks' and was himself a 'non-white'.

When Kente produced *How Long* the movement by and large dropped its criticism of him.[97] Being essentially a racial/cultural critique which, especially in its vulgar interpretation, rejected class as an important social factor within the black groups, the theory of Black Consciousness was unable – or unwilling – to characterize or analyse Kente's political work in order to reveal both the contradictions in it and the class reasons for them. Its tendency, too, despite its theoretical pronouncements, to be an intellectual, intermediate-class movement made it especially difficult for it to come to terms with a popular, commercial form such as that of Kente's political plays. Kente for his part never joined any of the Black Consciousness theatre organizations.

Essentially, the theory of the theatre of Black Consciousness followed the same pattern as the strategy that the movement had evolved for the resistance of cultural domination and liberation in general – withdrawal from association with whites, the creation of new structures and the conscientization of black people. A 'black theatre' group, as opposed to a 'non-white' or 'theatre presented by blacks' group, was a group that first and foremost was completely black. All aspects – administration, technical, artistic direction, acting, etc. – were to be controlled by and in the hands of blacks. Material had to be written or created by blacks and performed by blacks to black audiences, from which, in many cases, whites were excluded.

The creation of an all-black group was seen, though, as only the first step in the direction of the creation of larger black associations and the linking of these associations, where possible, to the national political and cultural organizations of the Black Consciousness movement and its aims. This process is what one means by withdrawal and establishment of alternative structures. The remaining function was that of conscientization. The broad outlines of this function were provided by the theoretical formulations of the BCM and followed the same principles. A 'black theatre' group would reverse the prevailing tendency to aspire to perform to white audiences in town, a tendency which made white critics and audiences the arbiters of black culture.[98] Instead, a 'black theatre' group would direct its attention to the various sections of the black community – i.e. the black Africans, 'Indians' and 'Coloureds' – and present to those sections material which would inform them about their real history and culture, prompt them to re-examine themselves as black people in the light of this and in the context of their environment, with the aim of bringing about that inner transformation which is Black Consciousness, without which they would be unable to embark on self-initiated projects of self- and mutual help and reliance. In addition to the psychological and spiritual transformation which a 'black theatre' group aimed to achieve, the audience was to be presented with problems arising from their situation as members of an oppressed group and stimulated to solve them. Not only were problems to be presented but solutions, revolutionary solutions, were to be suggested.

A 'black theatre' would not aim to hold up to its black audience a mirror of itself. It would not attempt to show it its degradation, the collapse of its

culture, its immorality, its stabbings, its drunkenness, its hopelessness — as
'non-white' and 'white' theatre might. A 'black theatre' group would, in the
words of a writer in the Mihloti newsletter, 'tell the people to stop moaning
and to wake up and start doing something about their valuable and beautiful
Black lives'.[99]

Apart from professing to reject 'white' forms, little attention was paid by
the 'black theatre' groups to the question of form — as a writer in *S'ketsh'*
magazine noted:

> So far Black Theatre has only undergone partial development, e.g. the
> relevant theatre of Mihloti, *Sizwe Banzi*, SABTU. Those who are looking
> for a true Black theatre will agree that relevance in material only is not
> enough. For people to identify with our theatre, it will have to be
> relevant in form as well as material. Forms that people are acquainted
> with as part of their lives, like the village dance under the tree.
> [Summer 1974/5, p.40]

Like other black artistic movements in capitalist societies, rejection of 'white'
cultural values tended not to go much further than content, sometimes no
further than dialogue.

In an article entitled 'Towards a National Theatre', the poet and editor of
the *Black Review* (1973), M. Pascal Gwala, expressed some ideas on the
function of 'black theatre' in the context of the creation of 'an authentic
national culture'.[100] He recognized that 'for a long time the black sub-culture
will act as counter-culture to the official white "culture". Until the completed
development of a national culture of Southern Africa, such prospect is only
possible after the social liberation of the black. Not before.' In this development 'white ethics', which have perpetuated 'hopelessness and cynicism' in
black society, have to be 'negated'. For this there has to be another 'identity
basis' — 'this identity basis is Black Consciousness', which Gwala saw as a
'temporary thing', 'a phase in the identification process leading to national
theatre'.

Once again, the main emphasis of the article is on the function of 'black
art' and its content. Gwala stressed the necessity of a 'socially critical ethic'
and particularly the integrated but progressive development of the traditional
and the urban cultures. 'Authenticity on black reality can only be achieved
through the calling back on the past and the forging of the future largely
through modern theatre techniques — plus the black ethic.' This reference to
'modern theatre techniques' and a passage on 'abstractionism' are his only
comments on the purely formal aspects of theatre. He writes:

> All we need now is to avoid the tendency of the obscure form in art;
> abstractionism. Since such avoidance may help blacks keep away from
> rigid patterns that make the different art forms a fashion instead of
> making them an expression of the time and of objective situation.
> Within the given context. There is no need to worry much about

whether your form of expression is futurist, structurist, concrete symbolist, expressionist or what have you. Epithets must be dropped. For the sake of Africa in art and art in Africa. Because epithets stem from a maddening disregard by critics for popular context. Many critics and journalists love to journalize tendencies. And either want to channelize those tendencies into their style of things or inveigh against them. Such a situation must be openly fought against by every black artist.

Here Gwala rejects the dilettantism of formalist aesthetics and implies that function should largely suggest form, i.e. if the playwright's art is 'an expression of the time and of objective situation' based in what he calls the 'theatre of the unattractive' and 'in the consciousness of all the people of the black community', he will not need to search for forms. The forms will follow. In saying this Gwala provides the probable explanation for the lack of concern of the Black Consciousness groups to delineate theoretically the formal attributes of their theatre·in the way they delineated function and content.

'White' forms were of course rejected. Gwala's essay and an examination of the work and pronouncements of TECON, Mihloti, PET and Obi (another Black Consciousness group and a member of Mdali) seem to suggest that 'white' forms were principally identified with *categorical* or puristic formal distinctions — in other words, a tendency to adhere to either a strict 'realism' or a strict 'abstract' or non-realist idiom. The function of Black Consciousness theatre suggested forms which combined elements of realism and non-realism. All these groups freely and at times arbitrarily discarded the illusion of reality and any artificial barriers between the action and the audience. Generally, meaning was communicated either in polemical speeches directed at the audience or in strong, harsh images, employing, especially in the work of TECON, sound, film projection, sculptural groupings, song, recitation and chant. To a large extent, such a form emerged organically from the relation of the audience to the performers. This was not a commercial theatre. The actors were not hired. They were angry members of a wronged community talking directly to others of that community about their common oppression. Artifice and the traditional embellishments of bourgeois realist or avant-garde theatre were not only unnecessary but would have interposed themselves damagingly between the performers and their audience.

The writer in *S'ketsh'* magazine, when writing about the search for new black forms to express black content, was clearly thinking of traditional African dramatic forms as a possible source for such forms. Credo Mutwa, in conjunction with Workshop '71, attempted to explore this source in the production of his play, *uNosilimela* (1973).[101] A reconstruction of the staging for performances of the traditional *umlinganiso* (acted representation) was adapted to modern conditions. This involved the collapse of the arena-type staging into a rectangular tennis-court arrangement, the erection of scaffolding and the use of lighting and sound. Five or six separate acting areas were created, which could be used simultaneously, together in different combinations or singly. In the main, the results were aesthetically interesting and suggestive, especially because they provided the episodic narrative form of the traditional epic with fluency and mobility — the whole epic being actable without a single break. Ultimately, however, in the context of the existing conditions in Soweto or any black *urban* area the form was inappropriate. It lent itself far better to the evocation of traditional atmosphere and forms — weddings, dancing and singing, journeys over vast distances, the appearance of gods, spirits and monsters, etc. — than it did to the urban scenes, which tended to take place in one relatively confined area — a shebeen, a bogus *inyanga*'s house, a street outside Baragwanath hospital, etc. The necessity to perform nightly for long periods, in order to pay for hall and scaffolding rental, made the staging itself impracticable. The conditions in the black urban areas dictate weekend performances, mobility, moving to one's audience; and long runs in one place are not feasible.

Mutwa's experiments were impracticable in the circumstances, though perfectly logical in terms of the BCM's concept of African communalism. Gwala, whose essay, though it did not specifically refer to African communalism, contained concepts which suggested it, attempted to solve this dilemma by rejecting white 'moral ethics' and 'domination' without rejecting the technology and forms of the white group's theatre. He saw these 'modern techniques' revivified and given new functions by an infusion of the 'black ethic' and Black Consciousness.

In some senses, the forms the 'black theatre' actually developed were the organically appropriate ones, given the content of the plays and the class of the performers and audience, in a modern urban society. The plays of the movement lent themselves to the one-night stand, performed with rudimentary, easily transportable equipment, requiring only a raised acting area and a large area for their audiences. The lecture-room structure of the church and municipal halls was perfectly suited to such performances, with their high unraked stages and flat auditoria, as it was to the didactic, direct presentation we shall be discussing later — however damaging they might have been to other forms of theatre.

In other respects, language, costume and musical instruments and especially the poetry and music form developed by the 'black theatre' groups were derived from the BCM's idealistic adherence to African communalism and Pan-Africanism. The movement's romanticism and religiosity can be heard in this extract from a poetry and music presentation, TECON's *Black Images:*

> i am the eyes, the ears, the voice
> the megaphone of the Brothers 83
> they were the beginning
> and the enemy tried to mute them
> but the power of our ju-ju
> our krishna
> the spirit of our gods

will enter my soul
and they will speak
with you
thro' my medium
come now brothers enter my
body take my voice
speak the BLACK TRUTH[102]

Mihloti performers wore *dashikis* and other 'Afro' clothing, and traditional drums and instruments were favoured rather than electrical or 'white' instruments.[103]

The poetry and music format as used by the Black Consciousness theatre groups illustrated quite clearly a contradiction inherent within the ideology of Black Consciousness itself. African communalism was a nostalgic notion, based on a vision of a society that never has existed and never will exist. Blacks had been irrevocably drawn into the structures of an economically integrated, though racially segregated capitalist state. The only way was forward, as the movement's theorists gradually came to realize, into modern capitalism or scientific socialism, not back to an ideal version of the traditional society with a bit of capitalism thrown in. The theory of Black Consciousness was elaborated to a large extent by students, some of whom, like Biko himself, had little experience of the large industrial communities of the Transvaal and the western Cape. They were intellectuals, unintegrated organizationally or by employment into the industrial and commercial structures. This was the context in which the African communalist utopia was evolved. The theatre groups, to the extent to which they genuinely faced the practical demands of communicating the movement's ideology to the workers and youth in the urban areas, simply ignored the concept. To the extent to which they did not, they favoured the poetry and music form in which there was considerable room for African romanticism — but audiences at such presentations, as we shall see later, tended to be made up of intellectuals and the élite.

Mthuli Shezi and the People's Experimental Theatre

Shanti was written by Mthuli Shezi, an influential member of the BCM and performed by the People's Experimental Theatre (PET), a theatre group which was directly connected with the movement. It did not receive many performances, but most of these performances were well attended and the impact of the play was considerable.

The *Black Review* of 1973 describes the establishment and activities of PET thus:

PET was initiated in Lenasia [an Indian 'township'] in early 1973. Before the creation of PET, there existed in Lenasia a movement called 'YOUTH' and among its aims was the hope to initiate a Black theatre group. YOUTH soon petered out and a few remaining active members convened a meeting to establish PET.

At about the same time a theatre group in Soweto called 'Shiqomo' (Spear) was launched. Both groups worked together very closely. Both groups also realized the importance of a merger. This realization was cemented when PET and Shiqomo presented 'An Evening of Black Thoughts' — a programme of poetry readings, music and extracts from Black revolutionary writers, which was extremely well received in Lenasia where it was presented.

Subsequently, a joint meeting of PET and Shiqomo was called and the new PET emerged with 'The Spear Lives on' as their motto.

PET's first major production was 'Shanti', a play written by the late Mthuli Shezi, vice-president of the BPC until his death in December 1972. 'Shanti' had a successful run in Lenasia and Soweto and was also promoted in Durban by TECON.

This was followed by a production called 'Requiem for Brother X', a play written by W. W. Mackay, a Black-American, and dedicated to the late Malcolm X, a Black Power leader in the United States.

Not content with just drama, this very energetic group brought out a newsletter. The newsletter was introduced to fill the vacuum that exists as far as original Black writing goes. Besides theatre, the newsletter discussed Black consciousness and published numerous poems written by young Blacks. This newsletter has been banned by the Publications Control Board. [p.109]

The following is an account of Mthuli Shezi, his writing of *Shanti*, subsequent death and the founding of Shiqomo, printed in PET's banned first newsletter:

Mthuli Ka Shezi, the ex-SRC president of the University of Zululand, decided to walk out of the University last year. It dawned on the mind of this young powerful Blackman that he could be more of an asset outside the tribal college than as a puppet student who was always expected to listen to 'His Master's Voice' and carry out instructions.

Education has to be relevant to one's situation. Mthuli realized that he needed education for self-reliance, not that which prepared him to be a better slave. He didn't want handouts or crumbs falling from the master's table, but education that would make him break the chains that bind us to perpetual servitude.

After Mthuli left University, he took it upon himself to do everything in his power to liberate the Black people. He was then elected the Vice-President of BPC. It was during this period that he sat down to write a drama called 'Shanti'. In this drama Mthuli portrays the true meaning of Black Consciousness, the odds and evils of oppression, the Blackman today and how these can be brought to a halt. Before Mthuli could see this play come to fruition, he was killed while defending the dignity of the Black people. His death hit the Black Community very hard. In him we saw an inspiring Black leader and his death, therefore, made us clench our fists and lift them even higher with determination ... It is on this note that we young people came together and formed a group called 'Shiqomo'. This means 'spear' and this we use as a symbol of fighting. We came together and decided to perform some relevant dramas like 'Shanti'. We cannot waste time on comical dramas. We live in times of war where a Black man cannot stop thinking of his liberation. We are determined to fight for our rights. [pp.1–2]

Mthuli Shezi died in December 1972, after being pushed onto the rails in front of an oncoming train by a white railway employee with whom he had quarrelled concerning the man's 'unacceptable treatment of some black woman at the station some day before the fatal "accident" '. At his funeral Mrs W. Kgware, the President of BPC, delivered an address and excerpts from his play, *Shanti*, were performed. In one of the speeches it was recalled that Shezi had said: 'Blacks can be liberated through the theatre.'

Sadecque Variava, allegedly the 'leader' of PET, was a Johannesburg teacher. uJebe Masokoane of Soweto directed *Shanti* and also played Thabo. Nomsisi Kraai and Victor Molathlegi Modise, both of Soweto, played Shanti and Koos respectively. Vusi Khumalo, a journalist on *The World* newspaper, played the guerrilla general, Mobu. Of the members of PET, Sadecque Variava and Solly Ismael were arrested and charged under the Terrorism Act in the SASO/BPC trial. The script of *Shanti* was included in the charge sheet as evidence that the accused had conspired to 'make, produce, publish or distribute subversive and anti-White utterances, writings, poems, plays and/or dramas'. Nomsisi Kraai was detained in November 1975.

Shanti was first performed some time before September 1973. In November 1973, it was in Soweto. On 27 November it was reported that the police had raided a performance of the play in the 'Coloured' residential area of Coronationville. A spokesman for the group said:

We don't know what the police did at the hall before the performance. But when we arrived we were told they had been there. There was a conspicuous absence of patronage.

The police returned after the performance and checked the reference books of the cast and took names. They then confiscated 'equipment, including the script, wardrobe, musical instruments and lighting system' (*The World* 27 November 1973). Other performances were given in November and December near Pretoria. At one performance three members of the Pretoria local branch of SASO were alleged to have assaulted some black security police in the audience. The magistrate in giving judgement pronounced that *Shanti* had 'a political theme'.[104]

PET had presented *Shanti* in Natal under the auspices of TECON. The close association of the two groups continued when PET, as already noted, followed *Shanti* with a production of the black American play, *Requiem for Brother X*, which had already been produced by TECON. The programme for that performance announced: 'This is it! True Black Drama! A dialogue of confrontation! It speaks to Blacks only, about Blacks!'

It is almost certain that the script of *Shanti* is not an accurate or complete record of the play as performed. There was a good deal of impromptu dialogue which included, for obvious reasons, much of the most militant material. It was also accompanied by other material, mostly poems.

The following is a summary of some of the theoretical and explanatory statements made by various members of the group to the press or in the group's newsletter, which are relevant to an analysis of the play.

Masokoane, the director, called the play 'a protest at the Black middle class for turning their backs on the Black masses still in bondage . . . *Shanti* differs from *Sizwe Banzi* in that it exposes these problems and hardships [arising from influx control regulations] and at the same time gives solutions'.

Vusi Khumalo, an actor in the play, became a theatre and music critic on *The World* and began to introduce a new form of arts coverage. Previously, the majority of articles on theatre in the 'black press' had amounted to little more than 'free' publicity or criticism or approval of plays in the vaguest and most hackneyed terms. Khumalo began making judgements about black art which throw useful light on the level of theory and consciousness which existed amongst PET members at the time.

Khumalo was active in church drama in Soweto and took part in the annual Soweto Anglican Drama Festivals, organized by the Anglican church. Khumalo was working as a journalist on *The World* when he joined PET. With the rise of Black Consciousness he had dropped the name Basil and was now Vusi Khumalo. By 1975 he was working on *The World*'s 'Showorld' section, for which he wrote a series of 'serious' or controversial articles. For instance, on 18 November there appeared an article on black theatre in which he wrote:

> Black playwrights have a moral duty to create theatre that depicts the people's struggle in terms of black awareness and to instil in them a sense of pride . . . the playwrights have to be proud of their Blackness first, then become playwrights. In this way they are in a position to carve a positive direction for the people and to give them theatre that will not only make them intelligent people but will 'conscientize' them.

In the same article he attacked popular theatre in the black urban areas with its 'obscenities, thugs flashing knives and bottles of liquor'. 'This is the kind of theatre,' he continued, 'that shows people how far their own system of culture and convention has been destroyed.' It is the duty of the playwright, he concluded, to 'awaken' the black audience.

This was very much in line with the main body of theory of the BCM and closely follows the thinking of the writer in the Mihloti newsletter quoted above. Later articles reveal contradictory positions, however. He wrote a eulogy on the tribal musical, *Ipi Tombi*, which almost all the basic principles of Black Consciousness required him to condemn, but criticized the *Malombo* jazz guitarist, Philip Tabane, for adulterating black music by the use of the 'wah-wah' pedal.

More appositely, however, for our study of *Shanti*, to his earlier criticism of popular theatre he added the complaint that now that 'there is a tremendous and overwhelming outbreak of youth interest' in theatre, 'young actors and drop-outs from some struggling township productions are taking up the play writing business' and in the process 'strangling' 'the Queen's language'. These playwrights, he complained, 'know little English' (25 March 1976). This was a stock criticism of popular black theatre, and journalists had made it since the growth of popular theatre activity in the 1960s. It should be borne in mind when we discuss the question of language in *Shanti* and in the theatre of the BCM.

To sum up, then, those involved in the creation and performance of *Shanti* were students and professionals who saw themselves at war with the white racialist establishment and felt that theatre was an effective weapon with which to fight it. They believed that the existing theatre groups were inadequate, demoralizing and 'irrelevant', being either white-dominated or popular and commercial. They therefore decided to form a theatre group, on behalf of 'the Black People of South Africa' and commit themselves to the performance of theatre which would authentically advance their political struggle. They determined, by informing all sections of the black groups of their position in society, to give them encouragement and to suggest political solutions to their social problems and awaken and conscientize them with a view to mobilizing them in the struggle for liberation.

Shanti — The Play

Plot Synopsis
Thabo, an African, and Shanti, an 'Indian', are in love but their parents oppose their marriage. Koos, their friend, is classified 'Other Coloured', a classification he is trying to get changed. Thabo is involved in a black political movement and he is supported in this by Shanti. While on a visit to Shanti's home in the 'Indian' area of Lenasia, he is arrested and sentenced on a false charge. On the way to the white farm where he is to serve his sentence, he escapes and crosses the border into Mozambique where he meets up with a Frelimo detachment. His attempts to contact Shanti there arouse the suspicion of Mangaya, a Frelimo guerrilla, and he meets his death at the bottom of a cliff. Koos goes to find out his friend's fate and writes the news of his death in a letter to Shanti, whose arrival is the final moment of the play.

Culture and Ideology
Shanti is placed in an inter-racial, student culture, which is hardly surprising

given the activities of the playwright and the origins and racial structure of the BCM in general and PET in particular. Until Thabo goes to prison and then escapes and makes his way to Mozambique, the world of the three main characters, Thabo, Shanti and Koos, is defined by three principal preoccupations. The first is student affairs. Koos is busy with exams. Thabo writes Private Law II. Shanti has an evening 'radio club'. They read books and sometimes quote Shakespeare.

The second is racial problems. Shanti and Thabo are in love and wish to marry. Their parents oppose the match since one of them is 'Indian', the other 'Bantu'. The character, Koos, who is classified 'Other Coloured', rather as in a Jonsonian comedy of humours, hardly amounts to much more than his obsession with the problem of his racial reclassification.

The third is political activities. Thabo is a member of a political organization and attends political meetings, an activity which Shanti supports, and is periodically subjected to police interrogation. He later joins a guerrilla group in Mozambique.

The play is not only about the main characters and their actions. It is also about the three black groups they represent — the 'Indians' (Shanti), the black Africans (Thabo) and the 'Coloureds' (Koos). Their private experiences and relations are intended to reflect those of their groups and their private problems are in this way projected as ones which millions of blacks share. Shanti points to this when she says:

> I am ... a layman, faced by the problem in terms of self — as a representative of a myopic component of the thirty million Blacks. [p.69]

At the same time, however, her words point to an implicit contradiction in her relationship with her own group and her group's relationship with other black groups. She seems to acknowledge that the problems of her friends and herself are personal ones and actually do not have all that much in common with those of the wider community. This is a contradiction which the play is not able to resolve. It accounts for many of the play's weaknesses and can ultimately be traced to the contradictions within the ideology of Black Consciousness itself.

The basic contradiction in the relationship of the main characters and the black groups they represent evidences itself most noticeably in certain cultural elements of the play. In *No-Good Friday* Willie Seopelo is an intellectual and a student. Although the play concentrates on his private struggle with the moral issues presented by the brutal activities of the gangster, Shark, it does situate his struggle in the wider community by placing it in a Sophiatown backyard. In *King Kong* the gregarious rise and fall of the principal characters are set in an even wider context by invoking the ordinary working world of Sophiatown in the persons of Pauline, Lena, Truffina and Dan. *Too Late*, as we have seen, demonstrates an idealized degree of social integration. In *Shanti* the action concentrates almost exclusively on the affairs of a small student circle. At times their activities take place indoors, as at Shanti's house, for example, where their privacy is realistic. At others, they are in public places, for example the street in Scenes Two and Five, though no indication as to its location is given in the latter case either in the stage directions or in the dialogue. As newspapers are usually sold on street corners, let us assume that it is indeed a street scene. Yet these streets are curiously deserted. One only has to compare them with the street scenes in *King Kong* (i.e. Sophiatown) and *Too Late* (i.e. Soweto). Where are these places that, apart from a newsvendor and Sandra in the case of Scene Five, are bleak and empty? In what area, what community are they set?

Nowhere in the play do we sense the real existence of a community — 'the thirty million Blacks' the play is intended to be about. In fact, they are actually referred to at one point as 'you faceless millions'. Only in the prison scene do we meet a handful of them, but here they are abstract and depersonalized. They are named first, second, third prisoner and so on, and at one stage function as nothing more than Thabo's echo:

Thabo: . . . The pass and the permit offenders suffer because of the laws that they have never made!
Other Prisoners: THE LAW THEY HAVE NEVER MADE. [p.76]

In comparison with that of Kente's work, the cultural world depicted in *Shanti* is artificial, unrooted and ephemeral. Though it purports to concentrate on the wider issues of a people's political struggle, it does not situate that struggle within the world or the culture of the people. Instead it shows a small student circle which is strangely isolated from the wider community. The reason for this is that though the three black groups are all subjected to a form of oppression, their social and economic circumstances are very different. They are oppressed in different ways and to different degrees. Their cultures, too, are very different. In reality the majorities of these groups have largely divided and separated social and cultural existences. These are social facts of which the ideology of Black Consciousness did not take adequate cognizance.

In the play, though each character might represent his or her racial group and its problems individually, the moment they begin to interrelate they involve themselves in activities and relationships which are quite unrepresentative of the relations of the groups they represent. There are few streets in modern South Africa in a residential area down which an 'Indian', a black African and a 'Coloured' can stroll and reasonably hope to 'bump into' each other. There are no more racially-mixed residential communities. Members of the different black racial groups now have to meet by appointment. This explains the unreal emptiness of the street in Scene Two. It is an abstract creation of the imagination which could only be peopled by a vision of a future alternative South Africa in which racially-mixed residential areas have been restored. The play does not attempt to portray such a world and hence the streets are deserted.

Another point is that the inter-racial intercourse presented in *Shanti* takes place in the relatively rarefied milieu of student association. Kente's plays portray a great deal more of what African communalism is about than *Shanti* does. We might recall Offside in this regard. Kente centred his plays in the life of the urban majority and the life of the urban majority is community-oriented and gregarious — and it is not inter-racial. In order for it to reflect the inter-racial ideal of Shezi and the BCM, *Shanti* presents a world which is far removed from the life of the urban majority of any of the black groups.

The ideological notion that the blackness of black South Africans, irrespective of race and class, is the mark of a common oppression, on the basis of which a common consciousness can be developed, breaks down in the play. Thabo, Shanti and Koos are all, according to the definition propagated by the BCM, 'black' and conscious. Yet the play cannot conceal the contradictions that such a definition produces. Racial, national and class factors render their problems and relations in important areas quite unrepresentative of the black groups they are intended to represent. For instance, the problems experienced by Thabo and Shanti concerning their marriage are idiosyncratic and, though central to *their* lives, quite peripheral to the lives of the groups they represent.

Then again, Shanti, in a speech we shall have occasion to cite in full later, says:

> Even when trying a stroll I am not free as they are — the Godlike
> I have to stop, produce a book, identify myself . . . [p.81]

Shanti, as an 'Indian' is not required to carry a reference book or pass. Her 'strolls' would therefore be much less likely to be interfered with than those of Thabo, though they are both 'black'. Indeed, this has already been revealed in an earlier scene when the police raid Shanti's house and arrest Thabo for not carrying his reference book.

In Kente's plays we discovered many of the cultural elements which we anticipated would characterize the authentic theatre of the majority. In *Shanti* we find a culture which, by comparison, is unreal and denuded.

However, though it is possible to fault the claim that the experiences of these students are necessarily those of the black groups they represent or that their individual experiences are the same — because all three are 'black' — it can nevertheless be demonstrated that the insistence on the fact of their blackness, as the key to understanding their oppressed condition, results in a play which contains some valuable insights and makes a very real and successful attempt, in some areas, to oppose the hegemony of the ruling sections of the white groups.

When Shanti, for instance, says the following she is describing not only her own experience but, with the exception of the last few lines already quoted, that of the majority of black Africans, 'Indians' and 'Coloureds' in South Africa:

What a life! Even at night
I no longer sleep the sleep they sleep.
Mine is short, wakeful and tiresome. Even my thoughts
are no longer peaceful as theirs of comfort.
Mine are monotonous, dreary and heavy. Even my vocabulary
is no longer pleasing as theirs of luxury.
Mine is oppression, increase, influx, police.
Even at rest I am at labour. I am unlike those at ease.
I think, I pine, I pray, I curse, I weep.
Even at prayer I no longer thank as they thank the Lord.
Mine is full of petitions, questions, expectations.
Even at founding a home, I no longer rejoice. I have no choice
of place — I would breed slaves, sufferers, Christians.
Even when trying a stroll I am not free as they are — the Godlike
I have to stop, produce a book, identify myself only because I'm Black!
or is it because of my patience? [p.81]

This lament is an impressive integration of personal and political suffering. As first it appears to refer to the pain Shanti has suffered since Thabo was taken away from her. The repeated 'no longer' reinforces this impression. But very gradually we realize that what Shanti is referring to is the distinct discrimination in the *quality* of existence itself which applies not just to Shanti but to the majority of blacks in South Africa.

The problem, identified by the BCM as 'white racism', so saturates the external and internal lives of blacks that sleep itself suffers a qualitative deterioration. In *Macbeth* Shakespeare uses the image of sleep, as a profound natural rhythm, in order to indicate how deeply the unnatural murders perpetrated by the Macbeths have disturbed and deranged them. Fanon describes similar psychological and cultural disturbances amongst Algerians and the population of the colonized countries. Here Shanti is attempting to describe the depth of disturbance a racialist ideology can cause in those it is directed against. It invades not only sleep, but thought, language ('vocabulary'), leisure, religion and contaminates even the joys of childbirth. As a description of the metaphysical (ideological) effects of racialism, this speech is remarkable. When, however, it attempts to account for it — 'only because I'm Black!' — it falls into the simplistic error that characterizes the ideology of the BCM. For instance, that Shanti will give birth to slaves is essentially as much a question of nation as of race or skin colour. Nevertheless a racism as intense as that experienced by black South Africans in apartheid South Africa makes such an explanation inevitable. As a reflection of Shanti's feelings and the prevailing consciousness in the society as a whole, it is also authentic. The more objectively accurate 'partly because I'm Black', even if it were not pure bathos, could hardly be expected in the circumstances.

The militant expression of the Black Consciousness ideology in the play produces two important cultural/ideological advances. The first is the important rejection of cultural associations attached to the concepts of 'black' and 'white' which Fanon, Baldwin, Biko and others identified in the consciousness of whites and the black intermediate classes. In Chapter Three we cited examples of this in Modisane's *Blame Me On History* and in Willie's speech in *No-Good Friday*. We referred to Nkosi's criticism of Fugard's image of the moth and the light in Fugard's *The Blood Knot*. In *King Kong* similar images exist (see nn.44 and 90). Kente revealed in an interview that his ambition was to perform his plays to a white audience in town. The BCM opposed this and projected an alternative, i.e. the opposite concept of colour. 'Black' became beautiful and 'white' was firmly associated with the ugliness of capitalism and racialism. In *Shanti* this is clearly projected at times. While blackness is celebrated, as in this example spoken by Koos:

> I am Black.
> Black like my mother.
> Black like the sufferers.
> Black like the continent. [p.72]

the question is asked: *'Abamhlophe bayini na?'* (What are whites then?). The answer is 'whites are not our friends', *'basilethela ubugqila'* (they brought us slavery). 'White' equals the enemy (p.76). Though not yet a fully acceptable position because of its inability to conceive of the enemy in anything but racial terms, it does constitute an advance on the traditional denigration of blackness.

The other important advance made by the movement was its exposure of cultural and psychological domination and the efforts it initiated to oppose it. *Shanti* consistently brings to the audience's attention the constant process of intimidation and indoctrination that members of the black groups in South Africa are subjected to. Koos refers to the propaganda that divides one black group from the other – 'the parliamentary speeches that the Coloured comes immediately after the white, then follows the rest' (p.72). Shanti refers to the effect that the fear of imprisonment, especially on Robben Island, has on those involved in political resistance (p.73). The function of the popular 'black press' is alluded to – 'Read all about the recent arrests, rape, murder, robbery and soccer' (p.75) – a press which, like the theatre which the movement condemned, projects images of a degraded culture in order to further lower the morale and justify the exclusion of blacks from 'civilized society'.

When Themba, who escapes to Mozambique with Thabo, refers to the Frelimo guerrillas as 'terrorists', their general, Mobu, replies:

> Leave him! This is what he has been taught to believe we are. Terrorists! To him, like his master, we are not patriots, lovers of our people, but terrorists. Mangaya! . . . Take this man and bind him next to that white spy we caught yesterday. He wears Black feathers but is white at heart. And please treat him with tolerance. [p.79]

Mobu understands why Themba believes him to be a terrorist. He recognizes the process of indoctrination Themba has undergone. Symbolically, Mobu sends Themba to join 'his master', a white spy. Though Themba is black, his mind is possessed by the concepts and values of the dominant 'white' ideology. Mobu's understanding of this phenomenon enables him to resist the temptation to treat Themba harshly for his insult. 'Treat him with tolerance,' he says.

Black Consciousness was particularly successful when dealing with the ideological relations of the black and the white groups. Its principal weakness lay in its inability (or unwillingness) to understand the interplay of the sections within racial groups and thus the relation between ideology and the economic infrastructure. Thus Black Consciousness as a theory effectively exposed the ideological dangers of ventures such as *No-Good Friday* and *King Kong* because they involved members of the white group. It proved less capable of understanding the real function of, say, Kente's political work, because an understanding of this required a recognition of classes and sections of classes within the black groups. Similarly, the BCM with its ideology of Black Consciousness and its concept of African communalism, like other racial/cultural movements and ideologies (the Black Power movement in the States, for example), was unable to begin to deal with the relations of men and women, because this too depends on an understanding of relations between sections within the black group. The society revealed by *Shanti* is one of entrenched *machismo*. It is the man whose liberation is being fought for, and it is the man who leads and fights the struggle — 'Black man, you are on your own'. The sign of Thabo's ability to fulfil these obligations is his 'manhood', a euphemism taken from black languages, which Shanti forces him to show her. Jokes like Koos's about the unsuitability of a lady imitating Hamlet embody a concept of what a 'lady' may and may not do which is never challenged, even by Shanti. Black Consciousness obviously does not predicate 'woman consciousness'. In this, Rebecca in *No-Good Friday* and Shanti are the same, equally dependent on their men and unconscious of the sexual dimension of oppression. *Too Late*, as with much of Kente's work, because it authentically reflects the society as it is, also reflects the increasingly dominant position occupied by women of the black working class — a development which in Marxist terms would seem to suggest the beginnings of 'new' structures within the 'old'.

Finally, the culture of the play is, like that of Kente's *Too Late* and Fugard's *No-Good Friday*, religious. This is once again hardly surprising given the importance of religion in the BCM and in the black community at large. We might similarly recall the development, embodied in the career of Vusi Khumalo, of Soweto church drama and the affiliation of sections of it to Black Consciousness. Though the ideology of the white groups was rejected by all writers of the movement, in a number of areas their rejection was not radical. They tended to suggest that what was needed were not new structures but a reinterpretation of existing principles in the spirit of 'black' culture and philosophy. For instance, they did not reject capitalism as such. It was 'white' capitalism they found objectionable. 'Black' capitalism was desirable. Similarly, as we saw in Gwala's essay, 'white' theatre techniques, if informed with the 'black ethic', were acceptable. Similarly, the religion of the white groups, Christianity, despite its function in colonial history and its important integration into the mechanisms of domination in South Africa, was not rejected. Instead, what was required was 'Black' Christianity or what the movement called 'Black Theology'. The social function of Christianity and other established religions in the context of 'hegemony' was not questioned or challenged in *Shanti*. Shanti, Thabo and Koos might have been ardent opponents of the establishment but they did not doubt the legitimacy of the established religions. As in Kente's world, in *Shanti* an irreligious remark is proof of the speaker's bitterness, his loss of courage, rather than an indictment of religion itself — as in the following interchange:

Shanti: And what do you do now?
Koos: Write a letter to heaven, I suppose.
Shanti: Koos! [p.70]

Religion is part of the problem between Thabo and Shanti, though Thabo recognizes that the more solid objection to the match on the part of their parents is race:

Thabo: Stop it, Shanti. We have discussed this many times now and we always arrive at the same point of the circle — religion! (*aside*) Still, it is not true that we are being tortured by religion. Shanti is aware of the truth but she dare not face it. Religion has never been an obstacle. [p.68]

Though he questions the justice of racial discrimination, Thabo does not criticize religion and its relation to racial discrimination as it functions in his case and in the society at large. Then the play opens with the song 'Zixolise', in which the first line is 'How long shall it be, Lord?', which recalls Kente's appeals to the deity in times of suffering. However, in this play such an appeal, and the religious attitudes elsewhere expressed by the protagonists, are not a symptom of the political conservatism which characterizes Kente's plays. In *Shanti*, while they do reflect the ideology of the society as a whole and the partial participation of the characters in that ideology, they do not inhibit the play's relatively more radical political purpose. In fact, the play ultimately advocates the painful necessity of resorting to armed struggle — a step which the dominant religious ideology in South Africa has traditionally opposed.

Like *Too Late* and unlike *No-Good Friday* and *King Kong*, *Shanti* consistently endeavours to project a positive vision and give its audience reasons to hope. In *Too Late* the community was shown to be mutually supportive and a conventional exhortation was 'Courage!' In *Shanti*, too, though the sustaining community is absent, the private circle of friends and later the prisoners perform a similar mutually supportive role. For instance, when Thabo is in prison:

Koos: We both feel for you, Shanti. Have a heart, take courage.
Shanti: Thanks, Koos. That's very kind of you. Please be with me on the day
    of the verdict. [p.75]

Even less than in *Too Late* is it the negative aspects of black culture that are
emphasized. *Shanti* stresses the strengths of the culture:

*(Voices of other prisoners heard singing softly. The singing appears to be
coming from all the cells in the prison.)*
Thabo: That sounds like singing right inside the cells of torture.
    Black man, your heart is so big that you are beyond torture.
    You sing even in suffering. [p.76]

The end of *Shanti*, too, like that of *Too Late*, avoids the defeatism of *No-Good
Friday* and *King Kong*. Shanti is reading Koos' letter informing her of Thabo's
death. She reads it aloud on stage:

. . . In his possession was a note, reading: 'If I should fail to meet you on the
day of liberation, in a country purged of racism, please know that the battle
is not lost but the victory is only postponed! I love you, Shanti. Yours and
all yours, Thabo. [p.84]

What we originally observed in Matshikiza's songs and saw developed in
Kente's work is therefore present in *Shanti* too. The function of theatre for
the authors of these works was to encourage and inspire their black audiences
so that they may be able to continue their struggles and possibly free
themselves from oppression — at the hands of the white groups at least. The
attitude to black suffering of these writers is in marked contrast to that of
Fugard and Bloom in *No-Good Friday* and *King Kong*, which were pervaded
by a sense of inevitability, by passivity or nostalgia. Matshikiza, Kente and
Shezi, on the contrary, tended to view the suffering of their group as
something temporary. This is an insight which Bloom possessed but failed to
embody in his play.

Also characteristic of the work of Kente was the balance he achieved
between the positive and negative elements of his society's culture, in
contrast to *No-Good Friday*'s and to some extent *King Kong*'s emphasis on
the negative. The movement specifically attacked theatre of the kind produced
by Kente because it did show an image of black culture in which there was
drunkenness, promiscuity, thieving, murder, etc. Black Consciousness in
effect called for an heroic form, which we might compare with Gorky's
'revolutionary romanticism'. Theoretically, it was believed that a play which
projected ideal conduct would inspire people to emulate the ideal. *Shanti* to
some extent embodies this. Thabo, Shanti and Koos are 'noble' examples for
black youth to follow. The black prisoners who sing in the midst of adversity
are examples of the heroic courage and resolution of 'the Black People'.

Of course, this is only partly true of *Shanti*. It is a subtler play than this.

We see Thabo wavering, for instance, on the brink of resignation from the party. Themba is neither an outright villain nor an exemplar. Even in the guerrilla camp, Mobu's lieutenant, Mangaya, demonstrates a deviousness which an ideal representation of the heroic 'freedom fighter' might have concealed. There is nevertheless a tendency in the play which reflects the idealism articulated in the Black Consciousness aesthetic, a point which the writer in the PET newsletter recognized when s/he wrote that in *Shanti* Shezi 'portrays the true meaning of Black Consciousness'.

However, as has already been intimated, it is not principally in the cultural sphere that the theatre of Black Consciousness suggested positive and progressive developments. Kente was a greater creative artist than Shezi and the members of PET, and the cultural richness of Kente's work is absent in theirs. It is in the more intellectual and political areas — areas where Kente was particularly weak — that *Shanti* is at its best.

Politics

Whereas in *King Kong* and *Too Late* political action was not mentioned, in *Shanti* it is the main topic, and unlike *No-Good Friday*, in which it was ridiculed, this play projects it as virtually the only acceptable commitment for 'a black man'. *Shanti* is packed with political comment and protest. Though it attacks racial oppression in South Africa on a wide range of issues, it concentrates its major energies on making three important statements: (black) men and women have the right to fall in love and marry, if they so wish, without the interference of law, race or religion; the oppressed racial groups in South Africa should come together in solidarity and resist all efforts to divide them; and oppression in South Africa can only be brought to an end by armed struggle.

The first of these admirably illustrates the political nature of the play and the political nature of Shezi's vision of South African society. At bottom *Shanti* is a variation of the 'Romeo and Juliet' theme. Shanti and Thabo try to surmount through their love the barriers erected by society to divide them. In the first place they are divided by the prejudice of their families. Shanti's 'Indian' parents do not take kindly to her marrying a black African and vice versa. They are further divided by religion. As Shanti says: 'It's not your being African, Thabo. It's your religion' (p.68). The play, however, takes on another dimension when we realize that, unlike in Verona, the two lovers are further divided by government policy and legislation as well. Though there is no law forbidding marriage between Indians and black Africans in South Africa, Indians are forced to live in their own areas and are not permitted to enter black African areas. The risk Thabo runs every time he visits Shanti in Lenasia is demonstrated in the scene in which he is arrested. The policies of separate development keep the communities so far apart that the policemen who find Thabo in Shanti's house cannot believe that he is merely 'visiting' Shanti:

1st policeman (to Thabo): Yes, you! What do you want here?
Thabo: Visiting.
1st policeman: After liquor again? Search this house. This must be a shebeen.
   I don't remember seeing a Bantu visiting a Coolie. [p.74]

Such a marriage would entail so many legal and other problems as to be
virtually impossible. Hence in the South African situation the 'Romeo and
Juliet' theme is transmogrified from being one of private tragedy to one of
political oppression.

Now, the 'love-across-the-colour-line' theme is not new in South African
literature. In fact, it is one of the most common themes in white liberal
literature generally — and in the writing of certain black writers. In works
like Alan Paton's novel *Too Late the Phalarope* and Fugard's play *Statements
After an Arrest Under the Immorality Act*, for instance, the love of man and
woman, cruelly interfered with by apartheid legislation, is treated in the
context of relations between black and white. The BCM, however, rejected
the traditional liberal interpretation of black-white relations. Indeed such
love (or lust) relationships between blacks and the 'enemy' were an example
of the kind of relationships with whites the movement wished to bring to
an end. Such relationships were seen as invariably exploitative, diversionary
and, especially in vulgar interpretation, immoral and almost treasonable. A
black woman who entered such a relationship was automatically regarded
as 'loose' (*isikeberesh'*). Typically (of the *machismo* of the society), the
same attitude was not adopted towards black men who entered into a relationship with a white woman.

In *Shanti* it is the restrictions which divide one black person from another
that are being deplored, not those that divide the whites from blacks. It is
these restrictions which, because they inhibit the development of genuine
black consciousness, i.e. a consciousness of sharing the oppression suffered by
all black people in South Africa, are protested against in the play.

This brings us to the second major statement of the play, the need for
black solidarity. This is allegorized not only in the love of Shanti and Thabo
but also in their friendship with Koos. Koos, so he tells us, was 'conceived
most probably in a bush'. His mother was a Mosotho and his father an
unknown white farmer by the name of Morgan. In South Africa not only are
blacks divided into groups, 'Bantu', 'Coloured' and 'Asiatic', but these groups
are further divided and subdivided. The 'Bantu' group is divided into ethnic
groups and the 'Coloured' group into subdivisions such as 'Cape Coloured',
'Malay' and 'Other Coloured'. Koos has been placed in the 'Other Coloured'
category and is attempting to have himself reclassified, though he says he
rejects classification of any sort.

Once again, works which protest at the artificial barriers erected by
political systems between human beings are numerous in the literature of
Europe and South Africa. Such protest, however, in the context of Black
Consciousness is restricted to barriers erected not between human beings but
between blacks. The ideology is not humanism, but black communalism. Koos

is not claiming the right to be a human being. He is claiming the right to be 'black'. He says:

> Yes, I am Black and inferior to no man.
> Why must I care what I am being called then?
> Coloured, Cape Coloured, Malay, 'other Coloured'?
> I am Black. [p.72]

According to the movement, the racialism that has divided people emanates in the first place from the 'whites'. They are the source of the disease, the plague itself, and therefore they must be shut out in order to effect a cure. Ultimately, Black Consciousness is the cure not only for the damage suffered by blacks at the hands of 'white racism', but also for the white racists themselves. The theorists of Black Consciousness make this clear. When the virus is stamped out and the 'open society' attained, there will be a place for 'healthy' whites at the table.

Shanti is full of anger, an anger which stems from outrage and betrayal. The same note is sometimes to be found in the theoretical writings of the BCM. African communalism, and indeed traditional African culture, stresses the quality of *'ubuntu'* or *'botho'* (the quality of being human). Blacks had believed that whites too were human. Their subsequent behaviour demonstrated that they lacked *'ubuntu'*. They were not human. The bitterness is that of faith betrayed. Take Thabo's speech in prison:

> My people sounding a low note again! What have we done that we are so oppressed? Our sin is Blackness indeed. The whites are not our friends. [p.76]

A few lines later he repeats this accusation: 'If whites are not our enemies, out to oppress us Blacks, why is it . . .' (p.77). The second prisoner recalls: 'A non-racial society was my idea before I was arrested, gagged and called an agitator' (p.77), and a few lines later he says: 'In all seriousness, whites are thugs, knaves, criminals.' To be read between the lines is the betrayed belief that whites are 'our friends', are human beings like us, and the frustrated hope (painfully suppressed) that they will still prove to be so.

Black Consciousness may have originated in the betrayal of such a belief, in NUSAS and the UCM, for instance, but it directed itself to the replacement of that belief with the concept of 'white racism' and the final extinction (in PET's *Shanti* not yet extinct) of that hope. The movement recognized in that hope the weakness that crippled self-reliance and the will to struggle for freedom by one's own unaided efforts.

The struggle for freedom is the third of the play's major concerns. Thabo attends meetings of an organization similar to BPC. Shanti calls it 'an overt or public movement' which 'may be formed, as long as it is not underground' (p.73). Thabo's participation in this organization earns him interrogation by the security police, who threaten him with imprisonment on Robben Island, a fate which two members of PET were actually to suffer three years later. Thabo's arrest and imprisonment are not, however, the result of these activities. He is tried and jailed, though innocent, for murdering a white shopkeeper during a robbery. This finally convinces him of the injustice of the law and in prison he learns that in South Africa *all* black prisoners (including criminals) are in a real sense political prisoners — thus heeding Biko's call for a recognition of the socio-political causes of black crime. This position should be compared with that of *No-Good Friday*, in which the relationship between crime in Sophiatown and political oppression is obscured, and with *King Kong*, in which black criminal activity functions to obscure white political responsibility.

Thabo's escape from prison delivers him finally into the hands of a Frelimo guerrilla detachment, fighting for the freedom of Mozambique from the Portuguese. It is here that he realizes his previous activities had been inadequate. He had wasted his energies in the typical activities of the black intermediate classes — the furthering of his education and career and the politics of negotiation. He comes to see that the armed struggle is both inevitable and essential. As Mobu, the guerrilla leader, says of Thabo after his death:

> You all know our aim is to eliminate all prejudice, especially the evil called 'racism'. I see no reason, therefore, why we should not give him a decent burial. His struggle was our struggle. It's only that we were in different countries and he believed in verbal confrontation, which we have sent to the museum. [p.82]

The ruling sections of the white groups have understandably been anxious to propagate the idea that violent means are not a legitimate way of effecting political change. Sections of the black intermediate classes have done like-wise. Mobu, as we have already noted, refers to one example of this, the insistence on the part of the ruling sections on the word 'terrorist' for anyone who does use such means, irrespective of his motives and the forms of violence he employs. In the effort to legitimate a non-violent position, the traditional intellectuals of the English-speaking white group — the 'white liberals' in Black Consciousness terminology — have been zealous and potent agents. The condemnation of violence embodied in the liberal Christian ideology is constantly reinforced by white writers and artists, the English-speaking press and the churches, despite the constant violence exercised by the forces of the state to preserve the status quo.

The BCM could not, for obvious reasons, publicly advocate the use of violent means of struggle. Instead, while respecting the decision of the ANC and the PAC to resort to violence, it committed itself 'to explore as much as possible non-violent means within the country'. It is impossible to ascertain officially (and to document) the extent to which the movement was prepared to resort to violence. In the above formulation, 'as much as possible' and 'within the country' allow for some flexibility on the point. The state clearly thought the movement was prepared to use violence and charged its members with conspiring to, among other things, 'transform the State by unconstitutional revolutionary and/or violent means' and to condition the black groups in South Africa 'for violent revolution'. *Shanti* was adduced as part of the evidence of this conspiracy.

By now the basic contradictions which the cultural and political ideology of Black Consciousness fails to reconcile should be manifest. Though these should continue to be borne in mind, it is important that we should not lose sight of how far forward the ideology carries the oppressed's consciousness of its own predicament and the means they might adopt to extricate themselves. *Shanti* clearly demonstrates the need for solidarity amongst those who are objectively oppressed by the system, but weakens this by defining the oppressed in terms of colour and refusing to take cognizance of the objective differences within and between black groups. The play likewise raises a number of 'grievances', and protests against them. For instance, the injustice of a legal system in which an adequate defence is denied to blacks (the poor), the inadequacy of higher education for blacks, official encouragement of drunkenness in the black urban areas, the indignity of passes and permits, job reservation and influx control, low salaries and high prices, exploitation of black labour, Bantustans, etc. Because its ideology does not transcend or penetrate the parameters of colour, the play does not (cannot) discriminate between disadvantages that are suffered for economic/class or national reasons and others that are suffered as a result of 'white racism'. For instance, Gibson Kente was quite able to afford legal advice when he appealed against the banning of his play *Too Late*, though he was black. Here the criterion is not race but an economic factor. Official encouragement of drunkenness is not caused by 'white racism'. It is a common aspect of class oppression in capitalist societies, whether the working class be black or white. The criterion here is again not race but class.

Because of this inherent weakness in the movement's ideology, it fails to offer a consistent and authentic analysis of oppression and therefore a rational theory of revolutionary change. Instead the fallacious (and dangerous) impression is imprinted on the consciousness of the supporters of the movement, and those influenced by it, that as 'white racism' is the source of all injustice, one only requires to abolish apartheid in its racial aspects in order to abolish injustice. Shezi, for instance, misrepresents Frelimo's struggle in Mozambique because of his blindness to factors other than race. He makes Mobu say: 'Our aim is to eliminate all prejudice, especially the evil called "racism".' Yet Frelimo was a Marxist movement and liberated Mozambique is now a Marxist-Leninist state. The abolition of racism was *one* of Frelimo's aims, but it was seen in the context of due consideration of class and nationality:

No one can claim that they are representatives of a race, ethnic group, region or religious belief. They represent the working People . . . We all fought and are still fighting for the same nation, for the single

185

ideal of liberating our land and our people. [Samora Machel[105]]

Abolish racial discrimination and 'white racism' and the poor will still be unable to procure legal defence and the legal system of the 'open' (or 'black') society will still be unjust. In the words of another 'black' leader, the late President Neto of Marxist Angola:

> What is the use of so much blood
> If in the end we remain subject to a state
> Which even if ruled by Africans
> Only serves the rich and powerful.

Individuals in the BCM were gradually moving towards an awareness of this when the movement was banned. Mthuli Shezi's *Shanti* shows no trace of this development. It is the intermediate classes who stand to benefit from the mistaken notion that the removal of racial discrimination is the key to the removal of injustice in South Africa and, as we have suggested, the BCM was fundamentally a movement of precisely these classes.

Aesthetics

Shanti is the only one of the four plays in our study which was expressly intended to function politically. We can assume that for PET artistic and commercial considerations were secondary, if they were taken into account at all. It was also the only one of the four plays that was conceived exclusively for black audiences (i.e. all three black groups) in black areas. These functional attributes together largely determine the aesthetics of the play.

Theatre that is intended to achieve predominantly political objectives subordinates aesthetic considerations to political effectiveness. A work of political theatre may be, at one and the same time, both a highly excellent piece of art and a politically effective instrument. In fact, to separate these two qualities, the aesthetic and the political, in the context of political theatre would raise highly debatable questions about the nature of art and aesthetics which we cannot possibly pursue here. The point about political theatre, however, is that it need use so-called 'artistic' methods only when these methods serve its political purpose. When they do not, it may resort quite legitimately to methods often considered 'inartistic' — slogan, manifesto, propaganda, polemics and statement, for instance. The use or rejection of methods of theatrical communication depend in political theatre on the nature of the material, ideas, message, motivation, etc. that is to be communicated, on the nature of the audience to whom it is to be communicated, on the precise political function of such communication, and so forth.

In the previous sections of this chapter we tried to clarify the ideas or statements which the play *Shanti* was intended to communicate. The audience to whom these statements were intended to be communicated was an audience of black people. The ideology of Black Consciousness determined that theatre groups whose activity was inspired by it would be unwilling to be more specific than that. Whether the black audience was rural or urban, educated or uneducated, intermediate or working class, 'Indian', 'Coloured' or black African was not 'relevant'. According to the movement its message was accessible to all blacks. The political function of *Shanti* would seem to have been to 'conscientize' this audience about their oppression and to demonstrate the need for armed resistance. That this can be assumed is suggested by PET's claim that, unlike *Sizwe Banzi, Shanti* not only demonstrates the circumstances of oppression, it also suggests the solution. In other words, theoretically *Shanti* aimed to show black audiences that the only way to win freedom was by armed struggle.

In order to evaluate the political effectiveness of such an aim, let us consider the effect of the 'solution' offered in *Shanti* on the black audience in the urban areas, in the context of the situation as it existed in 1973. Was the play asking, say, a married worker or a student to abandon his family, make his way to Mozambique and throw in his lot with a guerrilla organization? Would he not be afraid that he too might end up dead at the bottom of a cliff? What South African guerrilla organization existed in 1973 which would receive him and turn his commitment into militarily effective action?

No such organization existed, neither did the conditions for the successful prosecution of guerrilla invasion into South Africa. Clearly then some other 'solution' must have been intended. Was the audience intended to interpret Thabo's adventure and political discovery allegorically? In other words, is the play asking the worker or the student to prepare his mind for the necessity and justice — i.e. to 'legitimate' the concept — of armed struggle within the country? Once again, questions are raised. What kind of armed struggle? With what arms? Prepare his mind he might, yet in terms of the overthrow of the structures of 'white racism' the preparation of mental attitudes is hardly the 'solution', though it may be a necessary precondition of the 'solution'. And then, is the message of the play actually intended for the worker at all? Certainly much evidence, and the director's statement that *Shanti* was a protest directed at the 'black middle classes' for abandoning 'the masses', implies the contrary.

Once again, we come back to the basic weakness of the BCM, as a movement of the black intermediate classes unable to engage in action which would meaningfully affect the confrontation of the two fundamental classes in capitalist society, the bourgeoisie and the working class. The 'solutions' that *Shanti* or any other Black Consciousness play might urge on its audience were unlikely to be politically effective. With regard to the effect on PET itself of advocating such 'solutions', this, as we know, was disastrous.

If we assume, then, that basically we have a theatre group affiliated to an intellectual movement of the black intermediate classes, with roots in a black student movement, aiming to 'conscientize' black audiences about their conditions and to prepare their minds and their morale for an armed struggle — should favourable conditions come into existence — what means do they have at their disposal to do this?

Basically, two traditions in South African theatre are available to them —

the popular musical theatre of Kente and other commercial playwrights, and the 'serious' theatre of the educated intermediate classes. Much of this 'serious' theatre, like their own education, derived from European culture. Obi, for instance, performed Peter Weiss' *Marat/Sade*. Cornie Mabaso, a founder member of Mdali and director of *Black and Blue II*, had a long history of involvement in modern and avant-garde European and American theatre. Another 'élite' form available to them was the poetry and music presentation. This consisted of a series of poems or, in more developed forms, verse dialogue interspersed with poems and chants — as in TECON's *Black Images*. The verse was usually punctuated or accompanied by musical instruments, especially drums, and in some versions (*Black and Blue II*, for instance) by songs and dances. Usually the poems were by militant black American, West and East African and local black poets, mostly in English but also sometimes in African languages. The following are brief descriptions of Mihloti poetry and music performances, at the first Mdali Black Arts Festival in March 1973, in Soweto, and at the second the following year:

> The first group to climb the stage was Molefe Pheto's Mihloti Theatre group. The group presented poetry from writers like Baldwin, Franz Fanon, Diop, Serote and others. The poetry was overtly political and done with the necessary anger and emotion that goes with it. The second half was much more interesting with much more relevant poetry written in Zulu. Although the poetry was badly arranged, the overall performance was well done and the few people in the hall were really captured. [*S'ketsh'*, Summer 1973, p.43]

and

> Next in line was the Mihloti Black Theatre group. They recited poetry — almost exactly as they did in Mdali I. Only this time with a few poems added. The act itself was not very exciting . . . There was however an attempt at one stage of the act, where they all came together and with raised hands, each holding a weapon, froze into a beautiful image. [*S'ketsh'*, Summer 1974/5, p.34]

Whereas the first festival was said to have 'rivetted' the small audience present, the second did not:

> . . . the type of audience which did attend probably made the festival a success in the eyes of Mdali, success in that it was the kind of audience Mdali seems to want — a small group of conscious brothers and sisters, most of them would-be graduates who go to a play expecting their imaginations to be stirred to thrilling extremes by hair-raising slogans. And the tycoon's wife, who regards it an obligation to attend and parade her R75 wig and mink coat at such 'occasions'. This type usually sleeps throughout the show. Yes, one of them was actually sitting next

to me — sleeping. Where were all the thousands who go to Gibson Kente's plays and set the walls rocking with their responses? Big question. If Mdali can find the answer they'll be a success. [*S'ketsh'*, Summer 1974/5, p.33]

The above description seems to confirm that the form in the hands of Mihloti, at least, remained a relatively 'élite' one, tending to attract the 'conscious few' among students and intellectuals, and socialites.

As was pointed out in the last extract quoted, there was no doubt that the proletarian audience preferred the Kente musical to the 'élite' or 'serious' forms, just as there was no doubt that the educated intermediate classes preferred these to the Kente musical — or at least professed to do so. PET, like other Black Consciousness groups, was thus confronted with a quandary. As they professed to speak to blacks generally, they could not consciously opt either for a worker or an educated élite audience. But what pleased one group was unlikely to please the other.

In the event, though PET did not entirely dispense with music, their use of song was sparse and serious. There was no dance and little humour. The absence of these basic elements of the popular theatre would on its own be a serious handicap with popular audiences. It was, however, exacerbated by the presence of tendencies (relatively underdeveloped) towards a naturalistic drama of dialogue and ideas, derived from the tradition of 'serious' theatre as exemplified in this study by *No-Good Friday*. This is particularly true of the early scenes involving Shanti, Thabo and Koos.

Thus PET eschewed the musical forms favoured by the popular audience and partly adopted those of the high-brow 'serious' theatre as favoured by educated and 'élite' audiences. The situation is not, however, as simple as that, and Shezi and PET went some way towards developing a form of their own which in significant ways resolved this dichotomy. Structurally, *Shanti* contains many elements which suggest the African popular tradition rather than the European 'élite' tradition. *Shanti* reads like a series of extracts and images. Its episodic, narrative structure links it to *King Kong*, the work of Kente and the popular tradition. Again, the first six scenes, i.e. up to the imprisonment of Thabo, are drawn from areas of experience one can assume Shezi and the members of PET were reasonably familiar with. It is in this section that the naturalistic 'serious' elements are most pronounced. In the rest of the play, however, these elements give way to a structure of fantasy closely resembling the popular narrative genre, the photo-story. This becomes most pronounced in the scenes in the guerrilla camp, where the very short interchanges and the nature of the dialogue and language create the impression of a series of static photographs each with its snatch of dialogue, soliloquies, letters and asides, like the following of Mangaya's, encapsulated in speech bubbles:

General Mobu is being too careless. Mokgethi is a traitor. He must meet with an accident. [p.81]

It is difficult to demonstrate the photo-story quality of the action here. As the genre is probably the most popular reading matter amongst urban blacks, the style might easily have come unconsciously to Shezi, and the semi-educated sections of the audience would almost certainly have related to the idiom with ease.

The characteristic feature of the play, however, is the way in which these elements of popular African structure are transformed by style in order to emphasize the play's political statement. Although music as used by Kente in his earlier plays is rejected, both songs in *Shanti* are extraordinarily prophetic of the style Kente was developing for his new play *How Long*. Indeed the very title is contained in *Shanti*'s 'Zixolise':

> How long shall it be, Lord?
> How long must we carry this burden
> How long must we yield? [p.68]

The later prison song provokes Thabo's comment: 'Black man, your heart is so big that you are beyond torture. You sing even in suffering' (p.76). 'Africa sings' in *How Long* makes the same statement.[106] The prison song in *Shanti* itself is the transmogrification of the prison song, one of the most popular conventions of the popular theatre, from *King Kong*, through *Sikalo* down to *Zilo* and many others.

In addition, PET evolved a speech/acting form which resembled in function the music of popular African theatre. At moments in *Shanti* (and in other Black Consciousness plays) the action breaks through the fabric of the play's structure into a mode of communication for which there seem to be no previous South African models. This is the way in which at times of intense feeling, public political statement emerges out of naturalistic dialogue, much as song emerges from the action in the Kentian musical. At these moments statements are made which have the quality of manifesto. The actors cease wholly to maintain the stage illusion that they are Shanti or Thabo or Koos, and they turn to the audience and address it directly, making it clear that what they say is what they the actors think and what they expect the audience to think. At such moments they speak for themselves, for the audience and for all black South Africans — as well as for the characters in the play.

One such moment is when, in Scene Three, Koos interrupts Thabo as he begs Shanti to marry him, entering with the flippant: 'No, she won't kiss you, Thabo.' Koos jokes about his conception and his parents. Shanti is shocked: 'Koos, do not insult your parents.' It is this that jolts Koos out of his flippancy and he begins a speech which, in contrast to the naturalism of the previous dialogue, is immediately recognizable as verse:

> Parents, you say! I must not insult, you plead.
> But the world does not make me forget, the probable fact —
> born by both: not to belong to either.
> Who am I, Shanti? Am I not Black, Thabo?

Did not we two play marbles together?
Comes not my blood from the veins of a Black woman?
[p.72][107]

The speech progresses in a series of questions culminating in a moment of
manifesto in which Shanti and Thabo join Koos ritualistically, both by
repeating his words and by forming with him a defiant physical tableau:

I am Black.
Black like my mother.
Black like the sufferers.
Black like the continent.
(Koos stands centre stage, as he says this. Shanti and Thabo then kneel
on either side of him, facing the audience.)
Thabo and Shanti: Black like my mother!
    Black like the sufferers!
    Black like the continent! [p.72]

In performance these passages were chanted and accompanied by powerful
gesture and individual and group plastic effects — tableaux or human
sculpture, such as the Mihloti image described earlier.
    We have suggested that these moments of chant, of manifesto, are the
structural equivalent of song in the popular African tradition. They, like
music in this tradition, communicate the intensest feelings and invest the
play with its distinctive atmosphere. At times they perform the function of
bringing one scene to an end and preparing for the next, in much the same
way as music does in *King Kong* and Kente's work — as in the example
quoted above. The end of the prison scene is another example:

Second Prisoner: . . . How can the whites expect us to love them when we
    have turned both cheeks and at each turn they have slapped us?
All: Stand united, fight united, bring sense to the oppressors! [p.78]

As much as these elements might resemble, or perform functions similar
to, the forms and structures of popular African theatre, the form that
liberated PET (and other groups) from the constraints of naturalistic 'serious'
theatre, and enabled them to develop an episodic structure and non-realist
style, was almost certainly the poetry and music presentations which the
Black Consciousness groups found particularly suitable for their purposes.
The structure of such presentations was loose and allowed a direct polemical
relationship with the audience. The form itself, though it lacked the
narrative element, was sufficiently close (by virtue of its episodic structure
and the importance of music in it) to that of the popular musical to have
been itself popular. As used by the Black Consciousness groups, however, it
tended to attract an educated or student audience, as we have seen.
    PET had not only themselves performed a poetry and music presentation,

An Evening of Black Thoughts, but performances of *Shanti* itself appear to
have been accompanied by the recitation of poems, including one by Jebe
Masokoane, the director of *Shanti*, entitled 'Black Nana Avenge! Arise!'
The poem is not easy to understand, but it would appear to be about the child
of a black mother who has been raped and killed by a white man and who
grows up hating whites and determined to revenge his mother:

> You must live, to live you must die
> I will never give my eye to a white pig,
> When I clench my fist, beware white pig
> Black Nana hates Whiteman
> ARISE . . . ARISE IF YOU CAN
> SPIT THEM WITH BLACK VENOM
> RAPE THEM, FUCK THEM, SPOIL THEM IF YOU WILL
> BLACK NANA ARISE, ARISE BLACK NANA
> The white god is out of my heart
> Never will I hug him and say master
> I shall never speak to you white pig
> My Black back is turned against you
> Raise your BLACK FIST
> PUT it high, I BLACK NANA
> BLACK man you are on your OWN
> Power, Might, Love, Solidarity!
> I am the BLACK NANA!
> ARISE! BLACK NANA ARISE!
> THERE IS A CRY FOR YOU
> ARISE! BLACK NANA ARISE!
> I AM THE BLACK NANA!   [*The New Terrorists*, pp.27-8]

The moments in the play, referred to earlier, when the fabric of illusion
is broken and the 'actors' talk directly to (and for) the audience, were
performed with the same militancy and directness as the above poem suggests,
but the effect was the more startling and powerful because of the way in
which these moments emerged from realism, broke out from the 'frame'
of the play's more conventional 'serious' naturalistic form. In this way, as
used in *Shanti*, the effect was substantially a synthesis of popular and 'élite'
or 'serious' structures and styles.

Language

The language of the play reveals the same substantially successful synthesis
of popular and non-popular elements.

The BCM had committed itself to a form of inter-racial organization and
therefore African languages were seen as divisive.[108] The roots of the
organization in the student organizations, NUSAS, UCM and SASO, likewise
tended to favour the use of English in preference to African languages. Also,
there was the traditional preference of the educated and professional sections
for English. One of the members of PET, Vusi Khumalo, in an article already
cited, made it clear that he considered lack of knowledge of English, 'the

Queen's language', to be a disqualification for 'township' playwrights.

The suspicions concerning the use of African languages in projects involving members of the white groups was in many cases justified. Khumalo on one occasion rightly likened the increasing number of 'mother-tongue' films produced by white companies in the mid-'70s to Bantu education. Similarly, the use of African languages posed genuine problems within the black African community itself. For instance, in December 1973 the Transvaal United African Teachers' Association rejected mother-tongue education in black schools. They contended that 'English was the Black man's lingua franca used for basic communication across ethnic and tribal barriers'. 'It is not our intention,' they stated, 'to downgrade our languages but we deplore it when they are used to divide and separate us as people' (*The World*, 27 December 1973). This is of course an 'élitist' statement. English is the lingua franca of the *educated* black man, not of 'the Black man', as the teachers claimed.

In *Shanti* the dialogue is meticulously English, self-conscious, 'school', i.e. written, English at formal moments, relaxing only slightly at informal ones into a mild student slang. Take the dialogue between Shanti and Thabo in the opening scene:

Shanti: Thabo, stop living in a dream! You know we will never make it. Your parents cannot accept an Indian bride.
Thabo: Do not be unfair, Shanti. Your parents do not want an African son-in-law either.
Shanti: It's not your being African, Thabo. It's your religion.
Thabo: Stop it, Shanti. We have discussed this many times now and we always arrive at the same point of the circle — religion . . . We have seen Jews marry Christians, Moslems marry Christians and so on, but they always hit it. Darling, tell me. Why must we torture ourselves thus? [p.68]

Note the formality of Thabo's 'do not's' and Shanti's 'your being African'. Then Thabo's rejoinder 'Stop it', and his use of the word 'thus' in the last line, lack the colloquial quality one would expect of young people and friends, let alone, as Shanti and Thabo are, lovers. Thabo's 'but they always hit it', where 'off' is omitted, is informal and has the typical inaccuracy of second-language speech, spoken by black students, for example. Thus in the same piece of dialogue informal and formal elements are inconsistently mixed in a situation in which one would expect consistently informal language.

How far this kind of language echoes the literary culture of the students' education rather than that of the wider community — the language in Kente's *Too Late* — is illustrated even more emphatically by the terms Shanti has recourse to in the following speech, and by her lack of fluency, which would certainly have been available to Madinto or Offside:

Yes, that is what you think! You bastard, you lazy fool, you coward . . . you . . . You call yourself a Blackman. You are still brave to call yourself that. How can you? You stupid patience-ridden bugger, you dirty son of a . . . [p.74]

Here only the phrase 'you are still brave' bears the remotest resemblance to the organic English of the black urban areas, i.e. where 'still' is a literal translation of 'nog' (*tsotsitaal*/Afrikaans) meaning 'still', 'yet' or 'even'. The rest is made up of relatively archaic terms drawn from English literature.

Even the policemen in *Shanti*, invariably Afrikaans or Zulu-speaking in other plays written in English (compare Pelepele in *Too Late*), speak scrupulously in English:

Second policeman: No argument. You'll talk at the charge office.
Shanti: Leave him! He is my guest.
Second policeman: Shut your trap! [p.74]

To sum up, therefore, there is in comparison with the popular theatre of, say, Kente, a lot of dialogue, the dialogue is in English and in an English which is not organic to the culture of the majority of blacks. These factors would surely alienate a proletarian audience. Yet a number of factors reduced the likelihood of this happening. Though much of the dialogue in the earlier scenes is 'bookish', the later ones, after the prison scene, are narrated and spoken in the rather terse though simple English of the photo-story:

Mangaya: My apologies, general. There is a report that some three hundred soldiers are heading this way. Reports from base GK5 where we were last week are that all the mine bombs were easily evaded by the enemy. I begin to fear that there is a traitor in our midst.
Mobu: Yes, Mangaya, it is as I feared. I am beginning to believe the stories I hear about the stranger who calls himself Mokgethi. Call him here. [p.80]

As already noted, this idiom is a popular one. We have already mentioned, too, the dynamic direct acting style evolved by the movement in general and the politically sensational quality of the situations and much of the dialogue. Language (and situation) is pushed at times into a kind of violent recklessness, which elicited a powerful reaction from most sections of the black audience:

Shanti (to Thabo): Take off your pants and come here. Yeah, your pants, man. What are these? Decorations, indeed! You are no man in the sense positive. A man you are if it means having what you have before you. You call yourself a Blackman. What does it mean to you? Have you cared to ask? [p.74]

As we have seen in the case of *Too Late*, the radical elements in the black audience responded with enthusiasm to the expression of political defiance or revolutionary militancy. Others rushed to see a play of this kind because they believed it would soon be banned. Many must have watched the actors and their play — which boldly presented scenes across the border in Mozambique and guerrilla camps with captured white spies and called the black audiences to arms — with the fascination (and fear) of watching ritual suicide or self-incineration. They knew that it would only be a matter of time before the actors were arrested and the state extracted its vengeance.

      ★   ★   ★

Thus *Shanti* exemplified both the strengths and the weaknesses of the Black Consciousness movement. Tactically, PET's policy of direct confrontation was suicidal. In terms of offering political 'solutions' to black audiences it cannot be said to have been a success. Yet despite being so obviously a play of students and the intelligentsia, expressing in their idiom their particular needs and interests, the play in performance went some way towards achieving its objective of speaking to all (urban) blacks and preparing their minds for the demands the political and possibly armed struggle might make on them. Just as in the case of *Too Late* the black playwright was found to be a more authentic depicter of the culture of the black community than the whites who created *No-Good Friday* and *King Kong*, so the articulation in *Shanti* of the particular frustrations and disadvantages suffered by blacks in South Africa by a black playwright and a black theatre group is a more authentic articulation of these things than that found in those plays.

9. Conclusion: 'The Future in Their Hands'

'The Future in Their Hands' – Notes on Majority Theatre

In our introductory chapters we attempted to indicate that in order to understand the function of theatre activity in South Africa, it is necessary to understand the struggle for hegemony, both political and social, of the main racial/national groups and classes within these groups. Our analysis has suggested that all four plays functioned predominantly in the objective interests of groups and classes other than the majority. This was particularly clear in the case of *No-Good Friday* and *King Kong* because the structures and associations of individuals that produced these plays were linked to, and clearly espoused the ideology of, the dominant sections of the English-speaking white group. The intellectuals, black and white, who produced *No-Good Friday* and *King Kong* saw in the multi-racial nature of their work both a potential for political change and the model for an alternative society. In both, the white intellectuals dominated, and both embodied a certain invalidation of, or condescension towards, rural and urban majority culture. Behind *King Kong* – and ultimately behind the association which produced *No-Good Friday* – was the capitalist section which dominated the English-speaking white group and these plays largely functioned in the wider social interests of this section.

However, elements in the structures or associations which produced both plays pointed forward to a more independent 'black' theatre. The main concern of the makers of *No-Good Friday* was not commercial, but aesthetic and cultural. This freed them from the commercial constraints which obtained in the case of *King Kong*. It gave them a certain apparent 'independence' from the established structures, related to the 'independence' enjoyed by Gramsci's traditional intellectuals. This was taken up in the activities of a later generation of black intellectuals and utilized to produce the militant 'serious' theatre of the BCM – *Shanti*, for example.

In *King Kong* the cast was by and large neither intellectual nor firmly intermediate-class. It was largely drawn from marginal classes existing in the proletariat. In addition, there was in the production team an educated artist, Todd Matshikiza, who did not espouse, like others of his class, the ideology and culture of the English-speaking white group. These two facts, together with the commercial constraints imposed by the function of the union itself and the cultural attitudes of the white members of the production team, produced a 'popular' form which provided black playwrights such as Kente with a model which, with modification, was acceptable to majority audiences and ultimately capable of a nationalist expression which the union itself had certainly not intended.

The decade after *No-Good Friday* and *King Kong* saw an increase in the social hegemony of the Afrikaner nationalist group and the development of a powerful capitalist section in the group. These gains were at the expense of the English-speaking white group and their allies, the black intermediate classes. The reduction in the influence of the English-speaking white establishment in the cultural life of blacks gave rise to two new developments in theatre, an 'independent' black commercial theatre, e.g. Kente's work, and a new militant form of 'black' 'serious' theatre, e.g. *Shanti*.

Kente's *Too Late* was the product of a commercial structure created and owned by a member of the black intermediate classes. We found that 'independence' from the white groups in this case did not necessarily produce theatre activity that operated in the interests of the majority. We suggested that Kente's class interests, and even those of the (white) bourgeoisie proper to which they were related, were ultimately better served than those of the majority. Here, too, however, certain structural elements tended to modify the function of the work. First, Kente was himself a member of the racial/national group from which the largest section of the majority was drawn, i.e. the black African proletariat and peasantry. Second, his audience was, unlike that of *No-Good Friday*, largely drawn from this section. This resulted in cultural authenticity and a more radical function than Kente himself is likely to have intended.

Shanti was produced by a group related to the BCM, which we characterized as predominantly a movement of students and the educated and other sections of the black intermediate classes. As it was not a majority movement as such, the BCM did not function in the full interests of the majority. *Shanti*, it was suggested, functioned mainly in the interests of the classes that produced it. Nevertheless, the structure that produced it, PET, and the movement that PET was related to, the BCM, introduced a number of important new elements which suggested the basis for the establishment of an alternative hegemony in South Africa, namely that of the intermediate classes of the black groups. These were, briefly, the discrediting of the multi-racial ideology of the capitalist sections and the white English-speaking intellectuals, the identification of the latter as 'agents' in the domination by the white groups of blacks, and the evolution of a theory of cultural domination – and consequently of cultural struggle – which moved in the direction of Gramsci's concept of social hegemony. The result in *Shanti* was a play of a certain political radicalism in the 'serious' theatre tradition, with modifications in the direction of popular forms, but some cultural aridity derived from the limitations of the movement's class origins and preoccupation with race and colour.

If we pick up the positive elements in each of these activities we find we have the non-commercial 'independence' of Fugard, Nkosi and company, the 'popular' direction and proletarian presence in Union Artists, the 'popular' direction and proletarian audiences of Kente's companies and the theoretical advances of the BCM and the political militancy of PET. Clearly missing from this list are a number of factors for which our analysis has constantly suggested the need. All the structures and individuals which produced these plays conceived of their work (where ideological considerations were present) in racial or national terms. Our examination of cultural activity has suggested the necessity of recognizing the importance of class (as well as other factors such as sex, for example) as a determining factor. As we have seen, there was within the BCM a section which increasingly came to recognize the importance of economic and class factors. This recognition needs to be developed beyond the racial/cultural parameters of 'blackness' and 'black consciousness', without, however, negating the progressive and valid contentions of the movement or the importance of racial and national factors.

The introduction of a due recognition of class produces the concept of the 'majority' and develops the racial/cultural concept of blackness and black consciousness into the class concept of majority and majority consciousness. If we accept that it is the classes of the majority, i.e. the proletariat and the peasantry, who *fundamentally* oppose the bourgeoisie and are therefore the revolutionary classes and, in Gramsci's words, have 'the future in [their] hands', it is only these classes that are able to produce the basis for a genuinely alternative hegemony and a non-exploitative society. It is only these classes, then, that are able to provide the structures for a genuinely alternative theatre. Such structures would represent the next stage in the progression we have observed in this study, and would suggest organizations and associations in which the positive elements noted in the activities of previous organizations and associations are incorporated and complemented by other elements which would be supplied by the function of the new structures. The question then is: what is the nature of structures which will function in the society in the objective interests of the majority, what cultural action will majority structures engage in and what theatre activity will they produce?

The first part of this question cannot be answered here as it is largely a political one and concerns the form of political organization the majority needs to develop in order to effect a revolutionary change in the society. All that can be said here is that such structures will have to be based in the classes that make up the majority and not in any other. In attempting to answer the second part of the question we shall raise certain points which will also be relevant to the first. What should be stated categorically at this stage, however, is that to be really effective the cultural action of the majority has to be conducted as part of the wider strategy of the political organization of the majority. Cultural action, important as it may be, is not sufficient to bring about political change by itself. At the same time, the political struggle itself will be very much more effective if conducted with a due recognition of the political importance of cultural action.

Cultural Action of the Majority

Cultural action is cultural activity which is expressly and mainly intended to have a social function. The fact that those involved in a given cultural activity are conscious of their work having a social function does not in itself make of that activity cultural action. For example, Nkosi, Bloom, Gluckman and Kente were all to some extent conscious of the political and social implications of the plays they were involved in. Yet *No-Good Friday, King Kong* and *Too Late* could not be termed 'cultural action'. *Shanti*, on the other hand, could be so termed, because PET expressly intended it to have a distinct political and social function. The cultural activity of the *organized* and *conscious* majority would be expressly intended to have a political and social effect and therefore be cultural action. What is written here about the cultural action of the majority should not therefore be confused with its other general cultural activities and entertainments, such as music, dance, weddings, funerals, sports, etc., which obviously continue, being affected by and in turn giving substance and sustenance to the cultural action of the majority.

We have argued that, in order to serve the interests of the majority, cultural action would have to take cognizance of all the relevant factors — race, nation, colour, class and sex. We saw, in *No-Good Friday* and *King Kong*, white writers attempting to work in the culture of the black African group, and how this resulted in distortion and a loss of authenticity. To some extent the same was true of *Shanti*, in which a black African writer based his play in the ephemeral inter-racial world of students of different black groups. Kente, however, writing about his own racial/cultural group, though not his own class, produced in *Too Late* a rich and authentic (though still partially idealized) cultural world. This, then, would seem to suggest that a play is culturally more authentic when it is created and performed within integrated cultural groups by those who are of, or have an intimate knowledge of and empathy with, that culture. This in turn suggests that cultural action (even political action, as cultural factors are important here, too) would also be more effective if carried out in these conditions. Thus to be effective it would seem that the cultural action of the majority ought to be organized *initially* within the working class of each racial/national group separately. In this way it would be based on a due recognition of class *and* racial/national factors and the advantages, in terms of communication, of cultural cohesion and integrity would be utilized.

Cultural action which stopped here would, however, be counter-productive. To confine itself to organization restricted to classes within racial/national groups would be to conform with the dominant and oppressive ideology of separate development and reinforce the operation of existing social hegemony. A due recognition of the importance of class helps us to realize that there are essential considerations that link the working class of the different racial/

national groups. Additional and important cultural action would have to be organized, therefore, within the parameters of inter-racial working-class relations and experience, as an essential part of the struggle to replace ideology based on race and colour with a class ideology and thus generate class consciousness. Such inter-racial majority cultural action would parallel the activity of the BCM, but add to it the important element of class as opposed to national culture.

Such activity would not, however, fully take into consideration the strength of national factors — and not at all those of sex. The former raises the important issue of alliances between the working class and other classes or sections of classes. Previously, most organizations and ideologies in South Africa, with the exception of the Marxist parties and groups, have construed any attempt to organize in the black groups along class lines as divisive and in the interests of the white groups in the society. In so far as the struggle in South Africa is a national one, this is correct. However, it is not only a national struggle; it is also a class struggle and is becoming increasingly more a class struggle and less a national one.

This conjuncture of the national and the class factors — both important and valid in South Africa — suggests that, though the cultural action of the majority should be organized in the classes of the majority, it should also — while preserving a separate structure and character and serving primarily the interests of the majority — endeavour to win the support of the inter-mediate classes of the black groups, especially on national and racial questions, i.e. injustices and oppression suffered as a racial/national group, historical dispossession, etc., which are common to all blacks or to all black Africans.

The question of the liberation of women should also be seen as an important and valid one in the struggle for liberation in South Africa, and majority cultural action would have to include action based both within the sub-cultures of working-class women of the different racial groups and across racial barriers.

An important question raised by the organization of class action concerns the role of those who objectively belong to other classes but identify with the struggle of the majority. Are they excluded from majority cultural action? Can a member of the black intermediate classes or of any class of the white groups participate in the cultural action of the majority?

In this study we have seen that even 'sympathetic' whites have, when collaborating with blacks, produced work which has not been in the interests of the majority, that has in fact been a part of the general hegemony of the white groups. The writers of the BCM especially identified this phenomenon. We have also found that members of the black intermediate classes have, in various ways and to various degrees, produced work which does not primarily serve the interests of the majority and in fact operates directly or indirectly as part of the hegemony of other classes or groups over the majority. Does this mean, then, that individuals or groups of any class or section of class, racial group, nationality, etc. other than those of the majority ought not to be admitted to cultural action organized by the majority?

In our chapter on *No-Good Friday* we concluded that in this play Fugard and the others assisted the process of domination in South Africa. This assessment was not made because Fugard was white or because he and the others were members of the intermediate classes. The work of those who made *King Kong*, Kente, Shezi and the members of PET was not criticized because of their colour, their race, their nationality or their class. Their work has been criticized because it has been found to *function* ultimately in a way which was either quite against the interests or not in the full interests of the majority.

In other words, the criterion here is not membership of a racial/national group or class, but the actual function of the work produced. The work of non-members of the majority is not to be faulted just because it is the work of non-members of the majority. It is faulted if it works against the full interests of the majority and then *because* it works against these interests. If a non-member of the majority is able to switch his allegiance and transform the class character of his work so that it fully serves the interests of the majority, then his work ought no longer to be faulted but welcomed and supported. After all, as Gramsci wrote: 'One of the most important characteristics of any group that is developing towards dominance is its struggle to assimilate and to conquer "ideologically" the traditional intellectuals' (*Prison Notebooks*, p.10). The difficulty, if one belongs to an oppressor class or racial/national group, of making this change, can be very great — as Freire for example was very much aware:

> . . . another issue of indubitable importance arises: the fact that certain members of the oppressor class join the oppressed in their struggle for liberation, thus moving from one pole of the contradiction to the other. Theirs is a fundamental role, and has been so throughout the history of this struggle. It happens, however, that as they cease to be exploiters or indifferent spectators or simply the heirs of exploitation and move to the side of the exploited, they almost always bring with them the marks of their origin: their prejudices and their deformations, which include a lack of confidence in the people's ability to think, to want, and to know . . . Our converts . . . truly desire to transform the unjust order; but because of their background they believe that they must be the executors of the transformation. They talk about the people, but they do not trust them; and trusting the people is the indispensable precondition for revolutionary change. A real humanist can be identified more by his trust in the people, which engages him in their struggle, than by a thousand actions in their favour without that trust. [*Pedagogy*, p.36]

In South Africa this transformation is particularly difficult to achieve — so habitual is the practice of oppression. But Freire and even Biko[109] recognize that difficult though it may be, it is not impossible.

Though we have attempted to demonstrate that members of the black intermediate classes can function in ways which do not challenge the general hegemony of the white ruling classes and in some aspects positively assist it, their ability in the present situation to function oppressively is relatively limited. Their common experience, with the majority, of racial and national oppression, if coupled to a correct ideological grasp of the realities of majority interests, together with their intimate, first-hand experience of majority cultural forms, would qualify members of these classes to assist actively in the struggle of the majority. It is likely, then, that many of the cultural cadres and leaders active in the cultural action of the majority will in fact be drawn from these classes.[110]

Majority Theatre

Ideology and Culture

We discovered that, in each of the plays studied, the class position of the dominant structures and individuals determined to a considerable degree the play's cultural and ideological perspectives. This meant that, among other things, it largely accounted for the way in which other groups, sections or classes were represented in the plays. For instance, in *Shanti* the student characters were personalized while those of the 'masses' were generalized. In *No-Good Friday* the rural traditional character, Tobias, was stereotyped. In *Too Late* the doctor's class character was blurred. In each play, society was seen from a particular viewpoint, and as the viewpoint shifted from play to play, so cultural and ideological attitudes and values changed.

The plays we looked at revealed a number of characteristic preoccupations, most of which were related to the central question — that of the operation of hegemony, the way in which social groups and classes attempt to impose particular ideologies or cultural perceptions on other groups and classes. There was the attitude to the rural traditional culture, the attitude to urban popular culture, the dialectic of imposed and constituent elements in the urban culture, and moral and religious questions including the *moegoe/clever* ethic. The ways in which the cultures of different sections of the society are divided or integrated was also important, as in the case of Kente, who depicted an integrated black African society and culture and excluded elements which contradicted the homogeneity he projected.

The viewpoint of a play cannot only be related to the maker's particular class interests, but can also be related to the play's intended function, to who will perform it and to the audience for whom it is intended.

Thus the viewpoint in *No-Good Friday*, though substantially that of Fugard, was affected by the black intellectual actors and the English-speaking white audiences for whom the play would appear to have been predominantly intended. All these entertained contempt for the rural traditional culture. There was ambivalence about the urban culture, but Fugard's own emphasis on the imposed or negative aspects of it prevailed. The moral and religious criteria of the dominant English-speaking white group were applied and the entire 'meaning' of the play determined by them. The particular dilemma of the black intellectual in the 'ghetto' was personalized, while the experiences of the major part of the Sophiatown community were generalized.

The professional and commercial character of *King Kong* and the class of the performers to some extent modified the above viewpoint. For instance, *King Kong* was quite secular. It shared the attitude to the rural traditional culture, but expressed greater enthusiasm for and used the idiom of the urban culture to a larger extent than *No-Good Friday* did. There was a greater emphasis on the constituent element in the culture, as a result of Bloom's belief in its fundamental resilience and 'optimism'. But *King Kong*'s commercial intention to please large white audiences determined that 'optimism' would degenerate into 'good humour' and the real hardships and suffering of the society would be obscured.

Both plays embodied an implicit assumption that the culture and ideology of the white groups, particularly that of the English-speaking group, were superior to those of the black groups, and that the latter would inevitably (or at least ought to) give way to the former — an assumption articulated, as we have seen, by Oppenheimer, Huddleston and many others, in addition to those involved in creating the plays themselves.

The move away from white authors and audiences to black, in *Too Late* and *Shanti*, shifted the viewpoint. Instead of a society viewed from the perspective of the English-speaking white intellectuals, we had a society viewed from that of the black intermediate classes. In so far as these black intermediate classes subscribed to the culture and ideology of the English-speaking white group, the perspective remained roughly the same. In so far as they did not, it altered.

Whereas the images of black culture projected in *No-Good Friday* and *King Kong* were clearly distorted and often quite inauthentic, those projected in *Too Late*, though still not quite accurate, were very much less distorted and inauthentic. Yet, as in *No-Good Friday*, the play's morality was Christian. The attitude to the rural traditional culture was virtually the same as in the earlier two plays. Where the perspective altered most radically was the move from an individual-based society to a communal one, which was seen as virtually an extension of the family along the lines envisaged by the BCM in its concept of black communalism. There was also a more positive and affirmative attitude to the urban culture and a corresponding emphasis on its constituent elements. Kente's position in the black intermediate classes, and the need to reach a large black proletarian audience, prompted him to ignore or attack the white groups and draw the black proletariat into an integrated classless black African community, and it was fundamentally this that determined the above perspectives.

In *Shanti* the viewpoint altered yet again, and moved still further away from that of the English-speaking white intellectuals. It moved away from that of the commercial sections of the black intermediate classes, too. It became that of the black students, whose socially 'independent' position enabled them to adopt much more militant positions than other sections of the intermediate classes. White ideology and culture, lumped together as 'Anglo-Boer' culture, was rejected. The African pre-conquest traditional culture was revalued and co-opted to inform the urban culture with its traditional 'black' values and purify it of 'white' corruption. Yet because of the inter-racial 'black' perspective cultural authenticity was sacrificed. In the dialectic of imposed and constituent elements the shift initiated by Kente was carried still further and the ideal element magnified, so that what could or should be was projected rather than what is. All references to the negative aspects of the culture were to be excised. As we saw, however, this was more strictly observed in theory than in *Shanti* itself.

Despite the obvious gap reflected in the play between the students and the majority of the racial/national groups they represented, *Shanti*, like *Too Late*, attempted to project a classless community. It went further and projected a classless, raceless black community. Yet the Christian/religious perspective partly remained, as did certain ideological perspectives characteristic of the intermediate classes — attitudes to language, for instance.

The shift from Black Consciousness theatre to majority theatre constitutes another change in viewpoint. It is likely that a play written or produced by majority structures or individuals and inspired by 'majority consciousness', would result in more balanced, more differentiating perspectives than those described above. For instance, the *moegoe/clever* ethic and its conflict with Christian morality might be placed in perspective. The *moegoe/clever* ethic might be seen as the result of an environment in which survival depends on one's ability to prey on other people. It would be no good rejecting this by referring to the moral sanctions of Christianity. Instead, the political reasons for such a false morality might be demonstrated and a new morality evolved on the basis of political solidarity and action directed towards revolutionary change.

The imposed/constituent dialectic might also be handled in a different way as might the relation of black workers to the black intermediate classes. Just as it would not be in the interests of the majority either to suppress the truth concerning the negative and unflattering elements of the culture, or to ignore its positive and constitutive elements, so it would not be in its interests to conceal the national and racial circumstances which make the black inter-mediate classes its allies, nor to conceal the class factors which make them its class enemies. In both cases, therefore, the approach might be to present the dialectical situation as it exists, rather than suppress or exaggerate one factor at the expense of the other.

The balanced nature of this viewpoint is likely to be carried over into other areas as well. There would be no point in the majority pretending that the traditional ideology and culture of its pre-industrial ancestors was adequate in the modern industrial context, nor in subscribing to such notions as black communalism. Nor, on the other hand, would there be any need to be disparaging of it in its historical context, as the black intermediate classes and the white groups have tended to be.

Above all, the theatre of the majority would have as one of its tasks the raising of consciousness, the inculcating of 'majority consciousness'. The primary difficulty facing majority theatre in the performance of this function is the entrenched structures of 'false consciousness' erected and maintained by the intensive cultural action of the dominant groups and classes. No cultural action can be effective as a liberating force unless it assists in sweeping aside the false images, perspectives, values, snobberies, etc. that cultural hegemony has for so long fostered, and bringing the majority to confront the essential facts of its situation as an oppressed majority.

This study has raised a number of examples of false consciousness operating in social, cultural, political, economic, linguistic and aesthetic spheres. The entire system of social stratification in black urban culture, and what we have referred to as ideological geography and hierarchical ethnic attitudes, are based on false consciousness. In terms of language, we have observed the way in which English is associated with education and intelligence and with opposition to the government, and is considered the language of culture and sophistication; the way in which the majority languages are associated with ignorance, inarticulate expression, lack of sophistication, comedy, etc. We have touched on the distorted and inhuman morality of *clevergeid* and *moegoegeid*. And then overarching the entire system is the colossal ideological structure of racialism, racial categories and all the elements of false consciousness it embraces, in the shadow of which virtually all theatre in South Africa is produced and all thought and culture conducted.

Though itself trapped in this structure, the BCM began the process of identifying and eradicating certain areas of false consciousness. This process needs to be continued and pushed further than the racial ideology of Black Consciousness can take it. It needs to be pushed forward towards class (i.e. majority consciousness) and thus ultimately full human consciousness. The movement towards majority consciousness is a process which takes culture and thought out of the shadow of strictly racial ideology into the light of a completely new set of ideas and choices — as the following discussion of practical situations should reveal.

In South Africa there is a 'Manichean' tendency to characterize ideological positions as either one thing or the other, an ideological rigidity which derives from the complete absence in the society of dialectical patterns of thought. Four central areas of debate can be adduced as characterized by this tendency — language, culture, race relations and questions of class.

According to the dominant modes of thought among blacks in South Africa, liberal whites are either antagonistic to white domination and the Afrikaner nationalist government or part and parcel of it. This inability, or unwillingness, to recognize more complex relationships has led to a number of serious confusions, none more serious perhaps than the inability to understand how the two white groups are at one and the same time antagonistic *and* in partnership.

In terms of language, because the government advocates and enforces the use of 'Bantu' languages, the tendency is either to support the government and advocate the use of these languages or to oppose the government and use

English. The possibility of a third position, i.e. that one may oppose the government *and* use these languages in their democratic, organic form, is rarely entertained.

The same problem has inhibited fresh thought on the question of culture. The government advocates and enforces the practice of certain atrophied forms of 'Bantu' culture. Therefore valuing traditional African culture was construed as support for the government and rejecting it as opposition. In the 1970s the BCM began the important task of introducing and popularizing a third possibility, i.e. that one can oppose the government *and* endorse the value of traditional culture, though the ideological framework in which this was done — African communalism — was, as we have tried to show, inadequate.

Debate concerning race relations is particularly obstructed by this tendency towards categorical thinking. As the government enforces segregation, it was thought that to oppose it one must advocate integration. The government is racialist. To advocate anything but rejection of segregation, i.e. anything but multi-racialism, is to be racialist. Hence when the BCM rejected integration in the form conceived by the liberals, it was labelled 'racialistic'. The situation is further complicated by the fact that in the debate between white liberals and Black Consciousness intellectuals, once again two concepts have come to dominate and all attempts at formulating a third are stigmatized. In other words, one is compelled either to advocate racial separation, which in the context of that debate is the position favoured by Black Consciousness, or to advocate 'multi-racialism', which is the position of the liberals, both black and white. The possibility of a third, non-racial, i.e. socialist, position cannot find a voice in the debate, as all non-racial concepts are automatically confused with the liberal concept of 'multi-racialism'.

Attempts to introduce concepts related to the ideology of class and class struggle are similarly obstructed. For instance, to attempt to point out the historical tendency of nationalism, African or other, to carry oppressive élites to power on the backs of the majority is stigmatized as government-inspired. The government opposes African nationalism and, aided by the white liberals, it propagates the notion that blacks are not capable of government and that when they do govern they produce repressive and chaotic regimes. In order to propagate this notion they point to Zaire, Zambia and other parts of Africa. Therefore to express the class attitude of the majority vis-à-vis nationalism, and the role of the intermediate classes in nationalist movements, is to be labelled 'white', 'non-white', 'government agent', 'sell-out' or 'communist'.

This obstructive tendency will obviously persist while the debate on these issues is conducted between the white liberals and the black intermediate classes. Only the irruption into the debate of the majority can bring the impasse to an end and open up a way forward. Historically inarticulate and hitherto excluded from the debate, it is the only section of the population whose objective interests demand a series of 'third alternatives'.

The majority inhabits a culture to which important aspects of intermediate-class culture are alien, including its language, English. By rejecting English in favour of its own languages, the majority is not expressing its support for the government. By rejecting important aspects of intermediate-class 'Western culture' and African communalism, the majority is not expressing approval of government attitudes and policies. It is asserting its right to its own alternatives – a proletarian culture with African roots and languages which have developed organically within that culture, neither 'pure' in the traditional sense nor as dictated by the white government's linguistic experts.

The majority is also in a position to assert an authentic alternative to both multi-racialism and racial exclusivism. It 'knows', i.e. it knows in terms of its class consciousness, that political oppression and economic exploitation can be exercised by both white and black. Only *its* experience of non-racial oppression and exploitation can provide the primary insight that, though the present burden of racial/national oppression is taxing, the key to *ultimate* liberation is class revolution.

A new ideology is inherent in the objective conditions of majority experience. When the majority becomes conscious of the real nature of these conditions, this ideology becomes explicit. The role of majority theatre is to act as an agent in the process of the formation of majority class consciousness, participating in the majority's battle to strip away false consciousness and confront objective reality, to reveal and counter the various mechanisms and processes of cultural domination employed by other classes, sections and groups in the society to keep the majority in its place. In so doing, majority theatre will be participating in the establishment of a basis for an alternative hegemony in the society, i.e. in a society which the majority controls and which functions in its interests.

Politics

In our analysis of the plays, our evaluation of the politics of each play tended to divide into a consideration of the political content of the play on the one hand and its political function on the other. Whereas the former consideration could be based on an analysis of the text, the latter required the introduction of other factors, particularly relating to performance. For instance, in *Too Late* we saw how in the *script* the radical or militant content of the play was ultimately suppressed in favour of a moderate appeal to the authorities. And we saw how in *performance* certain sections of the audience ignored this and reacted with enthusiasm to the militant radical elements – so much so that local township superintendents refused to allow the play to be performed in halls under their jurisdiction – despite the fact that it had been cleared by the Publications Control Board and by the relevant minister himself after a reading of the script.

The central point concerning the political content of a play in South Africa must surely be the analysis it presents or implies of the oppressive system, and the methods it advocates (if indeed it advocates any) of either changing, enduring or preserving the status quo. All four plays studied include statements regarding the nature of crime, the function of the police and the existence of poverty and hardship in the black community. The perspective revealed in these statements proved to be a good pointer to the political position of each play.

For instance, in both *No-Good Friday* and *King Kong* crime was placed at the centre of the action and the gangsters were important figures. In *No-Good Friday* political action was discredited, the political reasons for crime suppressed, the police projected as the allies of the people in the fight against it, and poverty and hardship partly attributed to the apathy of the people themselves. In *King Kong*, though political action was not discredited, it was ignored. Crime was substituted for the oppressive forces of the state as the main cause of suffering and hardship. The role of the police was similar to that in *No-Good Friday*. Though *King Kong* contained some criticism of apartheid, the above remained the basic outline of its political content. This was further reinforced by the nature of the audience to which it was presented. As in *No-Good Friday*, this was predominantly drawn from the English-speaking white group. Both plays, in order to be successful, had to appeal to this group. This factor favoured an analysis in which the oppressive function of the white state and its police force was obscured and no possibility of revolutionary political change considered — let alone recommended. The multi-racial ideology of the play's makers further reinforced this tendency, since the political point of the performances, as Nkosi, Bloom and Gluckman all made explicit, was not to depict racial/national or class conflict, i.e. the real situation, but to improve 'race relations'.

In *Too Late* we saw a powerful dialectic at work between class and national factors and between Kente's politics and those of his audience. If we refer to our political touchstone — crime, the police, social suffering and the political solution — this dialectic is clearly seen. In *Too Late* crime was firmly placed in its social and political context, as, for instance, in the opening scene with the *majitas*. Similarly, the police were seen as the scourge of the 'township', not the *tsotsis*, who were themselves victims of the oppressive system and whose crime was merely a desperate attempt to survive. Social suffering was also shown to be caused by political factors, for example, the pass, unemployment, racial discrimination, etc., and this too was exacerbated by the actions of the police and the nature of the prison system. As we saw, such an analysis pointed firmly towards a revolutionary political conclusion. This conclusion Kente ultimately dodged. Though discrimination on a racial/national basis, and Kente's financial dependence on an audience which was becoming increasingly militant, suggested such an analysis to him, his class position and the necessity to continue functioning economically in the apartheid state made him unable to accept or project it. We saw the process by which Kente attempted to suppress the radical analysis and substitute a moderate reformist 'solution' in its place.

In *Shanti* the political content was more militant. Crime as a non-political category simply disappeared. Gone were the *tsotsis* and gangsters and the statement was made powerfully that all black prisoners and criminals were political prisoners. The police's role was unequivocal. They were the enforcers of apartheid. The sufferings of the people were projected as the direct result of it. The solution was the armed struggle and revolution. However, while this carried us forward, it remained the class position of sections of the intermediate classes. It provided the false analysis that suffering and oppression in South Africa are caused by racialism – though it did hint at other factors. Blacks suffer, we were told, because they are black. It therefore posited a false solution, i.e. that if racialism is removed, suffering and oppression will disappear. *Shanti* in performance posed other political problems. Plays which openly advocate armed revolution invite swift repression from the state. At the same time, it is not clear how an audience is expected to respond to a general and somewhat impracticable call to arms. Majority theatre would therefore not only be characterized by a more radical political content than that of *Shanti*, but it would also have to solve tactical problems which the theatre of Black Consciousness largely disregarded.

Majority theatre would clearly have to develop the position expressed in the political content of *Shanti* and its analysis of the South African situation by including other important factors such as those of class and the economic base of oppression in South Africa. For instance, in majority theatre crime might be related to unemployment, labour control mechanisms such as the influx control laws and the reproduction of cheap labour – as well as to the factors referred to in *Shanti*. The analysis would go beyond the political apparatus, the police, the superintendents, even the government, to the economic structures they represent and uphold. This would produce a 'solution' which would, like that proposed in *Shanti*, involve armed revolution and the abolition of racialism, but at the same time advocate the political organization of the majority as classes in the economic structures, and the abolition of the capitalist system itself.

Such content would, like that of *Shanti*, be faced with the problems entailed in expressing such radical political material in South Africa – censorship, police action, arrest, banning, life imprisonment and even death. We have already noted the fate of many members of the BCM in general and PET in particular. The danger of staging such material applies not only to those who present it, but to the audience to whom it is presented. This suggests that other methods of operating politically in theatre have to be sought – at least until the objective conditions alter. It is here that the understanding of Gramsci's analysis of 'rule' and 'hegemony' could be of great assistance. If it is realized that a play – in order to function politically – does not have to oppose the forces of 'rule' alone with confrontational political material, but that it can be especially effective as an instrument with which to oppose the operation of 'hegemony', a new conception of the radical potential of theatre is introduced.

The ability of revolutionary theatre in a repressive state such as South Africa to operate in an explicitly political way is almost as severely restricted as that of a revolutionary political organization. Majority theatre's prime political task would, then, seem to be to assist in the inculcation of a revolutionary majority consciousness and concentrate its attention in the area of cultural and ideological struggle, i.e. by opposing 'hegemony' in the first place, rather than by projecting overtly revolutionary 'messages' and calls to arms, i.e. by opposing 'rule'.

If our discussion of culture, ideology and politics suggests that majority theatre has, then, these two fundamental tasks — the inculcation of 'majority consciousness' in the place of false consciousness and the struggle to establish a basis for the alternative hegemony of the majority — the question is: what kind of theatre activity does such a function suggest?

Aesthetics and Language

Our discussion of the aesthetics of the plays in this study has revolved around two basic and related distinctions. The first was concerned with form and involved the distinction between 'serious' and 'popular' theatre. The second concerned function and involved the distinction between aesthetically, commercially and politically motivated theatre. For instance, *No-Good Friday* and *Shanti* belonged broadly speaking to the 'serious' theatre, *King Kong* and *Too Late* to the 'popular' theatre traditions. They were further distinguished by function. *No-Good Friday* was intended to function largely aesthetically, i.e. it was primarily produced to be enjoyed as art, though a concern for other factors was involved. *King Kong* and *Too Late* were frankly commercial, though once again other factors were involved. *Shanti* was frankly political in function. The function of each play was a major factor in determining its form and thus the questions of form and function were related. For instance, the non-commercial, i.e. aesthetic and political, functions produced 'serious' plays, while the commercial function produced 'popular' plays.

The 'serious' and 'popular' forms, in the hands of black artists, changed character. This revealed itself particularly in the endings of the plays, the ways in which the actors related to the audience, the nature of the feelings communicated to the audience, the structure, the language and a tendency to integrate 'serious' and 'popular' elements. For instance, *No-Good Friday*'s form was closely related to that of a certain trend in the theatre of nineteenth- and twentieth-century Europe, represented for example by Ibsen, Camus, Sartre, Anouilh's *Antigone*, etc. It was implicitly a realist play. It was verbal or literary and concerned with intellectual or moral problems. *Shanti* began clearly in the same tradition, but both form and structure were influenced by 'popular' elements. The 'laws' or conventions of European realism were not respected, and indeed the characteristic element in the play was the non-realist direct address to the audience by actors who had temporarily abandoned all illusion. Similarly, whereas the endings of the two plays that were written by whites were 'suspended' and 'cyclical' and the tone pessimistic and nostalgic, those written by blacks ended positively and were intended to encourage and inspire determination and optimism.

In terms of language, all four plays encountered but could not solve the abiding problems black or multi-racial drama in English is faced with in South Africa. In *No-Good Friday* the improvisatory method of evolving dialogue, in

King Kong the introduction of *tsotsitaal*, albeit in a distorted form, and the
importance of the visual and musical elements, in *Too Late* the use of phrases
from urban black languages, slang and 'Soweto English' and the effective
use of non-verbal elements, and in *Shanti* the photo-story narrative style
and the use of visual tableaux − all these were factors which helped to limit
the disadvantages of English as the language of dialogue in such plays without,
however, solving the central linguistic problem.

In the case of majority theatre − and one must caution that this is as yet
mere speculation − how might the 'serious'/'popular' distinction operate?
For the answer to this, one must refer back to the function of majority
theatre as enunciated at the end of the previous section. It then becomes
clear that the trend discernible in *Too Late* and *Shanti*, i.e. to combine
'serious' and 'popular' elements, points the way. This is in keeping with the
capacity, already noted, of majority theatre to deal successfully with dialectical problems. Theatre that is to raise consciousness and establish the basis
for an alternative form of hegemony cannot be all laughter, tears and music,
i.e. it cannot have the 'popular' form following from a commercial function.
It has to be able to carry the serious discussion of ideas. It cannot, however,
be all words and debate, as this, like the 'serious' form, would alienate it
from the majority. A form would have to develop − and this cannot happen
on paper − towards which many of the above-mentioned factors point, a
form which will be at the same time organic to the culture of the majority,
upholding its styles, structures and idioms, yet capable of launching the great
dialogue which must take place in order for it to liberate consciousness.

In this regard, we might consider in a little detail two questions: first, a
form already being developed elsewhere which suggests certain possibilities
for the development of majority theatre, and second, language.

The form of theatre referred to is what has alternatively been called
'popular theatre' or, more recently, 'theatre for development'. In a booklet
on the uses of popular theatre, designed for 'extension workers and others in
adult education in Botswana', 'popular theatre' is described thus:

> Popular theatre includes performances of drama, puppetry, singing,
> and dancing. These performances are called 'popular' because they are
> aimed at the whole community, not just those who are educated.
> They are open to everyone. They are performed in local languages and
> deal with local problems so everyone can understand them and find
> them useful.[111]

A fuller description is provided in a Unicef publication on 'popular theatre':

> Over the last decade there has been an increasing use of the performing
> arts as part of a two-way communication process in which performance
> is the catalyst for discussion. The purpose is no longer simply to put
> across information; it is to help people develop a critical awareness of
> their situation and a commitment to collective action. Used in this

way, the performing arts can help to demystify reality by challenging people's perceptions of their situation and rejecting the false definitions which normally influence them. People are encouraged to look at their problems, work out solutions, and take action themselves. The spectator is no longer a passive recipient of government messages; he is provoked by the performance and the educational programme to respond in an active way.

In this use of the performing arts, the performance is not the total experience. It is merely the initial catalyst for a programme of education and action. Art is used in a deliberately functional sense — not as an end in itself, but as a medium of social transformation. In this way art becomes socially relevant and part of a larger concern for the creation of a more humane and justly ordered society. It is more than 'high art occasionally toured around the boon-docks bringing culture to the deprived masses'.

This more functional and participatory use of the performing arts has been called 'popular theatre', which has been defined as 'people's theatre speaking to the common man in his language and idiom and dealing with problems of direct relevance to his situation'. It is 'popular' because it attempts to involve the whole community, not just a small élite determined by class or education. Its use of local languages and a participatory style and its attempt to reflect the audience's own situation from their perspective makes it their theatre rather than an imposition.

[Kidd and Byram, 1978]

Now, this clearly bears some similarity to majority theatre. The two cannot, however, be equated. The latter is defined specifically in terms of class and is an instrument of the political and cultural action of the classes that make up the majority. 'Popular theatre' is not defined in terms of class. In the above extract, for instance, we are told that 'popular theatre' is aimed 'at the whole community', 'open to everyone' and attempts to involve 'the whole community'. Nevertheless their related functions suggest useful uses of theatre and forms.

In Botswana, for instance, four different uses of theatre activity were identified and consequently four different forms evolved. A community education campaign, aimed at 'developing a rural development programme out of a *community* analysis of . . . local problems', produced a realistic play performed in the *kgotla* by a mobile team of 'actor-animateurs', followed by a discussion. Use of drama in 'Freirean literacy work' resulted in dramatization of problems by literacy-group members but particularly in story-telling by the 'animateur'. Extension work in 'appropriate technology' in rural areas aimed at 'dialogue with villagers on their problems, alternative ways of solving them . . . and strategies for action' resulted in 'single-theme', 'pre-packaged' puppet plays 'performed by their own staff'. Finally, in work amongst Basarwa (Bushmen), aimed at developing self-reliance amongst newly-established communities, a form of 'participation theatre' was evolved in which the entire group, both actors and audience, developed a play from an original stimulus by alternate improvisation and discussion, with members free to interject at any point (usually in character) in order to offer criticism, advice or suggestions.[112]

The 'democratic' and dialogic (i.e. dialogue-promoting) elements of such theatre activity appear to be particularly appropriate for the development of majority theatre in South Africa. These and other forms suggested by the positive elements identified in the four plays in this study provide a basis for the practical development of new forms in conjunction with majority audiences themselves. A crucial part of this development must surely be the solution of the language problem.

Only the majority, of all classes or sections in South African society, is able to go beyond the impasse concerning the use of language in South African theatre. To conduct majority theatre in English would not be democratic, and it would frustrate its dialogic intention. Most important, it would favour the emergence not of majority consciousness but of other élitist phenomena, which the emerging majority consciousness can be expected to oppose. It is one thing, however, to determine that the use of English in majority theatre is unacceptable, and another to solve the problems related to the use of other languages in its place.

In 1971, shortly after the establishment of its drama workshop, Workshop '71 took an important stand on language. First, it insisted that, at all drama workshops and in all meetings and discussions, members should feel free to express themselves in any of the main South African languages. Second, Workshop '71's first play, *Crossroads*, though still substantially in English, included large sections of action and dialogue in the everyday languages of the majority in the Witwatersrand, and did not restrict the use of these languages to comic effect only. Particularly prominent in this use of majority languages was the serious and substantial use made of authentic *tsotsitaal*. Towards the beginning of the play there is, as in so much popular South African theatre, a street scene. The following is an extract from that scene, which should be compared with dialogue quoted from other plays in this study:

(Seilaneng saunters up to Peter and accosts him saucily)
Seilaneng: Hello, Loverboy.
Peter (lowering newspaper slightly): Hello, Dudu. Go bjang?
Seilaneng: Ke teng. O kae wena?
Peter: Where you from?
Seilaneng: I'm from Diepkloof.
Peter: Jy jol weer in Diepkloof?
Seilaneng: Ya, ke jola le Madubula.
Peter: Moenie jol in Diepkloof. Ouens van da is moegoes.[113]

Here 'Soweto English', various colloquial dialects of Sotho and *tsotsitaal* are all used *exactly* as they might be in such a situation in real life.

Workshop '71 followed up *Crossroads* with a musical called *ZZZIP!!* After the experience of watching *Crossroads* become a great 'multi-racial' success, the committee took the decision to abandon performances to whites. Significantly, in order to ensure this, it was decided that *ZZZIP!!* would be acted entirely in majority languages. The company performed first in the Witwatersrand, and then took the play on tour to the Transkei and the Cape, where Xhosa is homogeneously spoken and Zulu, Sotho and *tsotsitaal* are imperfectly understood, if at all. In order to overcome this problem the actors, all of whom knew 'Soweto English' and some Xhosa, simply converted, sometimes during performance, lines originally delivered in Zulu, Sotho or *tsotsitaal* into Xhosa or English, depending on the context.

Workshop '71's stand on language suggests two things. It suggests that a democratic decision vis-à-vis language is practical and feasible both in group discussion and in performances anywhere in the country. It also suggests that such a decision solves important problems relating to the emergence of consciousness amongst performers and audience. When Workshop '71's meetings were conducted in languages other than English, the majority of white members who traditionally dominate 'multi-racial' gatherings began to drop out and members of other groups gained confidence. In other words, the use of majority languages in the context of black-white relations achieved a similar but more democratic result than the prescription offered by the BCM which, though it excluded whites, ensured the leadership of fluent black English-speakers, i.e. the educated intermediate classes, and inhibited the participation of non-English-speakers, i.e. the majority.

It is therefore difficult to conceive of majority theatrical activity being conducted in any language other than those understood and colloquially spoken by the majority. It is unlikely, too, that these languages would be used, except in linguistically homogeneous areas, in their pure forms, but rather in their colloquial organic modern forms. The question of language is important for the democratic dialogic nature of theatre activity. Only if each person involved is free to express himself in a language he can confidently handle, can the performers freely participate in discussion or in the performance and each individual feel that s/he, as much as anyone else, is free to control, influence, make suggestions and participate in the proceedings. It is also crucially important in the creation of consciousness. Language is a powerful lever of oppression. The class-cultural significances of language have revealed themselves repeatedly in this study. Thus by operating in majority languages, the majority discovers its powers and rejects an important element of the cultural domination exercised over it by other groups and classes.

★   ★   ★

The above suggestions concerning the future nature of majority theatre are of necessity tentative and speculative. But they derive from the concrete analysis of cultural struggle in South Africa in general, and four important and representative South African plays in particular, and from the firm and certain commitment which has informed this study, i.e. to the historic role of the majority in building a non-oppressive, non-exploitative society in South

Africa. Such a commitment, when applied to four given examples of theatre activity, has in the main been able to reveal the nature of each work and its ideological and political function. It remains therefore our guide when, as majority theatre develops, we are called upon to test new works and point the way forward to a theatre that will contribute to the liberation not only of the oppressed classes and national groups in South Africa, but ultimately of men and women everywhere.

> We go for (ward)
>> we will get the good things that
> We go for (ward)
>> things that every man on this earth
> Goes for (ward)
>> go for things that everyone alive can share
>
> We go for (ward)
>> we will get the sunshine when
> We go for (ward)
>> shining on our faces when
> We go for (ward)
>> air for all our breathing – let's
>>> go for the sun
>>> go for the air
>>> go for our share
> Go forward!

[Song from Workshop '71's *Survival* (1976)]

Notes

As far as possible, all references have been included in the text in as simple but clear a form as possible. When included annotation invariably implies additional sources, information or opinion, which though not requiring to be included in the text may be of interest to the reader.

1. See Frederick Johnstone, *Class, Race and Gold* (1976), numerous articles by Martin Legassik, including 'Race, Industrialization and Social Change in South Africa: The Case of R.F.A. Hoernle', in *African Studies*, 75, 299 (April 1976), 224-39, and articles by Harold Wolpe, including 'Class, Race and the Occupational Structure' in *Institute of Commonwealth Studies*, 12: Southern Africa, 2 (1970-1), 98-119, and 'Capitalism and Cheap Labour-Power in South Africa: From Segregation to Apartheid' in *Economy and Society*, 1 (1972), 425-56. Others who have written from this perspective include Colin Bundy, Stanley Trapido and Charles van Onselen. See also B.M. Magubane, *The Political Economy of Race and Class in South Africa* (New York/London, 1979) and 'No Sizwe', *One Azania, One Nation* (London, 1979).
2. As quoted by Lewis Nkosi in *South African Information and Analysis* (June 1968).
3. The title of Fugard's *No-Good Friday* refers to the fear with which Friday night was regarded in Sophiatown in 1958. This extract from Oswald Mtshali's poem 'Intake Night – Baragwanath Hospital' shows that Friday night 20 years later in Soweto was much the same. See Oswald Mtshali, *Sounds of a Cowhide Drum* (Johannesburg, 1971), p.41.
4. No detailed account of the politics and legislation of apartheid has been attempted here as this is an area with which one can assume the reader has some familiarity. The facts are readily available in the following, among many others: *Oxford History of South Africa, Laws Affecting Race Relations in South Africa, 1948-1976*, compiled by Muriel Horrell (Johannesburg, 1978), and *Racism and Apartheid*, based on material prepared by the Anti-Apartheid Movement (Paris, 1974).
5. The debate referred to in this paragraph has been argued in the context of the United States as well as South Africa. See Oliver Cromwell Cox, *Caste, Class and Race* (New York, 1948). Pierre L. van den Berghe, *South Africa: A*

Study in Conflict (Berkeley, 1965), has been the most influential 'pluralist' to write about South Africa. Of those who insist on the importance of class, H. Wolpe, Martin Legassik, Frederick Johnstone and the publications of the South African Communist Party have been possibly the most influential. Eugene D. Genovese wrote of certain Marxist historians who 'never see ideology as something partially autonomous and capable of affecting material interests profoundly' – *In Red and Black: Marxian Explorations in Southern and Afro-American History* (London, 1971), p.322. This is true of much radical and Marxist writing on South Africa. Harrison M. Wright has sketched out 'the liberal-radical controversy over Southern African history' in *The Burden of the Present* (Cape Town, 1977). Genovese is one of the few who recognized the importance of racial/national factors in the *Marxist* analysis of the black Americans: 'It is no longer possible to believe that a class can be understood apart from their nationality' and 'American blacks constitute not so much a class as a nation, and their experience in the United States has been unique' (pp.21, 57). This fact was pointed to in the South African context by a reviewer of Dan O'Meara's recent book *Volkskapitalisme: Class, Capital and Ideology in the Development of Afrikaner Nationalism 1934-1948* (CUP, 1983), who in recalling Lenin's caution on this question wrote:

> Lenin in his writings on the national question repeatedly stressed the need for communists to take account of national sensibilities. 'Nothing holds up the development and strengthening of proletarian class solidarity so much as national injustice; 'offended' nationals are not sensitive to anything so much as the feeling of equality and the violation of this equality'. . . [Z.N. in *The African Communist*, 96 (1984), p.88]

Problems of race, nationality and class are discussed in detail in 'No Sizwe', *One Azania, One Nation* (London, 1979).
6. See Harold Wolpe, 'Class, Race and the Occupational Structure', and 'Capitalism and Cheap Labour-Power in South Africa: From Segregation to Apartheid'. This quotation comes from the former, p.102. A recent article by the same author is 'Apartheid's Deepening Crisis' in *Marxism Today* 26, 1 (1983), 7-11.
7. These quotations are from Wolpe (1970-1), pp.103 and 98. Genovese writes of the 'conjuncture of class and national oppression, both of which become partly obscured when subsumed by the category "race" ' – Genovese (1971), p.58.
8. This fact, and the importance of the national question in South Africa, was recognized by the South African Communist Party in 1928 when it coined the phrase 'Native' or 'Black Republic'. Trotsky also recognized that the social revolution in South Africa has a national character: 'proletarian revolutionaries must never forget the right of the oppressed nationalities to self-determination, including full separation'; Leon Trotsky, 'On the South African Theses', in *Writings of Leon Trotsky* (New York, 1971), 250-1. No detailed historical background is given as this is relatively well known and

also readily available in numerous histories of South Africa, e.g. the *Oxford History* (OHSA).

9. For an account of the rise of Afrikaner capital, see R.W. Johnson, *How Long Will South Africa Survive?* (London, 1977) and, especially for the early stages of this development, Dan O'Meara (1983).

10. The development and activities of the African nationalist organizations are not gone into here, but information is readily available in numerous books including Peter Walshe, *The Rise of African Nationalism in South Africa: The African National Congress, 1912-1952*, (London, 1970), 'African Nationalism' by Leo Kuper in *OHSA*, Edward Feit, *South Africa: The Dynamics of the African National Congress* (London, 1962) Roux (1964), Simons (1968), etc.

11. It must be made clear that Gramsci's analysis is not used here in order to supplant that of the founders of Marxism. Marx and Engels laid the foundations, but Gramsci discusses modern capitalist society in terms which, though soundly based on Marx and Engels, suggest a readier application to present conditions. The extent to which Gramsci is simply re-stating in modern terms what they have already said is illustrated by the following quotation from *The German Ideology* which provides the precedence for Gramsci's concept of 'legitimation':

> For each new class which puts itself in the place of one ruling before it is compelled, merely in order to carry through its aim, to present its interest as the common interest of all the members of society, that is, expressed in ideal form: it has to give its ideas the form of universality, and present them as the only rational, universally valid ones.

The interests of a class expressed in ideal form includes art and literature, culture etc.

By 'culture (in both senses)', as expressed in the text, I mean the two main meanings attached to the word — as differentiated by Raymond Williams, for instance: 'the arts and intellectual life' and 'the social process which creates specific and different ways of life'; Williams (1977), p.17.

12. These statistics are from Johnson, p.27. Much of the economic information in this section was taken from the same book.

13. Donald Woods received much publicity at the time of the murder in detention of the Black Consciousness leader, Steve Biko, for his support of Biko and his condemnation of his death. He was banned and skipped the country with his family. In exile he wrote the book *Biko* (New York/London, 1978).

14. This process culminated after 1976 in the opening of all theatres to multi-racial audiences.

15. The minority black groups — the 'Coloureds' and 'Indians' — though their function in the economic and political life of the society is significant, have not been consistently included in this study. Therefore the term 'black' generally refers to black Africans unless there is the need to differentiate.

16. *Tsotsitaal*: see below p.54ff.; *stokvel*: a form of mutual-aid drinking club
in the urban areas; *umbhaqanga, ngomabusuku* and *marabi*: different forms of
music, singing or dance music in which traditional and modern elements
combine. *Umbhaqanga* music established itself strongly in the black urban
areas during the 1960s, as this grudging admission by a journalist on *The
World* (24 May 1970) testifies:

> The music might not be your kind of dish but the entertainment and
> the swinging value of these groups is something special and spectacular
> . . . This is not strictly African choreography but an amalgamation of
> the Afro with the West.

17. In the late 1960s a feature of Soweto life was the antagonism between
the Zulu migrant workers and the urbanized youth. The slogan *'ushay'
ikepisi, kuphum' utsotsi'* (hit a cap and out pops a *tsotsi*) recalls those and
earlier days. When in 1976, however, the state attempted to capitalize on
'tribalistic' antagonism and provoke a Zulu 'blacklash' against the students
in Soweto, they succeeded only in one hostel, Mzimhlophe. Inter-ethnic
solidarity in the rest of Soweto prevented this 'blacklash' from escalating and,
despite police protection and incitement, the Mzimhlophe hostel-dwellers
were forced to evacuate.
18. Fanon, quoted in Sivanandan, 'The Liberation of the Black Intellectual',
in *Race and Class*, 18, 4 (1977), p.334.
19. Mango Tshabangu, 'Mango Tshabangu Replies to Doreen Lamb', in
S'ketsh' (Summer 1973), p.37.
20. For drama in Bushman and Hottentot communities, see I. Schapera, *The
Khoisan Peoples of South Africa* (London, 1936) and C.M. Doke, 'Games,
Plays and Dances of the Khomani Bushmen', in *Bantu Studies*, 10 (1936).
For *intsomi*, see Harold Scheub, 'The Technique of the Expansible Image in
Xhosa *Ntsomi*-performances', in *Research in African Literatures*, 1, 2 (1970).
For other forms, see *The Bantu-speaking Tribes of South Africa*, edited by
I. Schapera (Cape Town, 1953), Hugh Ashton, *The Basuto* (London, 1967),
D.P. Kunene, *Heroic Poetry of the Basotho* (Oxford, 1971) and E.J. Krige,
The Social System of the Zulus (Pietermaritzburg, 1965). Note especially
the descriptions of dramatic and musical entertainment and ritual at the court
of Dingane, the Zulu king, in books by Delagorgue and Gardiner, summarized
in Krige (pp.342-4).
21.   See 'Drama and the African' in *South African Outlook*, 66 (1936) and
'African Drama and Poetry' in the same journal, 69 (1939). Also 'African
Drama and Research' in *Native Teachers' Journal*, 28 (1939).
22. See 'On the Theatre of Africa', in *S'ketsh'* (Summer 1973) and
'*Umlinganiso* . . . The Living Tradition', in *S'ketsh'* (Summer 1974/5). Also
uNosilimela in Kente, *South African People's Plays* (London, 1981).
23. For an account of the Lucky Stars, see T.C. Lloyd, 'The Bantu Tread the
Footlights' in *South African Opinion* (8 April 1935).
24. This was stated by the well-known poet Professor B.W. Vilakazi in 'Some

Aspects of Zulu Literature' in *African Studies*, 1 (1942).

25. The play was directed by the Belgian Communist director, Andre van Gyseghem. As an expert in 'mass theatre' he was invited to South Africa 'to organize a pageant on the history of the country . . . Involving over 2,000 actors with wagons, oxen and sheep. This was the first of a series of spectacular events for which he was responsible' – *Morning Star* (London).

26. Information on Mphahlele's dramatic activities in South Africa is available in his autobiography, *Down Second Avenue* (London, 1959), e.g. pp.129 and 180–2.

27. Research needs to be done on this episode in the development of South African political theatre. I have only found a tantalizingly brief reference to it in Roux, p.312.

28. Despite opposition from the various sections of the black African group, especially the intermediate classes, the government's efforts to discourage the use of English in favour of 'Bantu languages' were in many ways successful among sections of the proletariat. Not only were plays such as *Uqomisa Mina Nje, Uqomisa Iliba* by Andries Blose and *uNomalanga*, a dramatization of a novel by R.R.R. Dhlomo, performed in the black urban areas, but drama on Radio Bantu, especially serials, was immensely popular. In Zulu, K.E. Masinga, for instance, was responsible for many popular plays, adaptations and translations. In the 1970s, too, there was a great increase in films, produced by white-owned companies, in 'Bantu languages', e.g. *Inkedama, Ikati Elimnyama, uDeliwe, uNokukhanya* and *Ngwanaka*.

29. 'JP', 'African Drama in the Transvaal', in *Journal of the African Music Society*, 1, 5 (1952), p.8.

30. See Leshoai's account of the union's activities and his own activities after leaving South Africa in 1964, in 'Theatre and the Common Man', in *Transition*, 4, 19 (1965). Leshoai's published plays include *Wrath of the Ancestors* (Nairobi, 1972) and *The Weather Forecast* in *S'ketsh'* (Summer 1975), 16-7.

31. In, for instance, 'After Soweto: People's Theatre and the Political Struggle in South Africa', in *Theatre Quarterly*, 9, 33 (1979).

32. *The World* (8 July 1975). the previous month the People's Theatre Association (see p.68 below) called on Mr Pieterse to 'forget about American and Western influence in their plays' – *The World* (30 May 1975). Pieterse was applying cultural and aesthetic censorship and trying to impose on writers the official cultural policy of the government and steer 'Bantu' writers away from the culture of English capital towards a fossilized version of 'their own' traditional culture.

33. For more information on the theatre of this period, see Mshengu, 'After Soweto: People's Theatre and the Political Struggle in South Africa', and the Introduction to Kente, *South African People's Plays*.

34. In a PhD thesis entitled *Drum Magazine (1951–1961) and the Works of Black South African Writers Associated with it* (Leeds, 1975).

35. Sampson wrote that he found the support given *Drum* by Communists, African Nationalists and revolutionaries 'embarrassing' – p.52. *Drum* and

Post, like all the white-owned papers of the time, opposed the Africanists and devoted an issue to the influence of Communists in the African National Congress.

36. *Blame Me On History*, p.188. Ezekiel Mphahlele was one of those who most consistently disagreed with editorial policy. He pointed out that African taste had not yet formed and that Bailey's belief that pulp art and newspapers catered for the workers' taste would only degrade it – Rabkin, pp.89–90.

37. See Rabkin, Chapter 6. A novel in progress is also on the same theme – interview with Nkosi (1979).

38. May 1968 (Paris). Nkosi's incisive criticism is not included in an anthology of Fugard criticism, *Athol Fugard*, edited by Stephen Gray (Johannesburg, 1982). Of the 44 articles only two are by black writers. In addition, though one article from *S'ketsh'* magazine on the Serpent Players is included, Sipho Sepamla's critical review of *Sizwe Banzi* in *S'ketsh'* (Summer 1973) is excluded. One wonders whether the book is a critical anthology or uncritical idolatry.

39. *Theatre Quarterly*, 7, 28 (1977), 77–83. There is much additional information in Gray (see note 38 above).

40. Søren Aabye Kierkegaard was a 19th-century religious philosopher commonly regarded as the father of modern Existentialism; noted for his idealist critique of Hegel.

41. See Oswald Mtshali's poem, quoted on p.4 above.

42. 'The problem that Fugard set his hero – an educated African who must provide some leadership in the community', etc. – from Nkosi's critique of *No-Good Friday* in *South African Information and Analysis* (May 1968), p.3.

43. 'Not once in this play is the very morality of colour or *white* as a standard of what is beautiful or desirable, questioned' – this is Nkosi writing about Fugard's *The Blood Knot*. His comments in this context can easily and appropriately be applied to *No-Good Friday*. For the rest of this excellent criticism, see *South African Information and Analysis* (May 1968).

44. 'It is after all, through the enormous force, both civil and military that the law-abiding citizens are kept in the ghetto' – *South African Information and Analysis* (May 1968), where it is implied that freedom means leaving the ghetto rather than abolishing it.

45. For instance: 'In terms of one idea which is stirring [i.e. the idea for a new play] in me at the moment, it is a man alone again. Dimetos was a man alone. Marais, in the new film, *The Guest*, is a man alone – there are other people but the predicament is being alone' – *Theatre Quarterly*, 7, 28 (1977), p.83.

46. As in *Blame Me On History* and interview with Nkosi (1979) e.g.:

   In the final moment it was always Fugard who shaped the script.
       The final words are always captured by the playwright later on.
       It [language] was affected by what Fugard was hearing all the time he was writing the play.
       Fugard took over the writing of the play.
       Athol Fugard had accepted the principle [i.e. of not playing the

priest at the Brooke Theatre because he was white] without consulting with the actors . . . we became sentimental and relented because it seemed to be his whole life.

47. Nkosi recalls that whenever he delivered Father Higgens's big speech the rest of the cast burst out laughing – interview with Nkosi (1979).
48. J.P. Clark, the Nigerian writer, noted this in a similar context – *The Example of Shakespeare* (London, 1970), p.21.
49. Ian Bernhardt gives 1953 as the date of the founding of the Union – interview with Bernhardt (1977); Mona Glasser gives 1953 – *King Kong: A Venture in the Theatre* (Cape Town, 1960), p.7; a note in the *Emperor Jones* programme gives 1953, but another note in the Eoan Group programme gives 1952 – both programmes in *Dorkay House in Print*.
50. Bloom, p.10. Another example of such exploitation was that suffered by the world famous *kwela* musician, Spokes Mashiane. According to Nat Nakasa, Mashiane 'just makes the breadline and a little over many months, in spite of the miles of dough coined by his records here and overseas!' Mashiane told Nakasa: 'I've made over 30 records now . . . But, you see, I only got small money from them. For some of them I got a little over two pounds, a few about four quid and the rest up to £20 or nothing at all' – Patel, pp.80-90.
51. Interview with Ntshona (1979). Loder himself at first consented to be interviewed but then announced that he was too busy. He promised, however, to answer my written questions in writing. No such communication was received from him despite repeated reminders.
52. *Emperor Jones* programme in *Dorkay House in Print*.
53. Newspaper cutting in *Dorkay House in Print*.
54. H.F. Oppenheimer, 'Towards Racial Harmony', supplement in *Optima*, 6, 3 (1956).
55. This applied to many of the artists who remained overseas as well as those who remained at home. They were unemployed and many of them turned to drink and in some cases to prostitution – as the newspapers of the early 1960s poignantly record.
56. For instance, the designer of *King Kong*, Arthur Goldreich, had

had a highly successful year since his part in *King Kong*. He held an exhibition of paintings at Whippman's Gallery which furthered his reputation as a straight painter. The *King Kong* poster designed by him last year, resulted in his being commissioned to design an international poster for the launching, last month, of the film *On The Beach*; and he has become involved in designing fabric patterns for a Holland textile manufacturer. In 1960, he has to complete the redecoration project of a large department store in Durban, and is working for a group exhibition to be held in Johannesburg in April. [*Emperor Jones* programme in *Dorkay House in Print*]

Also it was largely the union's production of his play, *The Blood Knot*, which was subsequently staged on Broadway, which established Fugard in South Africa and internationally.

57. One musician was quoted as saying about the union:

> We thought it was yet another money-making project . . . and that it was yet another way to exploit African artists; another lot of promises that would never materialize. [Glasser, p.8]

58. It seems certain that white commentators exaggerate the shabbiness and lack of success of the black artists' world before the establishment of the union. What for them appears to have been a waste of talent was for blacks 'the fabulous fifties'. For instance, the account of the Manhattan Brothers' latest tour in *Umtetheli wabantu* (19 January 1952) does not appear to bear out Bloom and Glasser's descriptions of popular black music in the early 1950s:

> [The Manhattan Brothers and Shanty Town Sextet] have had such a successful tour of the Cape that they are extending their stay until the end of the month.

59. The following information about Leon Gluckman is taken from the following sources: Glasser (p.13), Bloom (p.15), the *Emperor Jones* programme in *Dorkay House in Print* and a newspaper cutting in the same.

60. See, for example, Nkosi (1965), p.32:

> It became a matter of the greatest surprise to us to realize that some of these people [whites] were leading appallingly empty lives, even in the midst of plenty, and perhaps because of this undeserved plenty, they were desperately impoverished; their lives had reached such a point of incoherence and fatuity that listening to their conversation was like listening to a cacophony of voices echoing other empty voices.

61. Quoted from Glasser, p.17 (our italics), Bloom, pp.15–16, Glasser, p.37 (our italics) and a newspaper cutting in *Dorkay House in Print*.

62. SAIA (May 1968), p.8. Nkosi also wrote of *No-Good Friday*: 'It was not after all the kind of play to alienate the white community. It did not suggest criminal culpability on their part' (p.4).

63. Nakasa, see chapter 'The Life and Death of King Kong'.

64. Mabel's comment about her white 'madam' is swiftly made palatable to the 'madams' in the audience when she says: 'Me? Leave my Madam? You're crazy. She's just a little bit impossible that's all' (p.30).

65. Nakasa, p.81. The black critic is Benny Bunsee.

66. The text has been corrected and the English translation is mine.

67. *Optima*, 9, 4 (1959), 219-29.

68. Conversely, the cultural factor, which gave Kente the advantage in live

entertainment for black audiences, probably at least as much as government policy militated against his plays being successful with white audiences.
69. *S'ketsh'* (Summer 1974/5), p.9.
70. *S'ketsh'* (Summer 1972), p.10.
71. Zulu traditional musical version of *Macbeth*, which made an impact at the Aldwych World Theatre Festival in London in 1970 and 1972.
72. *S'ketsh'* (Summer 1974/5), pp.28-9 and elsewhere in the press. As a note in *S'ketsh'* explains, this reputation was not entirely deserved: 'As a matter of fact, Peter Sephuma [who played the lead in *I Believe*] received intensive training with Workshop '71 . . . A wrong impression has also been created about Seth Sibanda, star of *How Long*. He is also no beginner, trained with Workshop '71.' Both these actors were in Workshop '71's *Crossroads* (1972).
73. *S'ketsh'* (Summer 1972), p.8.
74. None of Kente's plays has been published except *Too Late*, a complete version in Kente, *South African People's Plays*, and an abridged version in *S'ketsh'* (Winter 1975), pp.17-22. In this chapter almost all quotations and references are from the complete published version. When referring to the abridged version I have used the term, *Too Late* I. In my possession I have an unpublished manuscript of the complete play and when referring to this I have used the term *Too Late* II. Of Kente's other plays, I have seen performances of *Sikalo, Lifa, Zwi, How Long* and *I Believe*. Records are available of *Sikalo* (I and II), *How Long, Too Late* and *Can You Take It*.
75. *Majita* or *mjida* is a *tsotsitaal* word, meaning a young man who knows the ropes, i.e. somewhere between a 'clever' and a '*tsotsi*'. The *moegoe*/clever surrogate morality of the urban areas, remarked on in *No-Good Friday*, is thus that which defines the characterization of the *majitas*.
76. The message of *I Believe*, for instance, was expressed thus: 'Let there be peace, justice and fairness. Let us stand together and fight – but not by violent means' – *The World* (9 May 1974).
77. *How Long*, LP record (RTL 4033). Square brackets indicate lacunae resulting from indistinct recording.
78. Kente invented this catchphrase but it has its roots in traditional cultural forms, as in the Sotho greeting 'Kgotso' (Peace), for instance.
79. *S'ketsh'* (Summer 1972), p.9.
80. These comments on Kente are taken from *S'ketsh'* (Summer 1974/5), p.27, *S'ketsh'* (Winter 1975), p.9, and *S'ketsh'* (Summer 1972), p.9.
81. Stephen Bantu Biko, *I Write What I Like* (London, 1979), pp.8-16.
82. For instance, see the section entitled 'White Reactions to Black Consciousness' in *Black Review* (1972), pp.48-54.
83. For an account which recognizes and emphasizes these two weaknesses, but otherwise shows a conspicuous unwillingness to recognize the positive contributions of the movement, see Baruch Hirson, *Year of Fire, Year of Ash* (London, 1979), especially Chapter Four entitled 'Black Consciousness Politics, 1970-1974'.
84. Black Consciousness, though participated in by women, was a thoroughly

male-dominated, male-oriented ideology. See also p.178 below. The sexism of this slogan did not seem to occur to the BCM.
85. See 'Some African Cultural Concepts' in Biko, pp.40-7.
86. See, for a more detailed account of the leaders it attracted, their class and political affiliations, and especially the movement's attempts to establish a black workers' organization, see Hirson, pp.107-19.
87. Biko, p.50. Though Biko rejected Marx, he, like Marx, adopted from Hegel the concept of the dialectic and often expressed his ideas in terms of thesis, antithesis and synthesis. For example, in 'Definition of Black Consciousness' (Biko, p.51), he wrote: 'The overall analysis, therefore, based on the Hegelian theory of dialectical materialism [*sic*], is as follows. That since the thesis is a white racism there can be only one valid antithesis, i.e. a solid black unity to counterbalance the scale.'
88. Biko, p.96. See Woods, p.125, and Biko, pp.129-30, for an apparent defence of a kind of socialism in the SASO/BPC trial.
89. As Fugard himself described it:

> There was a knock on the door one night and in walked [some of those who were to become future members of the Serpent Players]. I despaired really. I was very tired after the tour [of *The Blood Knot*] and I didn't really feel like getting involved with actors so soon — it's very exhausting — but they persisted, and I felt guilty . . . so that was the beginning of Serpent' — *Theatre Quarterly*, 7, 28 (1977), 77-83.

90. See Biko in Woods, p.126. For *No-Good Friday* and *The Blood Knot* see p.72 ff., also n.43 on p.222 above. In *King Kong* we have the following example:

> King Kong — born as a fight man
> King Kong — built out of stone
> King Kong — could be a whiteman
> That's me. I'm him. King Kong [p.38]

where Ruth Williams, who wrote the lyrics, in her hyperbole seems to suggest that King Kong's excellence and the extent to which he towers over his fellows in Sophiatown can best be measured by referring to his potential — not more (note 'could') — to be a white man.
91. We shall be examining this point in the next section. It was allied too to a rejection of the kind of art which depicted vice and degradation in black society without relating it to the socio-economic causes, of which we suggested *No-Good Friday* is an example, as in the following words of Biko's:

> No one even attempts to relate these vices to poverty, unemployment, overcrowding, lack of schooling and migratory labour. No one wants to completely condone abhorrent behaviour, but it frequently is necessary for us to analyse situations a little bit deeper than the surface suggests. [p.57

92. *The World* (20 October 1972). Mdali also means 'creator' — therefore artist.
93. Countless other sources could be quoted for all these points, but as Biko is generally the most articulate spokesman in the movement, and as we have up to now referred to his writings a great deal, we quote him here. Attacks on blacks who collaborated with whites — often called non-whites, or in colloquial conversation 'ama-boy' — were made regularly in such publications as the *Black Review*, SASO, Mihloti and PET newsletters and in public speeches and conversations. 'Shame' is an expression of pity or sympathy in South Africa.
94. Quoted in a review of the Mihloti Newsletters 1 and 2 in *S'ketsh'* (Summer 1973), p.45. I have read those newsletters but unfortunately copies were not available for reference when I wrote this study.
95. From a Mihloti newsletter as quoted in the *Black Review* (1973), p.113. Sam Mhangwani's *Unfaithful Woman* was the story of a woman who is unfaithful to her man and as a result undergoes extreme humiliation and punishment for her sins, ending up an obscene and mad figure of fun and disgust.
96. Conversation with Pheto (London, 9 August 1979). Pheto was unwilling to furnish much information about Mihloti and Mdali because it was 'sensitive', and 'whites' cannot 'be as involved as we Blacks' — 'this area is better dealt with by those who were involved themselves' — letter to author (18 October 1979).
97. For instance, the *Black Review* of 1974/5 contains no criticism of his plays, and instead emphasizes the political protest in *Too Late* and its banning by the authorities (pp.212-13).
98. As we saw in the chapter on *King Kong*, this was a tendency much encouraged by the Union of Southern African Artists. With the granting of permits for performances by black casts in white theatres in the early 1970s, the tendency revived. Kente, as already noted, subscribed to it himself. The theatre groups (and artists in general) of the BCM firmly turned their backs on such a tendency and performed and organized art and drama festivals and exhibitions exclusively in black areas.
99. *Black Review* (1973), p.113. See also note 41 above.
100. *South African Outlook* (August 1973), pp.131-3.
101. Reviews of this play, and articles by Credo Mutwa on the traditional theatre of Africa and the staging of the play, can be found in *S'ketsh'* (Summer 1973, pp.38-41, and Summer 1974/5, pp.40-1 and 30-2). Extracts from the play were printed in *S'ketsh'* (Summer 1974/5) and the full script can be found in Kente, *South African People's Plays*.
102. Printed in *The New Terrorists: Documents from the SASO/BPC Trial*, published by International University Exchange Fund (June/July 1976), pp.29-47.
103. 'The 20-century old African dress worn all over independent Africa' — *Black Review* (1972), p.211. We quote this not as an objective explanation of the word, but as an indication of what the 'dashiki' meant to the BCM. As for the use of electrical instruments, see Vusi Khumalo's criticism of the

guitarist Philip Tabane for using the 'wah-wah pedal', cited on p.172.

104. All these performances were monitored by the security police and cited in the charge sheet at the SASO/BPC trial.

105. From his speech on the occasion of the investiture of the transitional government in Mozambique, as reprinted in *SASO Newsletter* 5, 2 (1975), 12–19. This extract is on p.13.

106. *How Long*, LP record. *Shanti* was rehearsed at the DOCC hall in Soweto where Kente also rehearsed, and it is almost certain that *Shanti* influenced his next play, *How Long*.

107. The original script moved quite freely from verse to prose and back again, much as in Jacobean drama. The script in *South African People's Plays* follows this but attempts to introduce a greater consistency.

108. In a conversation I had in 1972 with Saths Cooper of SABTU and TECON, he saw my insistence that the language of Soweto was not English as 'undermining', i.e. underestimating, the people of Soweto. He insisted that it was English and that English is the language of 'black theatre'. That he, as a member of the Indian black group who could speak no African languages, should so insist was understandable, but it did indicate one of the contradictions in Black Consciousness cultural thinking.

109. *I Write What I Like*, pp.22–3, where he suggests that it is both possible and impossible.

110. See, for example, Cabral's discussion of this in 'Identity and Dignity in the Context of the National Liberation Struggle', in *Return to the Source*.

111. Institute of Adult Education, *Laedza Batanani: Organizing Popular Theatre* (Gaborone, 1978), p.4.

112. *Popular Theatre: A Technique for Participatory Research* (Botswana), unpublished manuscript, pp.5–17.

A great deal of experiment and activity in the area of popular theatre/theatre for development has taken place in recent years, and an extensive literature is now available describing much of this work. The following are a few selected references:

Theatre for Integrated Development, report of the workshop on theatre for integrated development (Swaziland, 1981);

Third World Popular Theatre Newsletters (Jamaica);

Theaterwork Magazine (Minnesota);

Sonolux Information (6 September 1982, Munich);

'Post-mortem of Murewa Theatre Workshop', in *Moto*, 18 (Zimbabwe, 1983).

113. Workshop '71's *Crossroads* was never published, though extracts appeared in *S'ketsh'* (Summer 1972), 36–43. Other plays by Workshop '71 include *uHlanga: the Reed* (unpublished) and *Survival*, published in Kente, *South African People's Plays*.

Selected Bibliography

Selected Bibliography

1. Playscripts

Bloom, Harry, *King Kong* (London, 1961)

Fugard, Athol, *The Blood Knot*, in *Three Port Elizabeth Plays* (London, 1974)

— *No-Good Friday* and *Nongogo*, in *Dimetos and Two Early Plays* (Oxford, 1977)

Kente, Gibson, and others, *South African People's Plays* (London, 1981)

— *Too Late* in *South African People's Plays*

— *Too Late* I, abridged version published in *S'ketsh'* (Winter 1975), 17-22

— *Too Late* II, unpublished manuscript in my possession

Mutwa, Credo Vusamazulu, *uNosilimela*, in *South African People's Plays*

— *uNosilimela*, abridged version published in *S'ketsh'* (Summer 1974/5), 43-47

Nkosi, Lewis, *Rhythm of Violence*, in *Plays from Black Africa*, edited by Frederic M. Litto (New York, 1968)

Shezi, Mthuli, *Shanti*, in *South African People's Plays*

Workshop '71, *Survival*, in *South African People's Plays*

— *Crossroads*, abridged version published in *S'ketsh'* (Summer 1972), 36-43

— *uHlanga: The Reed* and *ZZZIP!*, unpublished manuscripts in my possession

2. Secondary material

Biko, Stephen Bantu, *I Write What I Like* (London, 1979)

Benson, Mary, 'Interview with Athol Fugard', in *Theatre Quarterly*, 7, 28 (1977), 77-83

Black Review, 1972, edited by B.A. Khoapa (Durban, 1973)

Black Review, 1973, edited by M. Pascal Gwala (Durban, 1974)

Black Review, 1974/5, edited by Thoko Mbanjwa (1975)

Bottomore, T.B., *Classes in Modern Society* (Birkenhead, 1965)

Brotz, Jeffrey, Robert I. Rotberg and John Adams, *The Black Homelands of South Africa* (Berkeley, 1977)

Cabral, Amilcar, *Return to the Source*, edited by Africa Information Service (London, 1973)

Carr, W.J.P., 'Raising the Standards of South Africa's Urban Natives', in *Optima*, 9, 4 (1959), 219-229

Couzens, Tim, 'The Social Ethos of Black Writing in South Africa 1920-50', in *Aspects of South African Literature*, edited by Christopher Heywood (London, 1976)

Cox, Oliver Cromwell, *Caste, Class and Race* (New York, 1948)

de Ridder, J.C., *The Personality of the Urban African in South Africa* (London, 1961)

Dhlomo, H.I.E., 'The Nature and Variety of Tribal Drama', in *Bantu Studies*, 13 (1939), 33-48

Dikobe, Modikwe, *The Marabi Dance* (London, 1973)

Doke, C.M., 'Games, Plays and Dances of the Khomani Bushmen', in *Bantu Studies*, 10 (1936)

Dorkay House in Print, unpublished presentation volume of programmes, posters, press cuttings, etc. in the possession of Robert Loder

Fanon, Frantz, *Black Skin, White Masks* (New York, 1967)
—   *Towards the African Revolution* (New York, 1967)
—   *The Wretched of the Earth* (Harmondsworth, 1967)

Feit, Edward, *South Africa: The Dynamics of the African National Congress* (London, 1962)

Finnegan, Ruth, *Oral Literature in Africa* (Oxford, 1970)

Freire, Paulo, *Cultural Action for Freedom* (Harmondsworth, 1972)
—   *Education: The Practice of Freedom* (London, 1976)
—   *Pedagogy of the Oppressed* (Harmondsworth, 1972)

Geiss, Immanuel, *The Pan-African Movement* (London, 1974)

Gerard, Albert S., *Four African Literatures* (Berkeley, 1971)

Genovese, Eugene D., *In Red and Black: Marxian Explorations in Southern and Afro-American History* (London, 1971)

Glasser, Mona, *King Kong: A Venture in the Theatre* (Cape Town, 1960)

Gramsci, Antonio, *The Modern Prince* (New York, 1957)
—   *Selections from the Prison Notebooks*, edited and translated by Q. Hoare and G.N. Smith (London, 1971)

Gray, Stephen, (ed.), *Athol Fugard* (Johannesburg, 1982)

Green, Robert J., 'The Drama of Athol Fugard', in *Aspects of South African Literature*, 162-173

Gwala, M. Pascal, 'Towards a National Theatre', in *South African Outlook* (August, 1973), 131-133

Hirson, Baruch, *Year of Fire, Year of Ash* (London, 1979)

Hoernle, R.F. Alfred, 'The Bantu Dramatic Society at Johannesburg', in *Africa*, 8 (1934), 223-227

Huddleston, Trevor, *Naught for Your Comfort* (London, 1956)

Institute of Adult Education (Botswana), 'Laedza Batanani: Organizing Popular Theatre, the Laedza Batanani Experience 1974-1977' (booklet for extension workers, Gaborone, 1978)

Institute of Race Relations, *Race Relations Journal*, 1958-1960 (Johannesburg)

  — *A Survey of Race Relations*, 1975 (Johannesburg, 1976)

'JP', 'African Drama in the Transvaal', in *Journal of the African Music Society*, 1, 5 (1952), 8-10

Johnson, R.W., *How Long Will South Africa Survive?* (London, 1977)

Johnstone, F., *Class, Race and Gold* (London, 1976)

Joll, James, *Gramsci* (Glasgow, 1977)

Kavanagh, M., 'South Africa', *World Theatre*, 7, 3 (1958)

Kidd, Ross, and Martin Byram, 'Popular Theatre as a Tool for Community Education in Botswana' (booklet published by Unicef, 1978)

Krige, E.J., *The Social System of the Zulus* (Pietermaritzburg, 1965)

Kuper, Leo, *An African Bourgeoisie* (New Haven, 1965)

Lenin, V.I., *On Literature and Art* (Moscow, 1967)

Leshoai, Bob, 'Theatre and the Common Man', in *Transition*, 4, 19 (1965)

Lestrade, G.P., 'Traditional Literature', in *Bantu-speaking Tribes of South Africa*, edited by I. Schapera (Cape Town, 1953)

Lloyd, T.C., 'The Bantu Tread the Footlights', in *South African Opinion* (8 March 1935), 3-5

Lukacs, Georg, *History and Class Consciousness* (London, 1971)

Magubane, B.M., *The Political Economy of Race and Class in South Africa* (New York/London, 1979)

Maine, Abbey, 'An African Theatre in South Africa', in *African Arts*, 3, 4 (1970)

Mao Tse-tung, *Mao Tse-tung: An Anthology of His Writings* (New York, 1971)

Marx, Karl, and Frederick Engels, *On Literature and Art* (Moscow, 1976)

  — *Selected Works* (London, 1968)

Mkele, Nimrod, 'The Emergent African Middle Class', in *Optima*, 10, 4 (1960), 217-226

Modisane, Bloke, *Blame Me On History* (London, 1963)

Mphahlele, Ezekiel, *Down Second Avenue* (London, 1959)

'Mshengu', 'Political Theatre in South Africa and the Work of Athol Fugard', in *Theatre Research International*, 7, 3 (Oxford, 1982)

Mutwa, Credo Vusamazulu, 'Umlinganiso . . . The Living Imitation', in *S'ketsh'* (Summer 1974/5), 30-32

  — 'On the Theatre of Africa', in *S'ketsh'* (Summer 1973), 38-39

Nakasa, Nat, *The World of Nat Nakasa*, edited by Essop Patel (Johannesburg, 1975)

Ngubane, Jordan K., *An African Explains Apartheid* (London, 1963)

Nkosi, Lewis, *Home and Exile* (London, 1965)

'No Sizwe', *One Azania, One Nation* (London, 1979)

Omer-Cooper, J.D., *The Zulu Aftermath* (London, 1966)

Oppenheimer, H.F., 'Towards Racial Harmony', in *Optima*, supplement to 6, 3 (1956)

Oxford History of South Africa, The, edited by Monica Wilson and Leonard Thompson, especially Volume Two, *South Africa 1870-1966* (Oxford, 1971)

Ossowski, S., *Class Structure in the Social Conseiousness* (London, 1963)

People's Experimental Theatre Newsletter, 1 (1973)

Potter, Elaine, *The Press as Opposition: The Political Role of South African Newspapers* (London, 1975)

Pityana, Barney, 'Power and Social Change in South Africa', in *Student Perspectives on South Africa*, edited by H.W. van der Merwe and David Walsh (Cape Town, 1972)

Rabkin, David, 'Drum Magazine (1951-1961) and the Works of Black South African Writers Associated with it' (unpublished doctoral dissertation, University of Leeds, 1975)

Roux, E., *Time Longer Than Rope*, second edition (Madison, 1964)

Sampson, Anthony, *Drum* (London, 1956)

Schapera, I., *The Khoisan Peoples of South Africa* (London, 1930)

Scheub, Harold, 'The Technique of the Expansible Image in Xhosa *Ntsomi*-performances', in *Research in African Literatures*, 1, 2 (1970), 119-146

Simons, H.J. and R.E., *Class and Colour in South Africa (1850-1950)* (Harmondsworth, 1968)

Sivanandan, A., 'The Liberation of the Black Intellectual', in *Race and Class*, 18, 4 (1977)

S'ketsh' (July 1972, Summer 1972, Summer 1973, Summer 1974/5, Winter 1975, Winter 1979) (Johannesburg)

South African Information and Analysis, edited by Lewis Nkosi, (May 1968, June 1968 and December 1969, Paris)

SASO Newsletter, 5, 1 (1975), 5, 2 (1975), 5, 3 (1975) and 6, 1 (1976); reprinted and distributed by International University Exchange Fund, Geneva.

Trotsky, Leon, 'On the South African Theses', in *Writings of Leon Trotsky* (New York, 1971)

Umteteli wabantu, January-December, 1952 (Johannesburg)

Unesco, *Apartheid* (Paris, 1967)

van den Berghe, Pierre L., *South Africa, A Study in Conflict* (Berkeley, 1965)

Vilakazi, B.W., 'Some Aspects of Zulu Literature', in *African Studies*, 1 (1942)

Weinberg, Sara, 'Political Change and Theatre in South Africa' (unpublished undergraduate dissertation, Middlesex Polytechnic, 1979)

Williams, Raymond, *Marxism and Literature* (Oxford, 1977)

Wolpe, Harold, 'Class, Race and the Occupational Structure', in University of London, *Institute of Commonwealth Studies*, 12: Southern Africa, 2 (1970-1), 98-119

— 'Capitalism and Cheap Labour Power in South Africa: From Segregation to Apartheid', in *Economy and Society*, 1 (1972), 425-456

Woods, Donald, *Biko* (New York/London, 1968)

World, The (Bantu World), 18 November 1965, 21 February 1967, 6 January 1971, 30 April 1976 (Johannesburg)

Wright, Harrison M., *The Burden of the Present* (Cape Town, 1977)

Index

QM LIBRARY
(MILE END)

AFRICA TITLES FROM ZED

Dan Nabudere
IMPERIALISM IN EAST AFRICA
Vol. I: Imperialism and Exploitation
Vol. II: Imperialism and Integration
Hb

Elenga M'Buyinga
**PAN AFRICANISM OR NEO
COLONIALISM?**
The Bankruptcy of the OAU
Hb and Pb

Bade Onimode
**IMPERIALISM AND
UNDERDEVELOPMENT IN
NIGERIA**
The Dialectics of Mass Poverty
Hb and Pb

Michael Wolfers and Jane Bergerol
ANGOLA IN THE FRONTLINE
Hb and Pb

Mohamed Babu
**AFRICAN SOCIALISM OR
SOCIALIST AFRICA?**
Hb and Pb

Anonymous
INDEPENDENT KENYA
Hb and Pb

Yolamu Barongo (Editor)
**POLITICAL SCIENCE IN AFRICA:
A RADICAL CRITIQUE**
Hb and Pb

Okwudiba Nnoli (Editor)
**PATH TO NIGERIAN
DEVELOPMENT**
Pb

Emile Vercruijsse
**THE PENETRATION OF
CAPITALISM**
A West African Case Study
Hb

Fatima Babikir Mahmoud
**THE SUDANESE BOURGEOISIE
— Vanguard of Development?**
Hb and Pb

No Sizwe
ONE AZANIA, ONE NATION
**The National Question in South
Africa**
Hb and Pb

Ben Turok (Editor)
DEVELOPMENT IN ZAMBIA
A Reader
Pb

J. F Rweyemamu (Editor)
**INDUSTRIALIZATION AND
INCOME DISTRIBUTION IN
AFRICA**
Hb and Pb

Claude Ake
**REVOLUTIONARY PRESSURES
IN AFRICA**
Hb and Pb

Anne Seidman and Neva Makgetla
**OUTPOSTS OF MONOPOLY
CAPITALISM**
**Southern Africa in the Changing
Global Economy**
Hb and Pb

Peter Rigby
PERSISTENT PASTORALISTS
Nomadic Societies in Transition
Hb and Pb

Edwin Madunagu
**PROBLEMS OF SOCIALISM: THE
NIGERIAN CHALLENGE**
Pb

Mai Palmberg
THE STRUGGLE FOR AFRICA
Hb and Pb

A.T. Nzula, I.I. Potekhin and A.Z. Zusmanovich
FORCED LABOUR IN COLONIAL AFRICA
Hb and Pb

Jeff Crisp
THE STORY OF AN AFRICAN WORKING CLASS
— Ghanaian Miners' Struggles, 1870-1980
Hb and Pb

Aquino de Braganca and Immanuel Wallerstein (Editors)
THE AFRICAN LIBERATION READER
Documents of the National Liberation Movements
Vol I: The Anatomy of Colonialism
Vol II: The National Liberation Movements
Vol III: The Strategy of Liberation
Hb and Pb

Faarax M.J. Cawl
IGNORANCE IS THE ENEMY OF LOVE
Pb

Kinfe Abraham
FROM RACE TO CLASS
Links and Parallels in African and Black American Protest Expression
Pb

Robert Mshengu Kavanagh
THEATRE AND CULTURAL STRUGGLE IN SOUTH AFRICA
A Study in Cultural Hegemony and Social Conflict
Hb and Pb

A. Temu and B. Swai
HISTORIANS AND AFRICANIST HISTORY: A CRITIQUE
Hb and Pb

Robert Archer and Antoine Bouillon
THE SOUTH AFRICAN GAME
Sport and Racism
Hb and Pb

Ray et al.
DIRTY WORK 2
The CIA in Africa
Pb

Raqiya Haji Dualeh Abdalla
SISTERS IN AFFLICTION
Circumcision and Infibulation of Women in Africa
Hb and Pb

Christine Obbo
AFRICAN WOMEN
Their Struggle for Economic Independence
Pb

Maria Rose Cutrufelli
WOMEN OF AFRICA
Roots of Oppression
Hb and Pb

Asma El Dareer
WOMAN, WHY DO YOU WEEP?
Circumcision and Its Consequences
Hb and Pb

Miranda Davies (Editor)
THIRD WORLD — SECOND SEX
Women's Struggles and National Liberation
Hb and Pb

Organization of Angolan Women
ANGOLAN WOMEN BUILDING THE FUTURE
From National Liberation to Women's Emancipation
Hb and Pb